Cuban Political Economy

Series in Political Economy
and Economic Development in Latin America

Series Editor
Andrew Zimbalist
Smith College

Through country case studies and regional analyses this series will contribute to a deeper understanding of development issues in Latin America. Shifting political environments, increasing economic interdependence, and the imposing problematic of debt, foreign investment, and trade policy demand novel conceptualizations of development strategies and potentials for the region. Individual volumes in this series will explore the deficiencies in conventional formulations of the Latin American development experience by examining new evidence and material. Topics will include, among others, women and development in Latin America; the impact of IMF interventions; the effects of redemocratization on development; Cubanology and Cuban political economy; Nicaraguan political economy; and individual case studies on development and debt policy in various countries in the region.

Other Titles in This Series

† *Rural Women and State Policy: Feminist Perspectives on Latin American Agricultural Development*, edited by Carmen Diana Deere and Magdalena León

The International Monetary Fund and Latin America: Economic Stabilization and Class Conflict, Manuel Pastor, Jr.

† Available in hardcover and paperback.

About the Book and Editor

This comprehensive and authoritative book assesses in theoretical and empirical terms some of the most widely debated issues in the study of Cuban political economy over the past two decades. Contributors discuss the Cuban economy's rate of growth, structural changes that have accompanied economic development, the extent of Cuba's economic and political dependence on the Soviet Union, the reliability of Cuban statistics, the performance of Cuba's system of central planning, and the progress Cuba has made in promoting equality for women. Without extolling or condemning the Castro government, these essays provide a timely analysis of the methods, theoretical approaches, and conclusions of the literature in Cuban studies since the 1960s and offer a new understanding of the Cuban reality.

Andrew Zimbalist is professor of economics at Smith College. He has written widely on the Cuban economy and has published several books in the fields of comparative economic systems and Latin American development.

Cuban Political Economy

Controversies in Cubanology

edited by
Andrew Zimbalist

Westview Press / Boulder and London

Series in Political Economy and Economic Development in Latin America

Copyright © 1988 by Westview Press, Inc.

Published in 1988 in the United States of America by Westview Press, Inc.; Frederick A. Praeger, Publisher; 5500 Central Avenue, Boulder, Colorado 80301

Library of Congress Cataloging-in-Publication Data
Cuban political economy: controversies in Cubanology/edited by
  Andrew Zimbalist.
    p.   cm.—(Series in political economy and economic
development in Latin America)
  Includes index.
  ISBN 0-8133-7424-3
  1. Cuba—Economic conditions—1959–   . 2. Cuba—Economic policy.
3. Cuba—Social policy. I. Zimbalist, Andrew S.   II. Series.
HC152.5.C818   1988
330.97291′064—dc19   87-22943
                                                                              CIP

Printed and bound in the United States of America

The paper used in this publication meets the requirements of the American National
Standard for Permanence of Paper for Printed Library Materials Z39.48-1984.

10   9   8   7   6   5   4   3   2   1

*With lots of love
to Lydia, Jeffrey, and Michael*

Contents

Tables

Preface

This book presents a broad critique of the mainstream scholarship in the United States on Cuban political economy. Mainstream Cubanology encompasses a wide range of theoretical approaches, methodological inclinations, intellectual backgrounds, and political preferences. It is as essential for the mainstream's critics to recognize this diversity as it is for the mainstream Cubanologists to recognize the same diversity among the critics. The contributors to the present collection are unified only by a common perception of inadequacy in the existing studies of Cuba's political economy.

Originally, I intended this book to include contributions from both the critics and the mainstream. The idea was stillborn, however, when Carmelo Mesa-Lago and Jorge Pérez-López, the two leading mainstream economists of Cubanology in the United States, turned down an invitation to participate. Lively discussions of the issues, I trust, will proceed nevertheless in other forums.

Many important and interesting topics related to Cuban political economy are not covered herein. For instance, a presently thriving controversy on human rights in Cuba receives little more than a few passing references in the chapters of this book. The Valladares book (*Against All Hope*), its problems notwithstanding, raised many vital issues. Much can still be learned about the treatment of political prisoners in Cuba.

Researching Cuba is no easy matter. The maze of hurdles one has to negotiate is well known to all who have tried to study post-1958 Cuba. Writing about Cuba, given the prevailing disinformation, ideological cascade, and emotional overlay, is also fraught with obstacles. One can scarcely run the gauntlet alone. I am indebted to too many friends, colleagues, and research assistants for their intellectual and emotional support to acknowledge here. I would, however, like to single out the following individuals: Lydia Nettler, Susan Eckstein, Carmen Diana Deere, Nola Reinhardt, Stuart Brown, Sinan Koont, Ophelia Yeung,

Gretchen Iorio, Lisa Genasci, Lisa Morris, Claes Brundenius, Arthur MacEwan, Roger Kaufman, Charles Staelin, Tom Riddell, Mieke Meurs, Marifeli Pérez-Stable, Ernesto Ortega, Fidel Vascós, José Luis Rodríguez, Jesus Molina, Miguel Figueras, Jean Stubbs, Juan Valdés Paz, Nestor Garcia, Juan Carlos Martínez Triana, Ariel Ricardo, and Armando Santiago. Finally, my deep gratitude goes to Jean and Harvey Picker for their personal encouragement, intellectual stimulation, and financial generosity.

Andrew Zimbalist

1

Cuban Political Economy and Cubanology: An Overview

Andrew Zimbalist

Mirroring the dynamism of Cuban political economy, scholarship on Cuba is in a period of debate and reformulation. Despite ongoing impediments, access to Cuban society has improved markedly in the 1980s. The consequent growth of an empirical base has facilitated a reexamination of existing interpretations of policy, performance, and structure.

Much of the extant literature is characterized by ideological dogmatism, from either end of the political spectrum, and gives a superficial and distorted view of Cuban reality. Given Cuba's geopolitical identity, few observers are able to regard Cuba dispassionately. The U.S. trade and travel blockade of Cuba and the research barriers confronted by the tenacious few who make it to the island further diminish the possibilities for penetrating and rigorous scholarship.[1]

The temporary thaw in U.S.-Cuban relations during the Carter administration resulted in unrestricted, though inconvenient, travel to Cuba for U.S. citizens. Many social scientists took advantage of the opportunity to explore the research terrain and make the requisite contacts to begin investigatory projects. At the same time, Cuban political institutions had stabilized, and the economy had developed sufficiently to allow the emergence of centers of academic research in Cuba. Further, from the early 1970s the Cuban economy entered a period of rapid growth, and authorities were obviously anxious that aspects of this economic success be appreciated and disseminated abroad. These auspicious conditions permitted many researchers to lay the groundwork for projects coming to fruition in the mid-1980s.

The mainstream interpretations of Carmelo Mesa-Lago, Jorge Pérez-López, Sergio Roca, Jorge Salazar-Carillo, Jorge Domínguez, Edward

1

Gonzalez, Cole Blasier, and other Cubanologists, previously unchallenged by serious research, have come under careful scrutiny from this new body of scholarship. This book brings together for the first time the work of various scholars who have participated in the reevaluation and critique of traditional Cubanology in the United States.

The underlying debates are encompassing, ranging from the use and understanding of statistics, to the conceptualization of political reality, to the dynamics of change and the interpretation of economic structure and performance. In the next section, I will summarize the state of our knowledge on the Cuban economy as it pertains to the most salient controversies.

Economic Structure and Performance

Economic Growth

Economic growth is probably the most common yardstick employed to assess economic performance. Thus it is not surprising that much of the debate on the Cuban economy has focused on this issue. In Chapter 3 in this book Claes Brundenius and Andrew Zimbalist point out many of the methodological and statistical questions that underlie this controversy, but they do not present their own estimates of Cuban growth.

From 1980 to 1985 real per capita gross domestic product (GDP) in Latin America fell at an average rate of 1.7 percent (for nineteen countries excluding Cuba), according to Economic Commission of Latin America (ECLA) calculations based on official government statistics.[2] In sharp contrast, again according to official statistics, constant price per capita gross social product (GSP) in Cuba grew at an average annual rate of 6.7 percent during the quinquennium.[3] If the official Cuban statistics could be accepted at face value, Cuban growth performance during the first half of the 1980s would be remarkable by Latin American standards.

Estimating Cuban growth or making it comparable to Western data, however, is not a simple matter. The largest problem resides in the Cuban system of national income accounting (referred to as the system of material balances or MPS), which is common to the countries of the Council for Mutual Economic Assistance (CMEA; the Soviet trading bloc) and quite different from the system used in the United States (referred to as the system of national accounts or SNA). MPS uses gross value of production instead of value added for several of its measurements of aggregate output, and it does not include the value of nonmaterial services (which account roughly for between 25 and 35 percent of national income). These methodological differences together with administered (as opposed to market) prices, the dubious meaning profits, changes in the Cuban accounting system over the years resulting in broken time series, and concerns over hidden inflation have created fertile ground for disagreement. These ambiguities notwithstanding, there are rigorous and acceptable procedures for estimating output growth in centrally planned economies provided that reasonable prices and weights are used.

Several Cubanologists have maintained that Cuban growth statistics are exaggerated because of hidden inflation. They point, in particular, to the wholesale and retail price reforms of 1981 as being more inflationary than officially acknowledged and argue that this bias engenders an overstatement of growth in the 1980s. Jorge Domínguez, for instance, in the September/October 1985 issue of *Problems of Communism*, asserted that "Cuba's statistical system has yet to generate credible data about the obviously economically troubled 1980–82 period, for which official figures unconvincingly suggest an economic boom."[4] One year later in the same journal a similar allegation appeared, this time authored by Jorge Pérez-López: "More important, there is reason to believe that a significant portion of the reported GSP growth in 1981–1985 may be attributable to inflation."[5] The "reason to believe" this, it turns out, is data about retail price increases for a limited sample of consumer goods. Among other problems here, this claim is a nonsequitur since Cuban national income measures are based on wholesale, not retail, prices. Wholesale and retail prices are separated by an extensive system of subsidies and turnover taxes and do not generally track each other very closely. The Cubans have published their own implicit GSP deflators based on a nearly complete sample of the one million plus goods produced in the country. Pérez-López provided no convincing argument to question these deflators.[6]

Elsewhere I have published an estimate of Cuban industrial growth based on constant prices and value-added branch weights over the period 1965–1984.[7] Although the procedure and data I used involved a net downward bias, the resulting estimate of a real average annual rate of growth of 6.3 percent suggests a very impressive performance. In light of the concerns about hidden inflation, it is important to underscore that since this estimate is based on constant 1981 prices it cannot be distorted by this factor. This estimate of 6.3 percent is below the official figure of 7.5 percent but considerably above the estimate of Pérez-López of 2.3 percent (for the period 1965–1982).[8]

In Chapter 3 of this book Brundenius and Zimbalist elucidate the improper methodology of the latter estimate. The difference between the official estimate and my estimate can be attributed largely to the restricted sample of industrial products included in the *Cuban Statistical*

Yearbook—a sample of some 200 commodities that has changed little since 1965 and hence significantly underrepresents the newest and most dynamic product groups in the Cuban economy. When this and other factors are controlled for, the inescapable conclusion emerges that there is little reason to distrust the presentation of output and growth data reported in Cuban official statistics. To be sure, if the national income statistics of other Latin American countries were subjected to the same scrutiny as Cuba's statistics have been, there is reason to suspect that the comparison would further enhance the credibility of Cuban statistics.

Cuba's industrial sector, of course, has grown more rapidly than the agricultural sector and the economy as a whole. Thus, overall national income growth has been slower than that suggested by the industrial figures.[9] Cubans have estimated the real average annual growth rate of the economy to be around 4.4 percent since 1959, though they acknowledge readily that data from the early years are incomplete. Although 4.4 percent strikes this writer as a bit optimistic, it does appear that the post-1959 growth record has been reputable overall and laudable since 1970. We shall discuss the sources of this growth in the following sections.

In light of this growth performance, it is ironic, though not unexpected, that U.S. press accounts, sustained by studies by Cubanologists, consistently denigrate the Cuban economy. A passing condemnation of Cuba's economy seems to have become almost obligatory, a litmus test of professionalism, for press stories about Cuba whether or not the piece deals explicitly with the economy. Thus, in a recent review of a biography of Castro in the *New York Times Book Review*, Susan Kaufman Purcell declared that Castro has presided over, no less, "the destruction of the Cuban economy."[10] And Stanley Hoffman, reviewing a different biography of Castro a month later in the same publication, passed a more moderate judgment: "The economy is in a wretched state."[11] As we shall see in the following sections and throughout this book, such assessments apply neither to Cuba's record of economic growth nor to other aspects of structure and performance.

Equity

The claim that Cuba has succeeded in achieving substantial economic growth along with distributional equity was first made rigorously by Brundenius.[12] As José Luis Rodríguez points out in Chapter 2, the claim has since been disputed by Mesa-Lago, Nicholas Eberstadt, and others.[13] The argument put forward by Eberstadt is that Cuba's accomplishments in the areas of education and health have been overstated and that when compared to the records for other countries in the Caribbean

Basin Cuba's record does not distinguish itself. To reach this assessment Eberstadt (1) misused Cuban statistics; (2) overlooked definitional and registration changes; (3) ignored questions of data reliability in other countries, and (4) selectively compared Cuba to those countries in the basin with the lowest infant mortality rates. In fact, given the diminutive size, colonial history, and the service orientation of these countries (e.g., Bermuda, Cayman Islands, Martinique, Guadeloupe), the comparison makes little sense. Eberstadt does not compare the Cuban record with that for any country in Latin America that has as much as one-third of Cuba's population; if he did so he would find that the Cuban health performance is unparalleled. In this regard it is interesting to note that the 1986 infant mortality rate in Cuba fell from 16.5 per 1,000 births to 13.6. In Chapter 6 Sarah Santana explores Cuban health statistics as well as Eberstadt's claims in considerable detail.

It is worth noting that Eberstadt's last piece was published in a special issue of *Caribbean Review* (15, no. 2, 1986) devoted to Cuba. Two other articles in that issue impugn Cuban statistics. In his article, Sergio Diaz-Briquets cited an interview by Sergio Roca of a Cuban exile living in Miami. The interviewee, an ex–public health worker, alleged that in one instance medical records were falsified to make it appear as if a dengue fever epidemic had been brought under control. The interviewee was promised anonymity by Roca, however, and cannot be held accountable for his extreme charge.

In the other article, Jorge Salazar-Carrillo argued that (1) the real Cuban economy is unknowable because of its indecipherable statistics and (2) Cuba's changes in statistical methodology reflect changes in Soviet dominance over the island. Ironically, from Salazar-Carrillo's discussion of indecipherable statistics, he appears to have at best a vague understanding of the MPS methodology: Many of his specific points are misleading; others are simply wrong. For instance, on page 25, he wrote: "The physical indicators reported in *Boletínes* and *Anuarios Estadísticos* represent value rather than volume indicators, the result of the inflationary process." Only 4 of the 206 products listed in the physical indicators are given in value terms. The rest are in physical terms—units, tons, cubic meters. The inflationary process has no effect whatsoever on these figures. The second contention regarding Soviet dominance is a powerful example of the extremes to which the Soviet-ization of Cuba thesis (analyzed in Chapter 8 by Frank T. Fitzgerald) can be carried.

Structural Change

For those analysts who have attempted to diminish Cuba's growth record, a standard corollary is that the Cuban economy has not diversified or industrialized and is still dependent. These arguments are analyzed by Brundenius and Zimbalist in Chapter 3. A few additional comments here, however, are in order.

Sugar has been dubbed the albatross of the pre-1959 Cuban economy. During the 1948–1958 period, sugar exports averaged 84.1 percent of total Cuban exports. Despite the beginnings of bagasse processing after 1956, forward and backward linkages to sugar production went largely undeveloped. Employment was seasonal, land use was wasteful, large profits were repatriated, and prices were volatile. Under these circumstances, sugar's ability to stimulate a broader economic development was nonexistent. Lack of diversification and dependency went hand in hand with underdevelopment and stagnation.

In a quantitative sense Cuba is certainly as dependent on the Soviet Union in the 1980s as it was on the United States in the 1950s. Dependency theory, however, whatever its limitations, is an effort at analytical explanation not just empirical description of the development process. It is impossible to conclude that the qualitative relationship of dependence on the Soviet Union is commensurate with that of the earlier dependence on the United States. Just as in a parent-child relationship dependency is to some degree unavoidable during early development and according to its nature can either nurture eventual strength and growing independence or lead to weakness and ongoing dependence.

Cuban dependence on the Soviet Union is not altogether benign, but its effects on Cuban development have been, on the whole, salutary. Terms of trade have been stable and favorable, technological transfer and training have been readily forthcoming, machine tool/heavy-industry production has been encouraged,[14] the nature of the sugar industry and its market has been transformed, spin-off industries have been promoted, and profit repatriation has ceased. These issues are addressed in greater detail by Fitzgerald in Chapter 8.

The main point is that a simple number like the share of sugar in total exports does not have the same implications for Cuban development today as it did thirty years ago. Depending on world market conditions, Cuba still sells between 10 and 40 percent of its sugar on the volatile world market, but the CMEA market provides a soft and reliable cushion. Sugar has also been the basis for significant forward and backward linkages since 1959, and harvest mechanization, production integration, and labor force reorganization have eliminated the noxious social and economic effects of seasonal *zafra* labor. Still the argument could be persuasively made, in my opinion, that given prospects for world sugar demand, Cuba is putting too many eggs in the cane basket.

Although Cuba continues to invest in expanding production and milling capacity, investments in other, nontraditional export products

TABLE 1.1
Share of Sugar in Total Exports (%)

1979	1980	1981	1982	1983	1984	1985
85.9	83.7	79.1	77.2	74.0	75.5	74.5

Note: Data are calculated from figures in Comité Estatal de Estadísticas, Anuario Estadistico de Cuba, various years.

have allowed for a significant diversification of Cuba's exports in recent years. Table 1.1 shows the downward trend for the share of sugar in total Cuban exports since 1979. As Pérez-López pointed out, several percentage points of this decreasing share are attributable to Cuban reexports of Soviet oil.[15] These reexports are made possible by an agreement with the Soviet Union that any petroleum shipments specified in the five-year trade protocol agreement that Cuba does not consume, because of energy conservation measures, may be exported by Cuba. Further supporting these exports has been a very rapid expansion in Cuban domestic petroleum output, which more than tripled between 1981 and 1985. Pérez-López, however, overstated the importance of oil reexports by almost two percentage points (and hence understated the decrease in the sugar share) by assuming that certain petroleum by-products exported by Cuba were from the Soviet Union, when, in fact, they were produced in Cuba.

More important, to qualify the sugar shares in order to gauge the true extent of production diversification, it is necessary to express the value of sugar and other exports in constant prices. That is, one would have to adjust for the manifold increase in sugar prices paid by the Soviet Union after the mid-1970s. If this were done, the diversification of the productive base for exports would be more extensive than suggested in the nominal sugar share. It should also be mentioned that one significant impediment to further diversification since 1980 has been the tightening of the U.S. blockade under President Ronald Reagan. Among other measures, the U.S. Commerce Department has prohibited the importation of steel and other products containing Cuban nickel from third countries. The Third World debt crisis and growing protectionism have also limited Cuban markets.

One very revealing indication of Cuba's success at diversification can be seen by comparing Cuba's efforts at increasing nontraditional exports with those of other nations in the Caribbean Basin—nations that have benefited from specialized tariff treatment and preferences by the United

TABLE 1.2
Annual Growth Rate of Nontraditional Exports,
1981-1985

Country	Growth Rate (%)
Cuba	39.3
Costa Rica	9.9
Guatemala	-5.4
Honduras	-6.1
Panama	5.1
Dominican Republic	7.9
Jamaica	5.6

Note: Data are from Banco Nacional de Cuba,
Informe Económico, March 1986, p. 10, and
from SRI International, Nontraditional Export
Expansion in the Central American Region.
Report prepared for the Agency for International Development, Arlington, Va., January
1987.

States under the General System of Preferences and Caribbean Basin Initiative (see Table 1.2).

The Cuban growth of nontraditional exports from 47.0 million pesos in 1981 to 177.0 million pesos in 1985 constituted an average annual growth rate of 39.3 percent, more than four times the growth rate of Costa Rica, the next best performer in the group.[16] These Cuban data include only merchandise exports and hence do not reflect the rapid growth in tourism and tourist services in recent years. Tourism revenues in 1985, for instance, grew by 33 percent. Nor do the data register the sizable service exports in the form of construction, educational, and medical personnel to other Third World countries that are discussed in Chapter 9 by Susan Eckstein. Finally, evidence from the first three-quarters of 1986 suggests continued growth in the nontraditional export category.[17]

Finally, the claim of Mesa-Lago's that Cuba's industrial share has actually declined while the commercial share has grown is a product of his incomplete understanding of Cuban national income accounting. This polemic is discussed fully in Chapter 3.

Soviet Aid

Those Cubanologists who have recognized Cuban accomplishments in the field of either social services or economic growth are quick to attribute these gains to massive doses of Soviet aid. Implicit in this doctrine is the idea that dependence on the Soviet Union has a different economic impact than previous dependence on the United States, although this is never made explicit. In fact, Soviet economic aid is enormous and the Cuban economy would scarcely be what it is without it. Yet several caveats must be made. First, as we shall demonstrate, the magnitude of this aid is vastly overstated by false methodology. Second, even if the exaggerated aid figures were accepted, on a per capita basis Cuba would still be getting less in CMEA aid than many other Latin America economies receive in Western aid. Third, if one is attempting to disentangle the sources of Cuban growth and to isolate its domestic and foreign components, it is hardly sufficient to consider only the beneficial effects of Soviet aid. One must also consider the monumental and ongoing costs to Cuba of the U.S. blockade. In 1982 the Cubans estimated these cumulative costs to be approaching $10 billion.[18]

Cubanologists have relied upon the Soviet aid estimates provided by the Central Intelligence Agency (CIA). The CIA estimates include not only direct balance of payments and project aid, but also price subsidies for sugar, nickel, petroleum, and other products. The sugar price subsidy is by far the largest component of Soviet aid in the CIA reckoning (e.g., 68.3 percent of total aid in 1983).[19] To estimate this subsidy the CIA (1) uses the official peso/dollar exchange rate (widely recognized to overvalue the peso), (2) ignores the tied nature of the aid (payments are overwhelmingly in ruble credits usable only for inferior Soviet goods), and (3) assumes the aid to be the difference between the converted dollar price paid by the Soviets and the free market price. Steps (1) and (2) have no economic justification and engender a significant upward bias. Step (3) is arbitrary and betrays either a political bias or a miscomprehension of world sugar trade.

Only roughly 14 percent of world sugar is sold at free market prices; the rest is sold under preferential agreements generally at above world market prices.[20] The free market price is thus not a true scarcity price because the subsidized prices of preferential trade cause the quantity of sugar supply to be higher and the quantity of sugar demand to be lower than would prevail under true market conditions. The world market price is, therefore, lower than the true scarcity price of sugar and cannot be employed properly as the opportunity cost (the price at which Cuba would have to sell its sugar if it did not have a preferential agreement with the Soviet Union) to calculate Soviet subsidies. Some have suggested that an appropriate alternative price might be the preferential U.S. market price, at which Cuba used to sell the vast bulk of its sugar exports prior to the U.S. embargo.[21] In mid-February 1987 the world market price is approximately $.075 per pound, in contrast to the U.S. preferential price of around $.21, the EEC preferential price of near $.20, and the Soviet price of approximately 30 centavos a pound for raw sugar.[22]

If the Soviet price is converted at the official (February 1987) exchange rate of 1 peso equals $1.25, then it becomes $.375, and when compared to the world price it constitutes a subsidy per pound, as computed by the CIA, of $.30. If the opportunity cost were taken to be the U.S. or European market, the subsidy would fall to around $.17 per pound using the official exchange rate. However, given Cuba's chronic current account deficit it seems that the Cuban peso is significantly overvalued at the official fixed rate, so even $.17 a pound would be too high an estimate. Further, given that the payment is in ruble credits, Cuba is tied to buying lower quality and possibly overpriced Soviet goods, lessening the real value of the subsidy further. To be sure, in all but three years between 1960 and 1974 the U.S. preferential price was above the Soviet price, implying a reverse subsidy until the mid-1970s. One author has estimated that Cuban sugar revenue would have been $800 million higher over this period had Cuba been trading with the United States instead of the Soviet Union.[23]

In his new book, Jorge Domínguez recognized the problems with the CIA estimates and made his own using the price Cuba receives for its sugar from Spain, Canada, and Japan as the opportunity cost.[24] Domínguez's method improved little on that of the CIA, however, because Canada and Japan, and Spain since 1979, have bought Cuban sugar at the residual world market, not preferential, prices. Hence, it is not surprising that Domínguez produced estimates similar to those of the CIA. In the end, there is no hard evidence whatsoever to support the claim that Cuba's economic and social accomplishments are entirely attributable to Soviet aid.

The Cuban Economy 1986–1990

After five years of strong economic growth, 1986 brought slow growth (under 2 percent in real terms), a temporary suspension of interest payments on foreign debt, restrictions on private sector activities spawned during the 1976–1985 liberalization period, and a package of new austerity measures. The year 1986 also saw continuous and intense discussions of economic policy and orientation, kicked off at the first sessions of the Third Party Congress in February, carried on at a variety of local, provincial, and national enterprise meetings, and culminating at the final sessions of the party congress in early December.

The discussions were open, candid, and critical. At times, leadership characterizations seemed to invoke a sense of economic and political crisis. At least many Cubanologists were quick to suggest and promote this interpretation. Along with this view came notions of cataclysm—

repudiation of the post-1976 planning system, abolition of material bonuses, return to the "Sino-Guevarism" of the 1960s, extreme recentralization, and so on.

The Cuban economy, like that of most Latin American countries, has been hard hit by conditions of the international economy and is passing through a very difficult period. This circumstance has made improvements in domestic efficiency more imperative and has accordingly provoked the current phase of self-examination. Yet the notion of crisis and cataclysm, following from Cubanologists' faulty conceptions and understanding, is fundamentally misleading.

Low sugar prices, plummeting petroleum prices, devastation from Hurricane Kate, several consecutive years of intensifying drought, drastic dollar devaluation, the tightening U.S. blockade, growing protectionism in Western markets—all combined in 1986 to reduce Cuba's hard currency earnings by nearly 50 percent, or $600 million. Cuba's failure at the summer 1986 Paris Club negotiations to obtain a new $300 million loan led to severe shortages of needed imported inputs. The ensuing shortages of outputs greatly diminished the possibilities for material incentives to function properly. This fact provides the objective backdrop to the subjective reexamination of the use of material and moral incentives.

Internally, the Cuban economy began to experience many of the same problems that have appeared in other centrally planned economies during periods of liberalization. Whatever might be its advantages, the torpidity and inefficiencies of central planning create an imperative to decentralize. The central state apparatus simply cannot plan and control effectively an entire economy. As this is realized and pragmatism dictates that local and private initiative be encouraged, a new set of problems appear. With opportunities for profit, state sector workers divert their energies to new activities. Lower work effort and higher absenteeism can result. Workers with access to resources from their state jobs are prompted to misuse them (e.g., using trucks to transport farm produce to peasant markets instead of making state deliveries, or pilfering building materials). Enterprises find new shortcuts to meet their profitability targets by violating or abusing pricing regulations. The majority of the workforce that spurns such behavior grow resentful, likely affecting the productivity of some.

Diverted resources compound the scarcity of imported inputs forcing many production lines to shut down temporarily. Affected workers (known as *interruptos*) are laid off at 70 percent salary until production is resumed, but this is costly and entails paying workers who produce nothing. That is, demand is created without supply and shortages are aggravated.

This dynamic began to take hold in Cuba during 1986, and the leadership acted to curb it. On one hand, some reimposition of central controls was necessary to deal with the severe shortages of foreign exchange. Limitations of private activities and the new austerity measures were directed, in part, at resolving this macroeconomic imbalance. On the other hand, the spirit of profiteering and the emergence of substantial inequities were undermining the balance between material and moral incentives. For a number of nonideological reasons (discussed in Chapters 4 and 8), the effectiveness of material incentives is constrained in socialist economies. Of course, if material incentives become dominant then ideological concern is also an issue.

The measures adopted in 1986 to limit private activities and redress the imbalance of incentives were based both in pragmatism and in philosophy. Taken together they denote a moratorium on the liberalization trend as well as a correction of excesses, similar to the Hungarian measures of 1972. They do not denote a reversal of direction, nor an espousal of Sino-Guevarism, nor a repudiation of the SDPE and material incentives.

Consider the following Cubanologist claims regarding the fate of the System of Economic Management and Planning (SDPE): "Thus, the economy overall will be impacted by the disorganization, paralysis and slowdown of the productive process caused by the reimposition of a highly ideological, centralized command socialized economy. . . . By now, the SDPE is under complete revision."[25] Or, the assertion by Jorge Pérez-López that the SDPE represented market socialism and that the "reinstitution of the microbrigades to work on housing construction was another assault of the principles of the SDPE."[26]

Indeed, if one views the SDPE as based on a market socialist model, then what Cuba has today is a repudiation of it. The problem, of course, is that the SDPE is a Liberman reform-type model that fully preserves central planning.[27] It is not by any stretch of the imagination a market socialist type model à la Lange or anyone else. It does not approach the market socialism of Yugoslavia nor even the intermediate form of plan/market socialism practiced in Hungary. The microbrigades were alive and well during the early years of the SDPE and are being reemphasized again because of shortcomings in the prevailing private contracting system.

The notion of centralization is partially accurate but really misses the point.[28] There is centralization in the sense that more activities are being brought back into the public sphere. There is also centralization with regard to control over resources linked to foreign exchange expenditures. There is, however, an ongoing effort at decentralization within the planning system. Direct contracting between enterprises for many inputs is being promoted, enterprise reports to their ministries are being cut back, the number of administrative personnel in the planning system is being reduced, enterprise self-financing of investment is being extended, worker participation in management and plan formulation is more extensive than before,[29] the decentralization of enterprise management into smaller units (brigades) with greater worker control is being universalized in agriculture and extended in industry, and the role of parallel markets where prices are set according to conditions of supply and demand is growing at an accelerated pace.

One of the more significant measures of 1986 was the May 19 decision to make the free peasant markets, which began in 1980, illegal. These markets had grown to fill an important niche in the provision of the population's food. In 1985, peasant market sales accounted in value terms for over 5 percent of food sales to the population, but according to official figures this share had been falling for three years. Price gouging and resource diversion, however, were generating sharp inequalities and resentment. Some truck drivers and private farmers, for instance, were earning over 100,000 pesos a year, whereas the country's top surgeons were paid 5,000 pesos. With potential incomes like these, the movement to cooperatize the private sector was being undermined. The state resolved to keep the same physical markets in place but to handle the distribution of food through the state supply network instead of private agents. This represented an enormous organizational problem. Among other changes, it meant distributing food with fewer vehicles because the illegal use of trucks for this purpose was being eliminated. After growing by 14 percent in 1985, parallel market sales grew by 42.8 million pesos during the first nine months of 1986.[30] Although there were problems in maintaining the supply of certain food items and inconveniences were reported, it does not appear that the dislocations that many predicted were forthcoming. To be sure, one of the most negative sources of anti-Cuban propaganda reported in fall 1986: "The effect of the elimination of the farmers' free market will not be felt until after December 15."[31] Though no evidence is available indicating that such a problem did in fact develop after mid-December, this quote suggests that prior to this time there were no serious effects.

Another argument that has surfaced in connection with the centralization thesis is that Cuba is moving in an antagonistic direction to that of the reforms instigated by Mikhail Gorbachev in the Soviet Union.[32] The latter stand for decentralization measures for the economy and *glasnost* (or opening) for the political sphere. Notwithstanding the immensity of the propaganda effort surrounding Armando Valladares's book on human rights in Cuba,[33] the balance of political currents in Cuba also seems to be tipped toward opening. Several dozen political prisoners were released last year in Cuba, and the media have devoted far more attention to in-depth, critical reporting than in the past. In Chapters 10 and 11 of the book Bengelsdorf and Valdés address the Cuban political process more fully. In the economic sphere it is interesting to note that the Cubans see the Gorbachev changes as following the Cuban approach to economic management. In particular, the Economist's Intelligence Unit report recently observed: "The Vice President, Carlos Rafael Rodríguez, in Bucharest for a closed session of Comecon representatives, recently drew specific attention to what he called the mood of imaginativeness and flexibility now abroad among the Moscow allies, with which he associated the Cuban process."[34] This comment is consistent with the ongoing Cuban efforts since 1976 to modify its planning system to make it more compatible with Cuban political culture. (The fact that Cuba no longer has free peasant markets while they exist in the Soviet Union and elsewhere in Eastern Europe has to be judged in relation to the size of private plots in the various countries. In the USSR private plots do not exceed a hectare whereas in Cuba the private farmer typically owns between 20 and 60 hectares.)

Changes in Cuba's incentive system have also been the subject of erroneous judgments by Cubanologists. Pérez-López, for example, claimed that Cuba had suspended worker productivity bonuses.[35] Actually, three forms of productivity-related bonuses are used in Cuba (normas, premios and primas), and none of them has been suspended. In the case of primas, however, certain types that duplicated other incentives, especially those related to export production, have been curtailed. Cuba's leadership has stated repeatedly that it is retaining material incentives. Its problem is that the incentive system developed many irrationalities and abuses. Thus, for instance, some radio announcers were working on piece rates, some mechanics in a maintenance factory were paid five times for repairing the same machine, and other workers were paid overtime bonuses and piece bonuses for the same work.[36] Overall, by the end of 1985 work norms had been set for 1.2 million workers with their pay tied to output. Most of these norms were several years old and not set according to technical standards. Four hundred thousand workers produced over 130 percent of their norms. There is a vital need to update and reform this system.

At the same time, Castro recognized the limits of material incentives under conditions of slow growth, full employment, and underdevelopment. Effective material incentives generally imply unemployment and substantial inequality, which in Cuba would mean accepting poverty and the lack of basic need fulfillment. Cuba is not willing to accept these consequences. It is clear that Cuba's commitment to egalitarian norms is not waning. Most of the December 1986 austerity measures bite hardest on the upper income groups. Some measures, such as doubling fares on public transportation (to 10 centavos), are supplemented by subsidies for retired people and students. The minimum wage has been increased from 85 pesos to 100 pesos per month, effective February 1, 1987.

Finally, the motivation issue is all the more pressing in 1986–1987 because Cuba's young workers today are a new generation. They did not experience the revolutionary struggle or the early romantic years of the Revolution. Castro's current exhortations about moral incentives, political consciousness, and socialist values are especially directed at these workers who entered the labor force at a time when material incentives were ascendent, if not dominant, and abuses were rampant. Yet, in every speech where the excesses of material incentives are criticized or the deficiencies of the SDPE are analyzed, the leadership has also made it clear that neither are being jettisoned. Thus, the comparisons made by Pérez-López, Domínguez, and others[37] between the present period and the 1960s—when there was budgetary financing, no unified central plan, no national budget and little record keeping, no individual bonuses, and no overtime pay—are misleading.

It only remains to point out that the present "rectification" campaign seems to be bearing fruit. Speeches and press accounts are increasingly referring to enterprises that have turned their productivity performance around, and recent aggregate productivity statistics are more encouraging. To be sure, although some improvements in work organization at the micro level may lead to modest productivity gains, the overall macro context in Cuba (resulting largely from the foreign exchange situation) remains difficult and prospects for healthy growth in the near future are dim.

Plan of the Book

The chapters contained in this book offer not only an antidotal polemic to existing currents in Cubanology but also a new framework for analyzing Cuban political economy. Chapter 1 is written by a leading Cuban economist, José Luis Rodríguez, who has been prominent in Cuban circles as a leading critic of U.S. Cubanology. In this chapter, the first of two by him in this collection, Rodríguez presents a Cuban perspective on the evolution of Cubanology in the United States and how it has reflected shifting political winds in this country.

This is followed by the Brundenius/Zimbalist chapter on Cuban economic performance. This chapter is a condensed version of the three-part debate with Mesa-Lago and Pérez-López that took place in *Com-*

parative Economic Studies in the spring, fall, and winter 1985 issues. It elaborates upon many of the themes invoked in Chapter 1. In Chapter 4 Zimbalist critiques several recent Cubanologist treatments of Cuban central planning. After offering a general interpretation of the experience of centrally planned economies, he attempts to show how Cubanologist writings on the subject lie outside of this context and, consequently, misconstrue the nature and dynamics of the Cuban planning problematic. This conceptual shortcoming is compounded, in the case of one author, by untenable methodology.

Chapters 5 and 6 deal with disputes about Cuban achievements in the area of basic needs and social services. Rodríguez argues that Cubanologists have overlooked the integral concept of development applied in Cuba since 1959, stressing simultaneous social and economic development. He also refutes the misinterpretation of statistics in several studies. The question of Cuban health statistics—their methodology, reliability, availability, and interpretation—is treated in the piece by Sarah Santana, an investigator from the School of Public Health at Columbia University who has spent much of the last two years on a university project at the statistical office of the Cuban Health Ministry (Minsap).

In Chapter 7 on interpreting the role of women in Cuban society Carollee Bengelsdorf explores the confrontation of the ideological commitment to gender equality and the Latin *machista* heritage. The outcome is more complex than suggested by existing analyses. Bengelsdorf identifies steady progress for women in the social, economic, and political spheres, but these gains are often less than they appear to be and certainly fall far short of equality.

In Chapter 8 Frank Fitzgerald explores three dimensions of the Sovietization of Cuba hypothesis: internal economic structure, external economic relations, and foreign policy. Fitzgerald argues that the claim of Soviet control over these aspects of Cuban society is oversimplifying and misleading. Susan Eckstein's Chapter 9 on Cuban foreign policy and economic assistance picks up where Fitzgerald stops, detailing several instances of independent Cuban international policymaking. Further, Eckstein argues that Cuba's extensive foreign economic assistance program can only be understood when one considers the weakness, as opposed to the strength and hegemony, of the Soviet bloc.

In Chapter 10 Nelson Valdés discusses some of the dominant premises, assumptions, and conclusions found in the U.S. literature on Cuban foreign policy and its national political system. He suggests that scholars should pay more attention to implicit paradigms, conceptual clarity, methodology, and the rules of evidence. Valdés exemplifies his points by reference to works concentrating on Fidel Castro and elite theory.

In her second contribution, Chapter 11, Bengelsdorf criticizes the analytical categories and conceptualizations of Cubanologist interpreters of Cuba's political reality. She maintains that the arguments of the "modernization theorists," "Havana watchers," "Sovietization and elite theorists" are without empirical basis and are often inconsistent and unhelpful in portraying the dynamics of change in Cuban society. Bengelsdorf grounds her discussion in the Cuban experience with Popular Power[38] and institutionalization.

As a group the authors in this book argue for reframing the analysis of Cuba's political economy. Existing interpretations not only distort the record but, by insisting on synchronic, simplified portrayals, provide little basis for comprehending the underlying dynamics of Cuban society. Regardless of its goals, to be effective U.S. policy toward Cuba must be founded on an accurate understanding of the Cuban system. In this regard, Cubanology has been an impediment to the formulation of rational and constructive U.S. policy toward the island. This collection will alert readers to the deeper complexities of Cuban society and, if successful, stimulate more thoughtful, balanced, and critical scholarship.

Notes

1. A very interesting discussion of the frustrations of doing research on Cuba is provided by Linda Fuller (1986).

2. CEPAL (1985), p. 8; *Latin American Weekly Report*, January 3, 1986, p. 8. ECLA or CEPAL is the Economic Commission for Latin America of the United Nations.

3. Cuban national income or net material product (which is based on value added and in theory eliminates double counting) grew even more rapidly according to official statistics, at 7.9 percent per capita per annum during 1980–1985. See the *Anuario Estadístico de Cuba,* 1984 and 1985.

4. Domínguez (1985:7).

5. Pérez-López (1986:18).

6. Pérez-López attempted to further impugn Cuban debt statistics. First he cited an August 1982 Central Bank study that reported a June 1982 foreign hard currency debt of $2.9 billion. Then he cited a February 1985 study that reported a 1982 debt of $2.7 billion. He then concluded that these divergent figures "bring into question the reliability of Cuban data" (ibid.:23). It is hard to take such commentary seriously. The figures could differ for a host of legitimate reasons: They might refer to different times in 1982; the later figure could be a revision; the dollar value could vary with changes in the exchange rate; the counting of trade credits could differ; the level of foreign deposits could have changed. Anyone familiar with Central Bank statistics on foreign debt in other Latin American countries would, if anything, comment on the consistency of these two figures, which are given thirty months apart.

7. Zimbalist (1987).

8. Pérez-López (1986a).

9. Estimating national income growth is a tricky matter indeed. This is elaborated upon in Brundenius (1984) and Brundenius and Zimbalist, forthcoming. A new estimate is proffered in the latter.

10. Purcell (1986:24).

11. Hoffman (1986:11).

12. Brundenius (1984).

13. Mesa-Lago (1986) and Eberstadt (1985 and 1986).

14. See the paper by Brundenius (1987) on the growth of the Cuban capital goods industry and the extension of this argument in Brundenius and Zimbalist, forthcoming.

15. Pérez-López (1986b:22). Also see Pérez-López (1986c).

16. The Cuban data are from the Banco Nacional de Cuba, *Informe Económico*, March 1986, p. 10. They do not include reexports. The data from the other countries come from their trade statistics, as reported in SRI International (1987).

17. Banco Nacional de Cuba, *Cuba: Quarterly Economic Report*, September 1986, p. 5; also see, Economist's Intelligence Unit, *Country Report* on Cuba, no. 4, 1986, p. 14. Nontraditional exports are projected to reach one billion pesos by 1990.

18. Banco Nacional, *Informe Económico*, 1982. Since no methodology is provided, this figure is cited only as illustrative of the magnitudes involved. In addition to curtailing imports from third countries of products containing Cuban raw materials, the Reagan administration has banned tourist travel to Cuba, illegalized dollar remittances to the island from the United States, instituted hefty dollar charges for visas, and forbade U.S. companies to trade with Panamanian companies having Cuban ties. See the Economist's Intelligence Unit, *Country Report* on Cuba, no. 4, 1986, pp. 12–13, for more details.

19. CIA (1984:40).

20. See Fry (1985:20).

21. Zimbalist (1982); Radell (1983).

22. The Soviet price has varied between roughly 22 and 39 centavos per pound over the last ten years. There have been several reports that the 1986–1990 trade protocol agreement with the Soviet Union calls for a 7 percent reduction in the average sugar price. See, for example, Economist's Intelligence Unit (1986), Staff of Radio José Martí (1986). Castro, speaking at the Third Party Congress on November 30, 1986, also alluded to the Soviet price as falling and below 30 centavos per pound. See *Granma Weekly Review*, December 14, 1987, pt. 2, p. 4.

23. Smith (1984:373).

24. Domínguez (1987).

25. Staff of Radio José Martí (1986, vol. 3, no. 3, sec. III, p. 13; sec. V, p. 4).

26. Pérez-López (1986b:34).

27. "Liberman reform-type" refers to the 1965 economic reforms in the Soviet Union that sought to put enterprises on a self-financing basis but did little to

alter the fundamental structure or performance of central planning. Today Gorbachev refers to that experience as piecemeal and abortive reform.

28. The prominent Cubanologist Jorge Domínguez (1986) also argued that the present changes represent recentralization and the reassertion of personalism. Among other curiosities, Domínguez asserted that Osmani Cienfuegos is the "new top official for the economy" (p. 210). In the absence of concrete evidence to the contrary, the top official is normally taken to be the head of Juceplan (the central planning board), José López Moreno. As head of the *Grupo Central,* Cienfuegos is indeed a key figure, but so are many others associated with the Council of Ministers and the new commission studying the SDPE.

29. See the commentary by Juceplan president, José López Moreno, in the *Granma Weekly Review,* January 11, 1987, p. 2.

30. These data are from the Banco Nacional's *Quarterly Economic Report,* March 1986, p. 6, and September, p. 7.

31. Staff of Radio José Martí (1986, vol. 3, no. 3, sec. III, p. ii).

32. This view has been presented, for instance, by Flora Lewis (1987).

33. Valladares (1986). This effort and the contents of the book itself are subjected to a careful and interesting analysis in a special issue of *Cuba Update* 7, nos. 3–4 (fall 1986).

34. Economist's Intelligence Unit (1986: no. 4, p. 10).

35. Pérez-López (1986b:16).

36. These abuses are discussed at length at the *Reuniones de Empresas* during late June and early July 1986, which were reported on at length in editions of *Granma* of that period.

37. See, for instance, Pérez-López (1986b:34), Domínguez (1986:121), Treaster (1987:28).

38. Briefly, Popular Power (Poder Popular) is the building block of Cuba's post-1976 formal political system. Although no organized opposition to the Communist party is allowed, local elections for seats in the municipal assemblies are contested. The provincial and national assemblies of Popular Power are generated largely from the municipal assemblies.

References

Banco Nacional de Cuba. *Cuba: Quarterly Economic Report.* Various issues, 1985 and 1986.

———. *Informe Económico.* 1982 through 1986, yearly.

Brundenius, Claes. *Revolutionary Cuba: The Challenge of Economic Growth with Equity.* Boulder: Westview Press, 1984.

———. "The Cuban Capital Goods Industry." *World Development.* January 1987.

——— and Andrew Zimbalist. *Essays on the Cuban Economy: Structure and Performance,* forthcoming.

Central Intelligence Agency (CIA). *The Cuban Economy: A Statistical Review.* Washington, D.C.: Government Printing Office, June 1984.

CEPAL. *Revista de la Cepal* 25 (April 1985).

Comité Estatal de Estadísticas. *Anuario Estadístico de Cuba.* 1984 and 1985.

Diaz-Briquets, Sergio. "How to Figure Out Cuba: Development, Ideology and Mortality." *Caribbean Review* 15, no. 2 (1986).

Domínguez, Jorge. "Cuba: Charismatic Communism." *Problems of Communism* (September-October 1985).

————. "Cuba in the 1980s." *Foreign Affairs* (fall 1986).

————. *To Make a World Safe for Revolution.* Cambridge: Harvard University Press, 1987.

Eberstadt, Nicholas. "Literacy and Health: The Cuban Model." *Wall Street Journal,* December 10, 1984.

————. "Did Fidel Fudge the Figures? Literacy and Health." *Caribbean Review* 15, no. 2 (1986).

Economist's Intelligence Unit. *Country Report: Cuba, D.R., Haiti and Puerto Rico,* nos. 1–4, 1986.

Fry, James. *Sugar: Aspects of a Complex Commodity Market.* World Bank Working Paper no. 19815-1. Washington, D.C.: 1985.

Fuller, Linda. "Fieldwork in Forbidden Terrain." Unpublished manuscript, 1986.

Hoffman, Stanley. "Power Unshared and Total." *New York Times Book Review,* November 30, 1986, p. 11.

Latin American Weekly Report. January 3, 1986.

Lewis, Flora. "Reverse Gear in Cuba." *New York Times,* February 23, 1987, p. A19.

Mesa-Lago, Carmelo. "Cuba's Centrally Planned Economy: An Equity Trade-off for Growth." In J. Hartlyn and S. Morley, eds., *Latin American Political Economy: Financial Crisis and Political Change.* Boulder: Westview Press, 1986.

Pérez-López, Jorge. "Real Economic Growth in Cuba, 1965–1982." *Journal of Developing Areas* 20 (January 1986a):151–172.

————. "Cuban Economy in the 1980s." *Problems of Communism* (September-October 1986b).

————."Sugar and the Cuban Economy: A Survey of the Literature." Unpublished manuscript, December 1986c.

Purcell, Susan Kaufman. "Was Communism an Afterthought." *New York Times Book Review,* October 19, 1986, p. 24.

Radell, Willard. "Cuban-Soviet Sugar Trade, 1960–1976." *Journal of Developing Areas* 17 (April 1983):365–382.

Salazar-Carrillo, Jorge. "Is the Cuban Economy Knowable?" *Caribbean Review* 15, no. 2, 1986.

Smith, John T. "Sugar Dependency in Cuba: Capitalism versus Socialism." In M. Seligson, ed., *The Gap Between the Rich and the Poor.* Boulder: Westview Press, 1984.

SRI International. *Nontraditional Export Expansion in the Central American Region.* Report prepared for the Agency for International Development. Arlington, Va.: January 1987.

Staff of Radio José Martí, Office of Research and Policy. *Cuba: Quarterly Situation Report* 2, nos. 1–3, 1986.

Treaster, Joseph. "Castro Recoils at a Hint of Wealth," *New York Times,* February 8, 1987, p. III-1.

Valladares, Armando. *Against All Hope*. New York: Knopf, 1986.
Zimbalist, Andrew. "Soviet Aid, U.S. Blockade and the Cuban Economy." *Comparative Economic Studies* 24 (winter 1982):137–147.
———. "Cuban Industrial Growth, 1965–84." *World Development*, January 1987.

2

The Antecedents and Theoretical Characteristics of Cubanology

José Luis Rodríguez

In the twenty-five years since the triumph of the Cuban revolution, the United States has not deviated once from its policy of undermining Cuba in all areas and by all means at its disposal. After an initial period when it seemed that the Revolution could be easily destroyed, the U.S. government began an increasingly significant and influential confrontation with Cuba on ideological and political levels.

In reality, the offensive initiated during those years has complemented the global anticommunist strategy undertaken by the United States and its allies around the world. The tactics they have employed have ranged from the most generalized means of diffusion to the most elaborate, refined theories developed in the resrictive atmospheres of academic communities and international universities.

Notwithstanding, in recent years such academic arguments have gained increasing strength in the Reagan administration's anticommunist crusade. The administration's policy objectives were made clear in the report issued by the Santa Fe Committee in May 1980.[1] Nevertheless, the origins of the most recent studies and correct interpretations of the Cuban Revolution can be traced to a school that developed in the 1960s, which it becomes indispensable to discuss.

Studies of Cuba Conducted in the United States up to the End of the 1960s[2]

It is evident that the triumph of the Revolution produced a significant change in U.S. studies of Cuba. Before 1959, investigations of Cuba possessed an exceptional character as part of the more general context of U.S. studies of Latin America. This does not mean that under certain circumstances studies were not conducted that revealed, at the time of their completion, a sufficiently comprehensive understanding of the problems affecting Cuban society at that moment.

Such was the case of the investigation entrusted to the Foreign Policy Association by the Cuban government in 1934 and published under the title of "Problems in the New Cuba."[3] This report offered a diagnosis of the convulsive situation Cuban society found itself in then and recommended certain reforms that would supposedly allow the government to avoid the repetition of revolutionary outbreaks in the country. At that time the neocolonial mechanisms of domination were adjusted as part of the New Deal policies instituted by the U.S. government.

On another occasion, an even more extensive study of the Cuban economy, known as the Truslow Report conducted by the World Bank in 1950, arrived at the same conclusions.[4] Throughout the prerevolutionary period there were as well a variety of individual studies on Cuban society.[5]

Beginning in 1959, the situation changed completely. When conditions in Cuban society led U.S. officials to question whether national security interests were being threatened, the need for a precise understanding of the Cuban scenario began to be felt. Nevertheless, the speed at which U.S.-Cuban confrontations developed coupled with the U.S. government's conviction that the conflicts could be quickly resolved in its favor greatly contributed to the fact that between 1959 and 1961 no academic studies of Cuba were undertaken with official support.[6]

The victory at Playa Girón caused this attitude to change. In 1961 the Pentagon had entrusted the Rand Corporation with the first officially endorsed academic investigations of Cuba.[7] Around the same time, similar studies were commissioned from the Special Operations Research Office of American University.[8]

Here, an important qualitative change may be appreciated. Once the Cuban Revolution had passed through the stage where its short-term failure had seemed possible it became the subject of prioritized study for the U.S government. In effect, midway through the 1960s, a center for Cuban studies at the CIA was formed, and in 1964 the Center for Latin American Studies at the University of Pittsburgh was founded and financed under the National Defense Education Act by the Ford Foundation and the U.S. government, among other sponsors. The center was to play an important role in the study of Cuba. At that time the center's studies had two basic objectives: the compilation of information on Cuba for the planning of future actions against the Revolution and the structuring of an expository and interpretative base argument of the phenomenon of the Cuban Revolution, with the goal of projecting a hostile depiction to the rest of the world.

In relation to this second aspect, it is important to make a few conceptual points. Propaganda techniques depend on the utilization of strategies that attempt to achieve certain individual or collective levels of consciousness and behavior. However, to attain such objectives, propaganda requires a level of information and analysis that only academic studies are able to supply.[9] Naturally, academic studies may also fulfill a specialized propagandistic function.

This chapter will concentrate on analyzing those studies that served as the basis for propaganda work, in other words, those studies that formulated the fundamental guidelines of action against the Cuban Revolution, particularly in the economic and social fields. Of course, not all of the investigations of the Cuban Revolution that have been conducted in the capitalist world have been designed or planned with the objective of undermining Cuba. Accordingly, in this chapter I do not attempt to examine all the multiple interpretations regarding the Cuban revolutionary process within the conceptual confines of the different currents of bourgeois ideology. Though these studies reflect the class positions of their authors, their elaboration is not necessarily conditioned to achieve the goals proposed by the ideological or political fight against socialism in the specific case of Cuba under the direct or indirect, overt or covert tutelage of the U.S. government.

Thus in this chapter I propose to evaluate work that conforms to what could be defined as the ideological matrix through which the specialized or massive propaganda war against Cuba was generated and which decisively influenced the focus of studies of Cuba in the area of the different schools of bourgeois ideology throughout the world.

Typical of the cold war period, basic studies of Cuba carried out in the first years of the 1960s reflected the anticommunist approach. As a socialist country, Cuba was examined using the openly anticommunist focus characterized by denial of all positive achievements of the Revolution, systematic challenge of official Cuban sources of information, and tendentious analysis of actual conditions and the generalized use of false information.[10] In this vein, the initial links between the so-called Sovietology[11] and the investigations of Cuba were expressed in those studies directed against the socialist system. Similarly, these studies clearly demonstrated the ties between the policy of counterinsurgency developed by the United States at that time and studies of Cuba.

An example of this class of work in the economic field is a 1962 article by Felipe Pazos, a Cuban who served as president of the Banco Nacional de Cuba (BNC) in 1959 and left Cuba in 1960. His study, "Comentario de dos artículos sobre la Revolución Cubana," was prepared as a reply to the work of Paul Baran, "Reflexiones sobre la Revolución Cubana," and of Juan F. Noyola, "La Revolución Cubana y sus efectos en el desarrollo económico," which were both published by the Mexican journal *El Trimestre Económico*. In his article Pazos attempted to demonstrate that an important part of the evident economic accomplishments attributed to the Revolution between 1959 and 1960 was the result of an intentional manipulation of statistical data. His thesis has been commonly used since those years.[12] On another count, he contended that the real economic advances achieved between 1959 and 1960 were produced in the "redistributing" stage of the Revolution and not during the "statist" stage. Instead, he attributed such advances to virtually the same factors that the Revolution had inherited and not those it created.[13]

Pazos concluded his critique: "The Cuban Revolution has ceased being an example that proves the rationality and efficiency of the socialist system; instead, it has become an evident demonstration of the failure of totalitarian socialism in a Latin American country."[14]

This article sufficiently reveals the traits common to the group of authors that emerged during the first years of the Revolution. This group represented different layers of the displaced Cuban bourgeoisie; their classist approach to Cuba's economic problems led to their confronting the Revolution by repeating the old and tired threats of the possible consequences of "totalitarian socialism" for Latin America.

Another author of significant importance in the ideological fight against the Revolution from its first years is the Cuban-born lawyer and economist Carmelo Mesa-Lago, who emigrated to the United States at the beginning of the 1960s. He later became director of the Center for Latin American Studies at the University of Pittsburgh, editor of *Cuban Studies/Estudios Cubanos*, and one of the most important figures in the group of scholars later known as Cubanologists.

Mesa-Lago's works embody the typical characteristics of the first stage in the ideological fight against the Cuban Revolution. An example of his studies may be found in his essay, "Availability and Reliability of Statistics in Socialist Cuba," published in 1969.[15] In this essay, Mesa-Lago analyzed Cuban statistics between 1959 and 1968 to determine their reliability. However, his conclusions are much more far reaching. From the data compiled and analyzed, he evaluated the level of economic and social development reached by the Cuban Revolution. He also assessed the possibilities of consolidating socialism in the country.

Some of the appraisals Mesa-Lago made in this work are far from objective evaluations of the economic and social realities in Cuba. First, if we consider Mesa-Lago's study as an analysis of statistical sources, he obviously omitted official Cuban sources. He also criticized sources relied on by international organizations such as the Economic Commission for Latin America (CEPAL), which produced studies of incontestable value and importance during these years.[16]

Furthermore, Mesa-Lago used biased criteria in his critical examination of statistics. Although he called the figures offered by socialist Cuba "abuses" of statistics, he considered Cuban National Bank statistics from 1950 to 1958 to be "reliable."[17] He made this distinction for the purpose of demonstrating that economic performance in Cuba after 1959 was worse than that of the 1950s before Castro's rise to power.[18] Mesa-Lago resorted to similar procedures in his evaluation of the phenomenon of unemployment. He considered figures prior to 1959 to be "inflated" whereas he considered data after this point to be deflated.[19] In the social terrain, the author contended that the policy of increasing the number of doctors with "inferior" training contributed to the increase of the mortality indices for the Cuban population during those years.[20] By the same token, Mesa-Lago considered that public health and education statistics were also inflated.[21]

In general, an absence of qualitative and objective analysis of the available statistical data may be noted in Mesa-Lago's study. At the same time, he discriminated in his use of official Cuban sources. All these factors reveal a work that produces conclusions of questionable scientific value.[22] During the 1960s this type of approach was historically determined by (1) the character of confrontation between socialism and capitalism as antagonistic systems and by (2) the particular conflict between the United States and Cuba.

The economic and social development attained by the Cuban Revolution in the first years of the 1970s—such as the political consolidation of this very process—illustrated that the changes the country had undergone were not solely attributable to opportune short-term factors. In this way, the permanence and the advances of the Revolution in Cuba created the conditions for displacing the ideological and political confrontation to another, more subtle and profound plane. At the same time, the change in the correlation of forces between capitalism and socialism that occurred during these years also favored changes in this same direction.

The Conceptual Location of Cubanology in the Framework of the Current Bourgeois Ideologies[23]

As a result of changes within Cuba as well as in the nature of ideological confrontation between capitalism and socialism, the focus of studies about Cuba changed in the 1970s. Thus, the traditional anticommunist formulations that characterized the majority of investigations of the

Revolution up to the end of the 1960s evolved into more sophisticated and supposedly objective forms of presenting the study of socialism in Cuba.

The International Conference on Cuban Acquisitions and Bibliography, organized by the U.S. Library of Congress in April 1970, played a fundamental role in this reformulation of positions.[24] This conference produced an overview of the studies on Cuba up to that moment, both inside and outside the United States, at the same time as it laid a strategy for the development of subsequent investigations.

In this respect, the general of the Army, Raul Castro indicated an element of great importance: "This Conference established the bases for an offensive against our country consisting of ideological diversion and cultural penetration."[25] After this conference the Center for Latin American Studies at the University of Pittsburgh became the coordinator and fundamental publicist of academic studies of Cuba done in the United States under the primary leadership of Cole Blasier and, after 1974, of Carmelo Mesa-Lago.

In this context, on the one hand, we can place the emergence of the first Cubanologist studies as the result of a transition from open to more covert forms of ideological and political confrontation in the process of combating the Cuban Revolution. On the other hand, this process, which had been—until the end of the 1960s—organically dispersed and up to a point incoherent, became centrally directed and strategically coordinated both within and without the United States. The center also served as a publishing house for dissemination of these studies.[26]

In this way, a group, self-denominated as "Cubanologists," was created that constituted the fundamental nucleus of those conducting studies on Cuba in the 1970s, not only in the United States but throughout the capitalist world.[27]

Strictly speaking, the term "Cubanologist" could be applied to anyone who is studying the Cuban reality, including those who come from diverging political and ideological positions. The definition given to the term "Cubanology" in this chapter—even if it seems too narrow— pertains to that group of Cuban scholars who play a central role in the studies of Cuba in the context of the ideological and political battle mounted against the Revolution. Naturally, this group holds an essentially negative vision of the political, economic, and social evolution of the Cuban Revolution.

Finally, it can be affirmed that Cubanologists' essential orientations evolved in conjunction with the U.S. government's positions toward the revolutionary process in Cuba. In other words, historical evidence confirms that the theses of the so-called Cubanology endorsed and were derived from—directly or indirectly, consciously or unconsciously—the

United States' political battle against socialism in Cuba. This last point is so important that it deserves additional attention.[28]

The link between Cubanology and U.S. foreign policy toward Cuba cannot be examined as a simple or linear relationship. On one level, a process of reciprocal interaction may be observed between Cubanologists and those responsible for formulating U.S. policies toward Cuba. On another level, the major part of the tie between Cubanology and the U.S. government has occurred in an indirect manner. In other words, the work done by specialists in Cuban problems has contributed to the creation of a state of opinion favorable to the development of U.S. policy toward Cuba.

Notwithstanding, the most distinguished ideologues of Cubanology have also directly participated in certain programs or official organizations concerning Cuba. It should also be indicated that U.S. positions toward Cuba have been formulated through the work of various Cubanologists in different international organizations. This especially has been the case with the Inter-American Commission on Human Rights of the Organization of American States (OAS)[29] and the World Bank.[30]

In general, since its emergence, we can speak of two stages in the development of Cubanology that correspond approximately to the positions adopted by the United States toward Cuba in those years. During the mid-1970s, political and academic circles close to the Democratic party adopted a more liberal policy regarding Cuba.

The opening that occurs in relations with Cuba during the Carter administration is supported by the ideas put forward in the study known as "Informe Linowitz II," published in 1976. It particularly recommended that "the new administration should look for ways to reopen a process of normalization in relations with Cuba, which should be both gradual and reciprocal," basing this process on the fact that "the North American policy of isolation with respect to Cuba did not promote the interests of the United States in any significant manner, and that these would be better served if the participation of Cuba in a constructive pattern of international relations were facilitated."[31]

Jorge Domínguez, the well-known Cubanologist, participated in the drafting of this report as well as subsequent ones,[32] along with the distinguished U.S. political scientist Samuel Huntington. Carmelo Mesa-Lago's work followed this same line of interpretation during these years.[33]

Nonetheless, when the Reagan administration came into power, relations with Cuba again changed signficantly as the most rightist positions of neoconservatism began to dominate the policy approach.[34] A link to the most influential currents of Cubanology and Sovietology again became apparent in administration positions: The theory of counterinsurgency resurfaced especially in regard to the analysis of the situation in Central America and the Caribbean and its implications for U.S. national security.

The character of the positions advocated by the most distinguished Cubanologists clearly illustrates these changes. In a 1982 study prepared for the State Department and the U.S. Armed Forces, Edward González wrote:

> Although the Castro regime continues to be viable, there are now new opportunities for the United States to exploit Cuba's interests and weaknesses, and as such, to moderate the behavior of Cuba. Recent international and internal changes have heightened Cuba's vulnerability and provide the United States with more possibilities for its exploitation.[35]

Further on he elaborates on these possibilities, pointing out that "the future transmissions of Radio Martí may create a instrument for the exploitation of political vulnerabilities and for putting the regime on the defensive."

In addition, the conclusions reached at 1984 discussions on Cuba held at Georgetown University with the participation of such distinguished Cubanologists—all inclined toward rightist positions—as Hugh Thomas, Cole Blasier, Juan Clark, Edward González, Irving L. Horowitz, Jorge Pérez-López, Sergio Roca, Jorge Sanguinetty, and Lawrence Theriot revealed academic support for the Reagan administration's policy toward Cuba.[36]

The National Cuban-American Foundation (NCAF) played a role of singular importance in the studies tracing the guidelines of neoconservative Cubanology in the 1980s.[37] The foundation tended to concentrate on promoting studies of Cuba that espoused an openly hostile and anticommunist approach to the Revolution—an attitude that recalls studies of Cuba published in the United States twenty years ago.

In this way, U.S. policy toward Cuba has found a source of support and diffusion in Cubanology since the 1970s. On another side, the changes in this policy have produced two well-defined stages in the guidelines for the ideological and political effort against Cuba: one that embraces the 1970s and another that begins with the advent of the Reagan administration. The distinct approaches and the differences they cause in the work of Cubanologists may be seen by looking at examples of Cubanologist study in diverse fields.

As in all ideological currents, Cubanology is heterogeneous and dynamic. Nonetheless, throughout the different stages of its development, a nucleus of common ideas has been present and is evident in the work of its fundamental representatives.[38] Hence, it is useful to insist on the fact that Cubanology possesses the characteristics to allow definition as an ideological matrix, through which the fundamental tendencies are generated that establish a value scale for the evaluation of the Cuban revolutionary reality.

General Characteristics of Cubanology

Cubanologists have conducted studies in practically all spheres in which they can analyze the work of the Cuban Revolution during the last fifteen years. In this section I shall treat only political studies as I deal with analyses of Cuba's economy elsewhere.

Cubanology's political approach[39] has always been determined by a goal that has remained essentially unchanged throughout the years: to prove the inviability of socialism as a political system for Cuba and to portray this system as totalitarian or, at least, undemocratic.

Regarding the analysis of domestic political structures, it can be said that all Cubanologist work stems from the bourgeois concept of democracy. Cubanologists limit themselves to emphasizing the absence of the formal features of democracy, those present in some capitalist societies. In this manner, the essential process of how the interests of the majority of the population are taken into account and the problems that result in practice are not seen or understood. Instead, analysis is displaced to considering only the formal mechanisms in the exercise of power without entering into the social conditions that determine them.

This leads to false perceptions of contradiction. For example, in 1983 Jorge Domínguez wrote:

> Authoritarianism in Cuba, thus, raises important empirical, analytical, and ethical problems. . . . The ethical problem is how to recognize and applaud the merits of a revolutionary regime that has accomplished a lot for its people and at the same time to condemn the abuses and restrictions that have caused death, pain, and suffering for many and have denigrated the Cuban population's right to be politically free.[40]

On the other hand, when other authors such as Irving Horowitz and Edward González have referred to "authoritarianism" in Cuba, they have increasingly emphasized the militaristic character of the Cuban state.

The debate on democracy in Cuba becomes particularly relevant with the Cuban socialist state's process of institutionalization that begins midway through the 1970s.[41] In general, Cubanology has tried to present the process "as a consequence of the failure of the 'elite's' absolute control and as a popular demand for a democratization of the process. . . . The process of institutionalization is presented as the 'consolidation,' 'legalization,' or 'routinization' of the 'elitist,' 'charismatic,' and 'centralized' regime."[42] This approach represents the predominant positions that appear in the most significant books of such authors as Edward González,[43] Jorge Domínguez,[44] and Carmelo Mesa-Lago.[45]

Human rights in Cuba have also been examined by applying bourgeois concepts to Cuban reality. On this issue, attention has been especially concentrated on problems concerning individual liberties and the freedom of expression, although it has also included the problem of religious and cultural freedom. In their analysis of these areas, Cubanologists have reiterated criticisms such as the following: "Considerable limitations exist regarding basic political rights, including those of speech, religion, other forms of expression, assembly, information and association. Although political participation is important, it is carefully monitored and controlled. Its principal effects have been consultative."[46] On this point, it should be noted that the topic of human rights came to occupy a central focus after the so-called exodus from Mariel in spring 1980.[47]

Cubanology's political approach has also been complemented by a historical reevaluation of the period prior to 1959. In this case, the predominant thesis consists in explaining the emergence of socialism in Cuba on the basis of "mistakes" committed within the framework of a bourgeois democratic system. Using this approach, the attempt is made to present socialism as an accident "at the margin of all objective historic determination."[48]

In the context of these generalizations, it is possible, nonetheless, to identify different approaches in the political appraisal of the Cuban revolutionary process. In effect, authors such as Jorge Domínguez temper their arguments with academic language whereas Cubanologists such as Edward Gonzalez or Irving L. Horowitz rely on traditionally anticommunist language—especially during the past few years. Accordingly, Jorge Domínguez classified the Cuban political system as a "consultative oligarchy,"[49] and Edward Gonzalez wrote that "the evolution of the Cuban political system since 1959, in effect, has modified certain traits at the same time that the basic character of Castro's dictatorship remain unchanged."[50] This last tendency gained more strength in the 1980s in correspondence with the policy of growing aggression toward Cuba developed by the Reagan administration.[51]

The interest in Cuba's external political relations gained more popularity after 1976. Until 1975 the Revolution's external political relations were examined by fundamentally taking into account Cuba's ties to the Soviet Union and the repercussions these implied for U.S. interests.

In the analysis of these relations, all Cubanologists started from the same premise: the existence of Cuba's political dependence on the USSR. Nonetheless, one group of authors emphasized the existence of a relatively independent Cuban external policy. In this vein, Jorge Domínguez wrote in 1983:

> Cuba maintains a considerable margin of autonomy within constraints established by Soviet hegemony in Cuba; but even more important, is the fact that Cuba has played a guiding and educational role in the formulation of Soviet external policy, and has perhaps contributed to the radicalization of Soviet policy toward the Third World, and especially toward South Africa and Central America.[52]

Other analysts of Cuba's external policies consider the country to be a Soviet satellite: such an approach identifies itself with the traditional anticommunist viewpoint and constitutes the basis for U.S. policy toward Cuba under the current administration.[53] Following the solidarity and support extended by Cuba to Angola and Ethiopia, beginning in the second half of the 1970s several studies have been conducted on relations between Cuba and Africa.[54]

Another area that has attracted a large amount of Cubanologists' attention after 1979 has been the political situation in Central America. This issue has largely been examined from the perspective of U.S. interests, and studies have concentrated on critically evaluating—with subtle differences—the so-called Cuban-Soviet connection in the area.[55]

Although the political analysis of Cubanologists has not been basically altered since 1970, we can observe the salience of relatively more moderate positions during the 1970s whereas openly hostile and anticommunist approaches become predominant in the 1980s. The National Cuban-American Foundation has played a singularly important role in the past few years. Thus, the work of Cubanologists has reflected the relations between the U.S. and Cuban governments, serving the ideological requirements of the modest shifts in U.S. policy toward Cuba.

Notes

1. The alternatives for other forms of aggression were also made clear in this document's various conclusions. One of them stated that "If propaganda fails, a war of national liberation will have be launched against Castro." See Santa Fe Committee (1981: 209)

2. Another interesting study of Cubanology during this period can be found in Zaldivar (1984).

3. See Foreign Policy Association (1935).

4. See International Bank for Reconstruction and Develoment (1951).

5. See Jenks (1929), Fitzgibbon (1935), Wallich (1950), and Nelson (1950).

6. This did not prevent—as would be the case in the future—nonacademic investigations from being conducted. Such is the case of the book written by Huberman and Sweezy (1960).

7. These studies were entitled *U.S. Business Interests in Cuba and the Rise of Castro* and *The Course of U.S. Private Investments in Latin America since the Rise of Castro.*

8. These studies were published collectively in 1961 under the title of *Case Studies in Insurgency and Revolutionary Warfare: Cuba 1953–1959.*

9. Presumably, these academic studies use scientific procedures to arrive at their conclusions in agreement with certain theoretical principles of bourgeois economy and sociology. In other words, not only do they propose to relate the facts but also to explain and interpret them conceptually.

10. Among the work representative of this period that may be consulted are the following: Cuban Economic Research Project (1965), Draper (1965), and A. Suárez (1967). It is interesting to note that the majority of studies with this focus has gradually lost scientific credibility even within the U.S. academic community.

11. The term "Sovietology" clusters together a set of disciplines directed at the analysis of the theory and practice of socialism in socialist countries.

12. Pazos (1962), pp. 3, 5.

13. Ibid., p. 11.

14. Ibid., p. 18.

15. See Mesa-Lago (1969). His work for the Cuban Economic Research Project may be seen in *Labor Conditions in Communist Cuba* (1963).

16. See CEPAL (1964), ch. 10.

17. These estimates were being criticized in those years as well, both in and outside Cuba. See Oshima (1961).

18. See Mesa-Lago (1969), pp. 42, 45.

19. Ibid., ch. 2.

20. Curiously enough, when the author examined public health indicators, he did not give major importance to the fact that thousands of doctors emigrated to the United States during those years.

21. Ibid., ch. 2.

22. Although Mesa-Lago returned to this point, in his later work there is only one partial critical evaluation of this study, despite the fact that numerous investigators later recognized the later improvement in the availability and reliability of Cuban statistics for the analysis of the 1959–1968 period.

23. On this issue see Zaldivar (1984), G. Suárez (1985), Yanes and Valdés (1984), and Rodríguez (1983).

24. See Library of Congress (1970). A similar, though more limited, conference had already been held by June 1968.

25. R. Castro (1972).

26. The first of these forms was the *Cuban Series Newsletter*, whose publication was begun in 1971. It later became the magazine *Cuban Studies/Estudios Cubanos* and was edited by Mesa-Lago at the Center for Latin American Studies at the University of Pittsburgh. The work of the so-called Cubanologists also appeared

regularly in important U.S. magazines such as *Latin American Research Review, Caribbean Studies, Current History,* and *Problems of Communism.*

27. This group was primarily composed of Cuban-origin academics who only joined together in the United States after the Revolution had triumphed. Actually, very few authors of the 1960s studies of Cuba maintained a stable organic relationship with this new group, which mainly included people from the United States and from European and Canadian universities.

28. Regarding this point see Hernández (1985), López Segrera et al. (unpublished), Martínez (1984), and García, Cervantes, and Hernández (1984).

29. See the Inter-American Commission on Human Rights (1983).

30. See Mesa-Lago and Pérez-López (1982).

31. See *Estados Unidos y América Latina Próximos Pasos* Segundo Informe de la Comisión sobre Relacines Estados Unidos-América Latina (Washington, D.C.: December 20, 1976), in the Informes Linowitz Documentos no. 2, Centro de Estudios sobre América (Havana: June 1980), pp. 100, 101.

32. See the Reports on Inter-American Dialogue, *Las Américas en una encrucijada* (Washington, D.C.: April 1983) and *Las Americas en 1984: un año para decisiones* (Washington, D.C.: May 1984). Because the discussions from which these reports emerged were presided over by Sol M. Linowitz, former U.S. ambassador to the Organization of American States (OAS), they are known as the Linowitz Reports III and IV. (This was obviously also the case for Linowitz Reports I and II.)

33. See "The Economics of US-Cuban Rapprochement," in Blasier and Mesa-Lago (1979).

34. The predominance of an ultraconservative approach did not entail a transformation in the same sense and of the same intensity in the opinions of some Cubanologists such as Mesa-Lago and Domínguez. See, for example, Domínguez (1983) and Mesa-Lago (1983). It cannot be doubted that the positions of both were influenced by the viewpoints concerning Cuba held by officials in the U.S. government.

35. Gonzalez (1982), pp. VIII, XII. As antecedents of this same line of reasoning, see also the less dominant/influential positions of Fontaine (1977).

36. To this respect see Thomas, Fauriol, and Weiss (1984).

37. The Bureau for Conferences of the FNCA especially stands out; its members included Hugh Thomas, Irving L. Horowitz, Juan Clark, Luis E. Aguilar, Sergio Dias-Briguets, and Carlos Rippoll.

38. Some Cubanologists have offered their own typology of approaches within Cuban studies. In this respect, see the opinions offered by Cole Blasier and Jorge Domínguez in the last conferences held in Cuba on this topic in the Centro de Estudios sobre América on May 28, 1984, and in the Departamento de Investigaciones sobre Estados Unidos on March 26, 1985, respectively.

39. Regarding this issue, see the already cited work of Zaldivar, Yanes and Valdés, and Martínez. The work of Yanes and Valdés (1985) and Fuentes (1984) may also be consulted.

40. Domínguez (1983), pp. 45–46.

41. In this respect, see "Cuba: The Institutionalization of the Revolution," reprinted from *Cuban Studies* 6, no. 1 (January 2 and July 1976) and "Forum on Institutionalization," *Cuban Studies* 9, no. 2 (July 1979).

42. Morales Pérez, n.d., p. 73.

43. See González (1974).

44. See Domínguez (1978).

45. See Mesa-Lago (1979).

46. Domínguez (1983), p. 42.

47. Regarding this issue see the studies published under the title, "The Cuban Exodus: A Symposium," in *Cuban Studies* 2, no. 2 (July 1981), and 13, no. 1 (January 1982).

48. A detailed analysis on this topic may be found in the already cited work of Domínguez (1978). The following may also be consulted: Aguilar (1972), Horowitz (1983), and Bonachea and San Martín (1974).

49. Domínguez (1983), p. 1.

50. See Thomas, Fauriol, and Weiss (1984), p. 19.

51. In a general sense it can be said that the more "moderate" criteria actually employed by Cubanologists such as Domínguez and Mesa-Lago found a more synthetic expression after 1980 in the report issued by the Interamerican Commission on Human Rights (OAS) (1983). On another hand, the currently dominant, more right-wing positions are summarized in Thomas et al. 1984.

52. Domínguez (1983), p. 20. This approach is also shared by Wayne Smith and William LeoGrande.

53. To this respect see González and Renfeldt (1975), Gonzalez (1974), Levesque (1978), and Cole Blasier (1983), ch. 5.

54. Among the numerous studies prepared on this theme, those published under the title, "Cuba in Africa," in *Cuban Studies* 10, no. 1 (January 1980), and no. 2 (July 1980), particularly stand out. See also Mesa-Lago and Belkin (1982) and William LeoGrande (1980).

55. Regarding this topic, see Domínguez (1983), Valenta (1982), Levine (1983), and "The USSR, Cuba, and the Crisis in Central America," *Orbis* 6, no. 25 (fall 1981).

References

Aguilar, Luis E. *Cuba 1933: Prologue to Revolution*. Ithaca: Cornell University Press, 1972.

Baran, Juan. "Reflexiones sobre la Revolución Cubana." *El Trimestre Económico*, no. 11 (1961).

Blasier, Cole. *The Giant's Rival*. Pittsburgh: University of Pittsburgh Press, 1983.

Blasier, C., and Carmelo Mesa-Lago, eds. *Cuba in the World*. Pittsburgh: University of Pittsburgh Press, 1979.

Bonachea, Ramón L., and Marta San Martín. *The Cuban Insurrection, 1952–1959*. New Brunswick, N.J.: Transaction Books, 1974.

Castro, Raul. "Discurso pronunciado por el General de Ejercito Raul Castro en el acto por el XI Aniversario del MININT." Speech, June 6, 1972.

CEPAL. *Estudio Económico de America Latina 1963*. New York: United Nations, 1964.

Cuban Economic Research Project. *Labor Conditions in Communist Cuba*. Coral Gables, Fla.: University of Miami Press, 1963.

Domínguez, Jorge. *Cuba: Order and Revolution*. Cambridge: Harvard University Press, 1978.

————. "Cuba's Relation with Caribbean and Central American Countries." *Cuban Studies* 13, no. 2 (1983).

————. "Las relaciones Cuba-Estados Unidos: el primer cuarto de siglo." Working paper for the Grupo de Estudio sobre las relaciones Cubano-Norteamericana de Relaciones Exteriores, February 15, 1983.

————. *Political Rights and the Cuban Political System*. Cambridge: Center for International Affairs, Harvard University, February 1983.

Draper, Theodore. *Castroism: Theory and Practice*. New York: Praeger, 1965.

Fitzgibbon, Russell H. *Cuba and the United States: 1900–1935*. Menasha, Wis.: Banta, 1935.

Fontaine, Roger. *US-Cuban Relations: A New, New Look*. Washington, D.C.: Council for Interamerican Security, 1977.

Foreign Policy Association. *Problemas de la nueva Cuba*. New York: Little and Ives, 1935.

Fuentes, Juan F. "Algunas tergiversaciones de la cubanología sobre la política internacional de la Revolución Cubana." Speech presented to the Seminar on Cubanology, DISEU-UH, Havana, March 2, 1984.

García, Raul, Lourdes Cervantes, and Rafael Hernández. "La Fundación Nacional Cubano-Americana y la conexión anticubana en Estados Unidos." *Cuadernos de Nuestra América* 1, no. 1 (January-July 1984).

Gonzalez, Edward. *A Strategy for Dealing with Cuba in the 1980s*. Santa Monica, Calif.: Rand Corporation, September 1982.

————. *Cuba Under Castro: The Limits of Charisma*. Boston: Houghton Mifflin, 1974.

Gonzalez, Edward, and David Rondfeldt. *Post-Revolutionary Cuba in a Changing World: A Report Prepared by the Office of the Assistant-Secretary of Defense*. Santa Monica, Calif.: Rand Corporation, 1975.

Hernández, Rafael. "Cubanologia y poder en Estados Unidos." Speech at the Mesa Redonda, Introducción al estudio de la llamada cubanologia, IV Conferencia Científica de Ciencia Sociales de UH, Havana: February 27, 1985.

Horowitz, Irving L., ed. *Cuban Communism*. New Brunswick, N.J.: Transaction Books, 1983.

Huberman, Leo, and Paul Sweezy. *Anatomy of a Revolution*. New York: Monthly Review Press, 1960.

Inter-American Commission on Human Rights. *La situación de los derechos humanos en Cuba*. Washington, D.C.: Organization of American States, 1983.

International Bank for Reconstruction and Development. *Report on Cuba: Findings and Recommendations of Economic and Technical Mission*. Washington, D.C.: 1951.

Jenks, Leland M. *Our Cuban Colony*. New York: Vanguard Press, 1929.

LeoGrande, William. *Cuba's Policy in Africa, 1959–1980*. Berkeley: University of California Press, 1980.

Levesque, J. *The USSR and the Cuban Revolution: Soviet Ideological and Strategical Perspectives, 1959–1977*. New York: Praeger, 1978.

Levine, Barry. *The New Cuban Presence in the Caribbean*. Boulder, Colo.: Westview, 1983.

Library of Congress. *Cuban Acquisitions and Bibliography*. Washington, D.C.: Government Printing Office, 1970.

López Segrera, Francisco, et al. *La política de estados Unidoes hacia Cuba (1959–1984)*. Unpublished book.

Martínez, Milagros. "Notas preliminares para la caracterización de la cubanología en el periodo 1980-1984." MIUREX-DISEU, June 28, 1984.

Mesa-Lago, Carmelo. "A Dissenting View." Paper Presented to the Western Hemisphere Stability, the Latin American Connection Worlds Affairs Council of Pittsburgh, 19th World Affairs Forum, Pittsburgh, 1983.

—————. "Availability and Reliability of Statistics in Socialist Cuba." *Latin American Research Review* 4, no. 1, and 4, no. 2 (1969).

—————. *Dialectica de la Revolución cubana: del idealismo carismatico al pragmatismo institucionalista*. Madrid: 1979.

Mesa-Lago, C., and June Belkin. *Cuba in Africa*. Pittsburgh: University of Pittsburgh Press, 1982.

Mesa-Lago, C., and Jorge Pérez-López. "Study of Cuba's MPS, Its Conversion to SNA, and Estimation of GDP/Capita and Growth Rates." World Bank Project on CPE's National Income Statistics, November 1982.

Morales Pérez, Arturo. *Crítica de algunas tergiversaciones de la cubanologia acerca del proceso de institucionalización y su incidencia en la esencia del Estado socialista en Cuba*. Escuela Superior del PCC Nico Lopez: trabajo de diploma.

Nelson, Lowry. *Rural Cuba*. Reprint. New York: Octagon Books, 1970 (originally published in 1950).

Noyola, Juan F. "La Revolución Cubana y sus efectos en el desarrollo económico." *El Trimestre Económico*, no. 11 (1961).

Oshima, Harry T. "A New Estimate of the National Income and Product of Cuba in 1953." *Food Research Institute Studies* (Stanford University) 11, no. 3 (November 1961).

Pazos, Felipe. "Comentarios a dos artículos sobre la Revolución Cubana." *El Trimestre Económico* (Mexico), no. 113 (1962).

Rodríguez, José Luis. "La llamada cubanología y el desarrollo económico de Cuba." *Temas de Economía Mundial* (CIEM, Havana), no. 7 (1983).

Santa Fe Committee. *Las relaciones interamericanas: escudo de la seguridad del nuevo mundo y espada de la proyección del poder global de Estados Unidos*. CIDE Cuadernos Semestrales Estados Unidos, Perspectivas latinoamericanas, no. 9 (first semester 1981).

Suárez, Andrés. *Cuba: Castroism and Communism 1959–1966*. Cambridge: MIT Press, 1967.

Suárez, Georgina. "Hacia una caracterización de "cubanología" burguesa en los años sesenta." Speech presented to the Mesa Redonda Introducción al estudio de la llamada cubanologia, IV Conferencia Científica de Ciencias Sociales de la Universidad de Habana, Havana, February 27, 1985.

Thomas, Hugh, George A. Fauriol, and Juan C. Weiss. *The Cuban Revolution 25 Years Later.* Boulder: Westview Press, 1984.

Valenta, Jiri. "Soviet Strategy in the Caribbean Basin." *United States Naval Institute Proceedings* 108 (May 1982).

Wallich, Henry C. *Monetary Problems of an Export Economy.* Cambridge: Harvard University Press, 1950.

Yanes, Hernán, and Gilberto Valdés. "Notas para una caracterización de la "cubanología" burguesa." Seminar on Cubanology, speeches, Departamento de Investigaciones sobre Estados Unidos, University of Havana, March 2, 1984.

————. *Breve comentario a "Derechos políticos y sistema político Cubano" de Jorge Domínguez.* Speech presented to the Mesa Redonda: Introducción al estudio de la llamada cubanología. IV Conferencia Científica de Ciencias Sociales de la UH, Havana, February 26, 1985.

Zaldivar, Andrés. "Algunas consideraciones sobre el surgimiento y desarrollo de la cubanología." Paper presented to a seminar on Cubanology. Ponencia Departamento de Investigaciones sobre Estados Unidos (DISEU), University of Havana, March 2, 1984.

3

Cubanology and Cuban Economic Performance

Claes Brundenius
and Andrew Zimbalist

In this chapter we shall review three recent major studies on Cuban economic growth. The papers were written by Carmelo Mesa-Lago, the most prolific and prominent U.S. interpreter of the Cuban economy, and by Jorge Pérez-López.

Our purpose is twofold. First, we will identify and correct several blatant methodological and theoretical errors in these three papers. As these studies are already being cited as authoritative in both the academic literature and media coverage on Cuba, we feel it is important to set the record straight. Second, we offer some new evidence and analysis regarding Cuban economic performance. We shall discuss these papers in chronological order.

The World Bank Study:
Methodological Confusion

In November 1982 Carmelo Mesa-Lago and Jorge Pérez-López completed a study for the World Bank's project on centrally planned economies' (CPEs') national income statistics, entitled *Study of Cuba's MPS, Its Conversion to SNA and Estimation of GDP/capita and Growth Rates.*[1] Although the study provides an adequate and useful survey of existing work in this area, it is marred by a deficient understanding of Cuba's

---

This chapter is a condensation with some updating of two articles originally published in *Comparative Economic Studies* 27, nos. 1 and 3 (spring and fall 1985).

system of material balances (MPS), improper methodology, confusing presentation, and lack of focus. A discussion of this study will enable us to highlight and clarify certain relationships in the Cuban growth process.

The Mesa-Lago/Pérez-López World Bank Study (hereafter MLPL) begins with the assertion that the Cuban statistical yearbook's *Anuario Estadístico de Cuba* section on macro-indicators (*indicadores globales*) usually has only one page of data and no discussion of methodology (with the exception of the 1972 edition). In fact, the 1980 yearbook has six pages, the 1981 yearbook has seven pages, and the 1982 yearbook has fifteen pages in the macro-indicators section. Each yearbook has an introductory, multipage (one page in 1980) discussion of methodology that serves to qualify the opening statement that Cuba uses the MPS of the Council for Mutual Economic Assistance (CMEA). That is, the yearbook makes it clear that the statistics are aggregated by MPS procedures with the qualifications and elaborations specified.[2] Curiously, the MLPL study overlooks this clear methodological statement at points and is thereby forced to guess at the meaning of certain terms when, in fact, the meaning is evident.

The MLPL study correctly notes that a process of enterprise mergers during the 1960s significantly reduced the number of enterprises and that a process of enterprise disaggregation in the 1970s increased the number of enterprises from approximately 300 to 3,000. (Actually, the number of enterprises peaked at 3,058 at the end of 1976 and has been subsequently reduced. At the end of 1982, there were 2,231 enterprises, national and local [Martínez 1983:81].) The authors go on to note that as enterprises merge (through vertical integration) there is less opportunity for double counting. Hence, gross social product (GSP), which counts intermediate inputs, tends to be reduced during trends of enterprise mergers and to be increased during trends of enterprise disaggregation. Gross material product (GMP), however, is not in theory subject to double counting and is not affected by enterprise aggregation and disaggregation, or, at least, not by as much as is GSP. An important caveat should have been (but was not) added at this point by the authors. That is, GSP is affected only if the accounting system is not adjusted to (or does not already) compensate for the change in industrial organization. As we shall see, this is a potentially important oversight.

The authors write: "In 1963–70 the ratio of GMP to GSP declined (from 62 to 50 percent) as enterprises merged, while in 1971–78 it increased (from 54 to 62 percent) partly due to the disaggregation of enterprises" (p. 6). A moment's reflection will reveal that the authors have the causality backward. Since mergers lower GSP and do not alter GMP, other things equal, the GMP/GSP ratio in the 1960s should have increased, not declined, as the MLPL study asserts. Conversely, for the 1970s the ratio should have decreased, other things equal, not increased as the study claims.

How then does one account for the fact that the official GMP/GSP ratio actually decreased in the 1960s when the change in industrial organization should have made it increase (and conversely for the period 1970–1978)? Although never acknowledged by the MLPL authors, the MPS system does have a built-in flexibility to compensate for changing industrial organization. In particular, there are four methods for dealing with intermediate inputs in aggregating gross output: the gross turnover method; the enterprise method; the trust method; and the branch method.[3]

In the gross turnover method all intermediate inputs are counted in the gross output of industry. In the enterprise exit method all intermediate inputs except those produced by the enterprise itself are counted. In the trust (association of enterprises) method all intermediate inputs except those produced within the given trust are counted. In the branch method all intermediate inputs except those produced within the given branch are counted. Thus, the branch method involves the least double counting, followed by the trust, the enterprise exit, and the gross turnover methods, respectively. If, as the enterprises are combined into trusts or associations the accounting practice is to use the trust method, then the gross output value would not be affected. It is likely that such accounting practices were followed for purposes of keeping accurate and consistent records. If so, part of the GMP/GSP discrepancy would be thereby explained.

Overlooking or ignorant of these distinct MPS accounting methods, the MLPL authors do not understand the Cuban references to their own practices as *circulación completa* and *a la salida de empresa*. The MLPL authors speculate incorrectly on the meaning of these terms, which they complain the Cubans do not explain. The meaning of these terms is apparent in the context of the MPS methodologies. *Circulación completa* refers to the gross turnover method and *a la salida de empresa* to the enterprise exit method. The Cubans used gross turnover for most industries between 1970 and 1976 and then switched to the enterprise method in 1977. They continue to use gross turnover in agriculture, and the Cubans use the branch (*rama*) method in construction.

Having misunderstood both the relationship of GMP to GSP and the accounting of intermediate inputs, the MLPL authors conclude, without providing any documentation: "Although it is difficult to accurately estimate the net effect of the two trends, our educated guess is that the two roughly offset each other" (p. 8). As we have shown, their guess is based on a fundamental misunderstanding of the methodology employed to generate the data.

Survey of Conversion and Growth Estimates

Fortunately, the subsequent sections of the MLPL study are sufficiently unconnected to the first section so that they can be discussed separately. In the MLPL discussion of the Cuban effort to convert Cuban GMP to gross domestic product (GDP) for the year 1974, the authors make an interesting observation. The basic conversion procedure is to add non-material services (NMS), such as culture, government administration, and health, which are excluded from GSP and GMP, to GMP to arrive at GDP.[4] Since NMS does not appear in Cuban national income accounts, the authors derive an estimate for NMS based on the share of social service expenditures in the state budget. They conclude that the value of NMS relative to GDP grew from 21 to 23.6 percent in 1963–1965 to 30 percent in 1978.[5] Although the authors make no note of it, this increasing share of NMS in national income implies that the traditional measures of Cuban national income (e.g., GSP, GMP) that exclude NMS yield an underestimation of the actual economic growth rate, other things being equal.

The MLPL study leaves the Cuban GMP/GDP conversion exercise rather abruptly without drawing any conclusions. The next section reports on various other estimated series of Cuban economic growth in terms of GDP or GNP. First, the authors consider Soviet estimates that they dismiss as being inconsistent and having no explicit methodology. Next, they discuss the CIA estimates. The CIA briefly outlines its methods, but it provides no details on its calculations. According to the MLPL authors, the various CIA growth estimates are inconsistent with each other, and they significantly underreport NMS in their benchmark calculation.

The MLPL study then turns to consider the estimates made by the U.S. Arms Control and Disarmament Agency (ACDA). The ACDA does not specify its sources or its methodology and the MLPL authors note that: "Personal communication with ACDA staff responsible for the yearbooks has failed to throw any light on the origin of the Cuban GNP estimates."[6] The MLPL authors also say the ACDA estimates are "highly inconsistent."

The estimates published in the *World Bank Atlas* are reviewed next. This is the only long-term series of estimated dollar GNP per capita growth for the Cuban economy and hence has been widely used by the press and by scholars. Unfortunately, these estimates are also clouded with a methodological fog. Staff members of the relevant World Bank department could not explain to the MLPL authors how the estimates were made and virtually no documentation on method is available. Moreover, there are serious anomalies in the estimates for certain periods.

Thus, the *World Bank Atlas* estimates are probably as unreliable as those of the ACDA, the CIA, and the Soviets, and the brief MLPL review of the existing estimates takes us back to square one.

Original MLPL Estimate and the Role of Sugar

At this point, the MLPL authors introduce their own method for estimating Cuban GDP per capita growth. Following the lead of the UN Economic Commission for Europe, the MLPL authors employ the so-called physical indicators (PI) method. Briefly, the univariate version of the PI method, as applied in the MLPL study, entails generating separate regression equations of GDP per capita growth on each of twenty-four different commodities (in units of physical output) across twenty-five underdeveloped economies. The regression equations are then used to obtain a series of per capita GDP values each corresponding to the given physical indicator. The composite GDP per capita value is then arrived at by taking a simple arithmetic average of the individual estimates. The MLPL authors used dollar GDP per capita figures from 1958 as their benchmark.

The univariate physical indicators method, of course, is rather rudimentary, but since it sidesteps knotty issues of currency conversion, it has proved useful as a rough estimator in its application to various industrial economies. The results of the MLPL univariate physical indicators estimate are as follows: 1977 GDP per capita in Cuba was $1,355, measured in constant 1958 dollars; real GDP growth per capita was 5.1 percent per year between 1965 and 1970, 14.8 percent per year between 1970 and 1975, and 9.6 percent per year between 1975 and 1977. The MLPL authors also estimated Cuban growth using the more sophisticated multivariate PI method, but this exercise produced even higher growth rates than the univariate method and was dismissed immediately.

It should be noted that the univariate PI growth estimates are higher than official GSP growth estimates. This difference can be explained in part by the earlier finding of the MLPL study that the service sector grew more rapidly than the rest of the economy from the early 1960s to the late 1970s (since GSP does not include the nonproductive services). This explanation, however, is overlooked by the MLPL authors who instead use questionable reasoning to reject the estimate altogether:

> But Cuba is a monoculture type of economy in which sugar plays a key role: wide, erratic fluctuations of the sugar price in the international market have a significant impact on Cuba's economy and growth rate. In the 24 physical indicators used in the Cuban case only one deals with sugar and it is based on consumption per capita. Sugar production at world prices

would have been a more significant indicator but inconsistent with the PI approach. (p. 58)

Let us consider this argument. First, if the monocultural nature of the Cuban economy in fact made the PI approach unreliable, then the proper procedure would be to reject the PI method at the outset. To run the test, get an estimate not to your liking, and then find a post hoc rationalization why the test was inappropriate in the first place obviously cannot be justified even by the most liberal interpretation of the scientific method.

Second, even if one grants that the Cuban economy is monocultural and that erratic sugar price fluctuations have a strong impact on Cuban growth, it is not clear why this should invalidate the PI method. If higher sugar prices mean more foreign exchange and hence more imports and greater resource availability (and vice versa), then this would be reflected in higher physical output levels of the relevant commodities. It would not matter, particularly in measuring growth over five-year periods, that sugar is reckoned in consumption per head rather than production value at world prices. Furthermore, insofar as the PI method is really used for estimating standards of living, it is precisely consumption of sugar per head, and not production per head, that is relevant.

Third, greater caution is appropriate when speaking of alleged monoculture and the major role of sugar prices. The decline of monocultural traits in the Cuban economy has been elaborated elsewhere and is discussed briefly in the last section of this chapter.[7] Here we wish to consider the assertion made in the MLPL study that "fluctuations of the sugar price in the international market have a significant impact on Cuba's economy and growth rate" (p. 58). In Mesa-Lago's November 1983 paper (to be discussed in the third section), he further elevates the role of sugar prices to "an enormous impact on the Cuban economy . . . largely explaining the economic boom of the first half of the seventies" (p. 13).

The available statistical evidence does not directly support this claim. In Table 3.1 we show the simple correlations between the official growth

TABLE 3.1
Correlation Coefficients Between Economic Growth Rates and Sugar Prices

	World Raw Sugar Price	Sugar Price Paid by Soviet Union	Weighted Average of World and Soviet Prices
Official growth rate	0.182	0.068	0.113
Wharton growth rate	0.034	-0.041	-0.017

rate of GSP, the Wharton estimated growth rate of GSP, and various measures of sugar prices for the years 1962–1981 inclusive (1965–1980 for Wharton estimates). The Wharton estimates, made by Pérez-López, are discussed in the second section of this chapter.

Clearly, none of these correlations comes close to being significant at the 10 percent level. Whereas one might attribute the weak relationships to an unreliable official growth series, it is noteworthy that the correlations are considerably weaker and even have the wrong sign in two of three cases when the Wharton estimates of Cuban growth are employed. The statistical insignificance of sugar prices remains when various lag structures are tested.

It is arguable, however, that the simple correlation coefficient is based on a mis-specified relationship. For instance, one might argue that changing sugar prices do not directly influence growth rates; rather, they increase resource and consumer good availability and thereby reduce bottlenecks, raise morale (and x-efficiency), enhance the efficacy of bonuses, and so on. Accordingly, higher sugar prices tend to raise the efficiency level of what is, in an aggregate production function, variously referred to as the Hicks-neutral technical change term, the total factor productivity term, or the residual, in other words, A (t). In this alternate specification, the aggregate production function might appear as follows:

$$Y = A_1(P_s)K^{\alpha} L^{\beta} \tag{1}$$

where

Y stands for GSP;

A_1, a subset of A, is all residual influences except world sugar prices;

P_s, also a subset of A, is the world raw sugar price;

K is the capital stock, and

L is the size of the civilian labor force.[8]

Assuming constant returns to scale,[9] this function can be simplified as:

$$\ln (Y/L) = \ln A_1 + \ln P_s + a\ln(K/L) \tag{2}$$

Constructing a capital stock series based on official gross investment data under the assumption that the capital stock equaled two times GSP in 1961, we estimated equation (2) for 1961–1981 using the official GSP series (equation 3) and for 1965–1980 using the Wharton GSP estimates (equation 4):

$$\ln(Y/L) = -.29 + .09\ln(P_s) + .66\ln(K/L) \quad \text{adj. } R^2 = .84 \tag{3}[10]$$
$$\quad\quad (-1.14)(2.76) \quad\quad\quad (5.38)$$

$$\ln(Y/L) = -.37 - .02 \ln(P_S) + .181 \ln (K/L) \quad \text{adj. } R^2 = .02 \qquad (4)$$
$$(-14.31)(-.73) \qquad (1.44)$$

First, we observe that the fit of the Wharton estimates is extremely poor: Both the independent variables are insignificant at the 0.10 level. Second, we observe both plausible coefficients and a very good fit in equation (3) that uses the official Cuban GSP series. The world sugar price variable is significant at the 0.05 level and the capital-labor ratio variable at the 0.001 level. The coefficients can be interpreted as follows: A 10 percent increase in the world sugar price is associated with an approximately 1 percent increase in (Y/L) or in labor productivity; and a 10 percent increase in the capital-labor ratio is associated with an approximately 7 percent increase in labor productivity. Finally, if we add an exponential time trend to the aggregate production function (equation 5) reflecting a constant rate of technical change as a detrender, the coefficients on the independent variables are rather stable and remain significant at the 0.05 level (equation 6).

$$Y = A_1(P_S)e^{rt}K^\alpha L^\beta \qquad (5)$$

$$\ln(Y/L) = -.49 - .004t + .10 \ln(P_S) + .82 \ln(K/L) \quad \text{adj. } R^2 = .84 \qquad (6)$$
$$(-.69)(-.303) (2.66) \qquad (2.14)$$

The Wharton Econometric Study

In November 1983 under contract to the U.S. Department of State, Wharton Econometrics Forecasting Associates (WEFA) published a voluminous study entitled *Construction of Cuban Activity and Trade Indexes (Final Report of Study to Develop a Methodology for Estimating Cuba's GNP)*. The principal author of this study is Jorge Pérez-López, who coauthored the World Bank report just discussed. The study gives at first glance the impression of being the result of very serious and solid work. The main objective of the exercise seems to have been to present some reliable alternative estimates of Cuban economic growth after the Revolution or, in other words, more reliable estimates than those presented officially in Cuba or by other Western specialists such as those by Brundenius.[11] The objective as such is very laudable, and a summary result of the exercise is presented in Table 3.2. There are some intriguing differences between the official growth rates of key economic aggregates and estimates by Brundenius and WEFA.

TABLE 3.2
Average Annual Rates of Growth for Selected
Indicators of Cuban Economic Activity

	1965–1969	1970–1974	1975–1980
Industry			
Official	2.2	7.7	3.8
Brundenius	1.7	8.0	2.9
WEFA[a]	3.0	5.2	0.8
Agriculture			
Official	4.7	1.6	7.7
Brundenius	−0.3	−0.6	4.3
WEFA	2.5	0.9	4.3
Material Product			
Official	2.2	8.6	4.0
Brundenius	0.3	8.3	3.6
WEFA	2.4	5.7	0.9
GSP			
Official	1.7	12.6	4.8
WEFA	0.9	7.2	2.2
GNP			
Official	n.a.	13.9[b]	6.9
WEFA	1.3[c]	4.9[b]	3.4

[a]Wharton Econometric Forecasting Associates.
[b]1971–1974.
[c]1965–1970.

Sources: Jorge Pérez-López, Construction of Cuban
Activity and Trade Indexes (Final Report of Study to
Develop Methodology for Estimating Cuba's GNP)
(Washington, D.C.: Wharton Econometric Forecasting
Associates, November 1983); Claes Brundenius,
Revolutionary Cuba: The Challenge of Economic Growth
with Equity (Boulder: Westview Press, 1984); and
Comité Estatal de Estadísticas, Anuario Estadístico de
Cuba, various years.

According to WEFA, official Cuban sources, as well as Brundenius, grossly exaggerated real growth, particularly in the period 1970–1980. If the WEFA estimates were accurate it could indeed be argued that Cuban economic growth in the 1970s has been far less impressive than suggested by the official statistics and by Brundenius.

The WEFA methodology is essentially the one employed by Brundenius; that is, a so-called bottom-up procedure that uses indexes for various economic sectors, starting with disaggregated levels based on nonmonetary indicators. Since official Cuban sources list output series for several hundred agricultural and industrial products as well as various types of services, this method is certainly plausible in principle. To arrive at aggregate indexes for broad sectors, total material product, gross material product, and gross national product, two steps must be taken: (1) The various product indexes must be aggregated into branch/sector indexes using a set of base year weights (such as prices) that reflect the relative importance of each product or service within branches or sectors of the economy; and (2) these branch/sector indexes must be combined into an overall index of production using base year weights (such as value added) that reflect the contribution of each branch/sector to national income in the base year.

In the case of branch weights, WEFA has chosen to estimate value added by branch/sector for 1974.[12] This approach appears to be sound because there was an attempt in 1982 by the Cubans to convert the Cuban system of balances of the economy (MPS) to the system of national accounts (SNA) as practiced by the market economies of the West for 1974. Although WEFA makes the rather extravagant assumption that the value added/gross value of production ratios is constant over time, there are more serious problems with its methods.

WEFA's basic procedure for establishing branch weights was to apply the ratio of value added (va) to gross value of output (GVO) for each branch during the first half of 1963 (data from an official 45 by 45 input-output matrix published in 1965) to the branch distribution of gross value of output in 1975 (used as a proxy for 1974) and the actual industrial GVO in 1974. As WEFA reports on page 68, however, the sugar industry was subordinated to a separate ministry and was not included in this 45 by 45 matrix published by the Ministry of Industries (neither was the food processing branch). WEFA apparently used a 1965 ECLA study, which relies on branch value-added data provided by the Cubans for 1961, to estimate the va/GVO ratio for the sugar industry. The curiosity here is that WEFA dismissed the ECLA estimates earlier in the study as being too aggregated and subject to various errors. The actual procedure WEFA employed is further muddled by the following statement:

The branch distribution of output for 1975 has been used as a proxy for the distribution in 1974 since it was the closest year for which data were available. (The objection could be raised that the selection of the branch distribution for 1975 as a proxy for 1974 understates the role of the sugar industry since the world price of sugar plummeted in 1975 after recording historical highs in 1974.) (p. 62)

This passage gives the impression that WEFA either weighted sugar using world prices instead of domestic wholesale prices or believes that the Cubans do this. The Cubans, in fact, use domestic wholesale prices for valuing their output. These prices are generally fixed for long periods (several years) before being adjusted to reflect international price movements. In the interim, subsidies or turnover taxes are used to preserve the domestic price.

Another problem is WEFA's puzzling decision to weigh the non-productive service sector as 13.8 percent of the gross value of output. This share is out of line with the estimate made by Mesa-Lago and Pérez-López in their November 1982 World Bank study that this sector's share in 1978 GDP was 30 percent. Because the authors acknowledge that this sector grew at a considerably faster pace than the material goods producing sector, this lower weight diminishes the aggregate growth estimate.

Bigger problems, however, are still to come. A key element in using the WEFA methodology is finding adequate relative product weights, that is, prices. In the absence of Cuban prices some proxy prices, or shadow prices, have to be used. Brundenius also had to resort to proxy prices in his estimates (using Cuban official prices in branches where such prices were available and Peruvian prices in branches where Cuban prices were not available, mainly in investment goods branches). WEFA, however, rejects using official Cuban prices because "Cuba is not a market economy, the prevalent system of prices does not provide the basis for meaningful product/service weights" (p. 82). This is a highly questionable statement. One might ask "meaningful for whom" or "meaningful for what purposes"? There is no a priori set of prices that is more "meaningful" than another.

In conventional economic theory competitive market prices are the proper ones to use in measuring welfare changes. The problem is how does this theory apply to real world comparisons? Market prices do not reflect externalities, are not used to value public goods, do not convey the distributional preferences of the society's welfare function, and so on. Moreover, the societies at hand are hardly perfectly competitive. Hence, the real world problem boils down to the question: Does a given set of prices produce a growth bias?

WEFA relies heavily on 1973 Guatemalan prices as proxies for Cuban prices. Why did WEFA choose Guatemala of all countries? The answer can only elicit wonderment: "[Because] the structure of the [Guatemalan] economy shared important features with Cuba: small, predominently agricultural and eminently open" (p. 94). But Guatemala belongs to the Central American Common Market, which set a common tariff averaging above 25 percent for industrial products in the early 1970s. Through its National Agricultural Market Institute, the Guatemalan government plays a significant role in agricultural price formation and regulation, affecting the prices of milk, cream, butter, cheese, cereals, and meat, among other products. Interest rate controls and ceiling prices on medicines, dyes, basic clothing items, and other goods further distort Guatemalan prices away from free, competitive market prices. Moreover, with 55 percent of Guatemala's labor force in agriculture in 1980 (compared to 23 percent in Cuba), secondary school enrollment of 16 percent of the relevant age cohort in 1981 (compared to 75 percent in Cuba), an illiteracy rate of 53.9 percent in 1973 (compared to around 5 percent in Cuba), and a 1981 manufacturing share in GDP of 16.2 percent (compared to roughly 30 percent in Cuba), it is hard to see how Guatemalan factor endowments are similar to Cuba's anyway.[13] Given these problems with Guatemalan prices and given the small, irregular sample of Guatemalan prices obtained by WEFA, we are uneasy about the choice of this price set. Further, WEFA does not explain when or why they use wholesale prices for some goods and retail prices for others, or why they use U.S. prices for some branches and Guatemalan prices for others.

Let us, acknowledging the difficulties of data collection, settle for this collection of prices and weights and turn to consider the WEFA results. In its Table 46 (see Table 3.3) WEFA shows a production index series for twenty-one goods-producing branches. Between 1974 and 1980 overall goods production increased by only 18 percent and industrial production by only 13 percent—indeed, a rather poor performance. Looking more closely at the WEFA estimates, however, one notices, for instance, that branches containing products with supposedly high growth rates according to official statistics seem to have very sluggish growth according to WEFA—particularly investment goods branches such as metal products and construction materials. Starting with metal products (its branch G) we found the following strange result. According to WEFA, this branch had a 1980 output index of 0.46 in relation to 1974 (1974 = 1.00); that is, output of metal products would be less than half in 1980 what it was in 1974. An examination of the goods included in this branch (we are using the same physical output series as WEFA throughout this chapter) reveals the following index for 1980 (again, 1974 = 1.00). In

TABLE 3.3
1980 Production Index for Metal
Products Branch (1974 = 1.00)

Steel structures	5.80
Stainless steel tanks	1.46
Steel cans	0.96
Aluminum cans	0.88
Electrodes	1.05
Bottle caps	1.13
Pressure cookers	0.25
Nails	0.93

Source: Jorge Pérez-López, Construc-
tion of Cuban Activity and Trade
Indexes (Final Report of Study to
Develop Methodology for Estimating
Cuba's GNP) (Washington, D.C.:
Wharton Econometric Forecasting
Associates, November 1983.)

other words, the only product in the output mix that has a lower index than 0.46 is pressure cookers! It goes without saying, however, that steel structures should have an important weight in the output mix whatever price one puts on pressure cookers, so it was necessary to probe deeper.

We scrutinized WEFA's list of proxy prices (its Table 45) and discovered that WEFA had included only two of the eight products in its index estimate, namely, pressure cookers and nails. This selectivity represents a gross misuse of the data and methodology and is highly misleading. As such, it is a severe methodological limitation that should have been explicitly acknowledged by WEFA. Using Peruvian prices of 1967 (*Estadística Industrial*, 1967, pp. 125–165), we calculated a new index series for metal products using WEFA's output series but now including all eight products. We arrived at an output index for Cuban metal products that is compared to WEFA's index in Table 3.4.

The difference is striking. While WEFA claims that output of metal products declined considerably between 1974 and 1980, our approach, including all products and not only an arbitrarily chosen few, suggests that output actually more than doubled in the same period.

Let us now turn to another branch in question, construction materials (WEFA's branch L). According to WEFA, this branch output increased by only 11 percent between 1974 and 1980—not a very impressive growth for such a key investment goods branch. Repeating the earlier exercise, we found output indexes for 1980 for the products included

TABLE 3.4
Comparison of Metal Products Production Indexes

Year	WEFA[a]	CB/AZ[b]
1965	.16	.03
1966	.32	.26
1967	.25	.36
1968	.30	.67
1969	.24	.45
1970	.31	.33
1971	.70	.64
1972	.81	.75
1973	.86	.61
1974	1.00	1.00
1975	.94	.85
1976	.29	.65
1977	.27	1.19
1978	.44	1.94
1979	.25	2.25
1980	.46	2.27

[a]Wharton Econometric Forecasting Associates.
[b]Claes Brundenius/Andrew Zimbalist.

Source: Jorge Pérez-López, Construction of Cuban Activity and Trade Indexes (Final Report of Study to Develop Methodology for Estimating Cuba's GNP) (Washington, D.C.: Wharton Econometric Forecasting Associates, November 1983).

by WEFA in the construction materials branch (1974 = 1.00) as shown in Table 3.5.

Nine of twelve products have indexes higher than WEFA's overall index for the branch, 1.11. Given the source of the low growth rate estimates by WEFA in the case of metal products we now suspected that in this case also there would be important products, such as cement, excluded. However, we found that eight of twelve products were indeed included, and cement was one of them. So the strange branch index had to have some other explanation. Looking at the list of proxy prices for the branch's goods (reported in WEFA's Table 45) we discovered that the unit value of cement is put in metric tons and not in thousand metric tons as it should have been. This error has resulted in giving cement a weight of only 0.24 percent in the total index when the correct weight is 70.4 percent. Adjusting for this mistake we obtained a new

TABLE 3.5
1980 Production Index for Construction
Materials Branch (1974 = 1.00)

Sand	1.20
Crushed stone	1.32
Cement	1.56
Terazzo tiles	1.16
Floor tiles	1.13
Bricks	1.63
Pref. concrete blocks	0.89
Refractory materials	1.08
Concrete pipes	1.66
Fiberglass roof panels	1.05
Fiberglass pipes	6.05
Cinder blocks	1.60

Source: Jorge Pérez-López, Construction
of Cuban Activity and Trade Indexes
(Final Report of Study to Develop
Methodology for Estimating Cuba's GNP)
(Washington, D.C.: Wharton Econometric
Forecasting Associates, November 1983).

index of 1.40 for 1980 for the construction materials branch. Recalculating
the branch's index using Peruvian 1967 prices for all twelve products
we arrived at the results shown in Table 3.6 compared with WEFA.

We do not claim that the data have been deliberately manipulated
in order for WEFA to prove the point that growth in Cuba has been
slower in the 1970s than claimed by the official statistics and other
authors, but the errors previously discussed are sufficiently serious to
disqualify the report. The more likely explanation for WEFA's unrepresentative price sample is that the Guatemalan economy is considerably
less industrialized than the Cuban, and hence a 1973 Guatemalan price
set is unlikely to include many of Cuba's newer and more rapidly
growing industrial products. Such products are thus excluded from the
WEFA calculations, systematically biasing these downward.

This interpretation gains further support as we consider additional
branches. In the chemicals branch with a weight of 0.11 WEFA has
prices for only eleven of twenty-nine products. The branch's output falls
by 8 percent between 1974 and 1980 according to WEFA; yet there are
no prices for anhydrous ammonia, sulfuric acid, ammonium nitrate, urea,
mixed fertilizers, granulated fertilizers, or torula yeast, products whose
output increased between 36 and 469 percent.

TABLE 3.6
Comparison of Construction Materials
Production Indexes

Year	WEFA[a]	CB/AZ[b]
1965	.22	.41
1966	.22	.41
1967	.33	.46
1968	.28	.43
1969	.24	.37
1970	.27	.39
1971	.47	.59
1972	.73	.79
1973	.90	.94
1974	1.00	1.00
1975	1.18	1.14
1976	1.21	1.32
1977	1.22	1.38
1978	1.09	1.11
1979	1.08	1.11
1980	1.11	1.44

[a]Wharton Econometric Forecasting
Associates.
[b]Claes Brundenius/Andrew Zimbalist.

Source: Jorge Pérez-López, Construction
of Cuban Activity and Trade Indexes
(Final Report of Study to Develop
Methodology for Estimating Cuba's GNP)
(Washington, D.C.:   Wharton Econometric
Forecasting Associates, November 1983).

In the nonelectrical machinery branch with a weight of 0.05 there are prices for only five of ten products, and the output falls according to WEFA by 26 percent between 1974 and 1980. There are no prices for industrial air conditioners and refrigeration equipment whose physical output increases 262 percent, for combines whose output goes from zero to 502 units, for sugarcane carts whose output increases 13.7 percent, or for kerosene stoves whose output increases 3.5 percent. Fishing boats are the only product without a price whose output fell, in this case by 8.5 percent.

There are questions with nearly every branch. Overall, using both Guatemalan and U.S. prices WEFA found prices for only 128 of the 206 goods in the output series. For perspective, it is useful to keep in

TABLE 3.7
Comparison of Estimated Growth Indexes for Selected Branches (1974 = 100)

	1965	1970	1974	1980	1983
Construction Materials					
(12 products in sample)					
WEFA (8 of 12 products)	22	27	100	111	--
CB/AZ (12 of 12)	48	41	100	134	149
Metal Products					
(8 products in sample)					
WEFA (2 of 8 products)	16	31	100	46	--
CB/AZ (8 of 8)	12	30	100	153	230
Nonelectrical Machinery					
(11 products in sample)					
WEFA (5 of 11 products)	10	21	100	74	--
CB/AZ (9 of 11)	21	26	100	185	228
Electrical Machinery					
(8 products in sample)					
WEFA (6 of 8 products)	58	34	100	129	--
CB/AZ (8 of 8)	39	47	100	184	219
Chemicals					
(29 products in sample)					
WEFA (11 of 29 products)	57	77	100	92	--
CB/AZ (23 of 29)	50	64	100	151	150

Note: WEFA--Wharton Econometrics Forecasting Associates. CB/AZ--Claes Brundenius/Andrew Zimbalist.

Source: Jorge Pérez-López, Construction of Cuban Activity and Trade Indexes (Final Report of Study to Develop Methodology for Estimating Cuba's GNP) (Washington, D.C.: Wharton Econometric Forecasting Associates, November 1983), and calculations of the authors.

mind there are over one million goods produced in the Cuban economy today.

To extend the coverage of products we have applied official 1981 Cuban prices to the output sample used by WEFA. In Table 3.7 our growth estimates are compared with those of WEFA for five industrial branches. We have selected only those branches for which the WEFA estimates appear abnormally low given the underlying production data presented by WEFA for those branches.

Table 3.7 shows that the product coverage in our estimates using 1981 Cuban prices is almost complete, relative to the WEFA production sample, in contrast to the partial and erratic product coverage by WEFA using 1973 Guatemalan prices. The extended coverage yields higher growth estimates in all five sectors. In three sectors that were estimated by WEFA to have negative growth, our estimates suggest rapid, positive growth: Between 1974 and 1980 metal products output grew 53 percent, nonelectrical machinery by 85 percent, and electrical machinery by 51 percent.

When we used the restricted WEFA product coverage with Cuban prices and compared the resulting output index to the WEFA estimates, the Cuban price weighted index yielded slower growth over the period 1965–1980 than the Guatemalan price weighted index in three of the five branches. In one of the remaining two branches, the Cuban price weighted index grew more slowly from 1974 to 1980. These results are consistent with the hypothesis that Cuban price weights do not produce an upward bias in the growth estimate.[14] In these five branches at least, it appears that extended product coverage, rather than the use of Cuban prices, accounts for the higher growth estimates. That is, the fuller the product coverage within a branch, the closer the growth estimate corresponds to the official growth figure. We must caution, however, that this type of sensitivity analysis does not inspire high confidence levels due to the restricted sample sizes. It must be recalled that the WEFA coverage in the metals products branch, for instance, includes only two products, pressure cookers and nails, which together accounted for only 2.5 percent of the gross value of output in the branch in 1980.

Although our product coverage is nearly complete for these five branches with respect to the products reported in the official statistical yearbooks and used by WEFA, it is much less complete with respect to total branch output. In value terms, our products cover the following shares of the total 1983 branch output in Cuba: chemicals, 75.6 percent of GVO; construction materials, 64.6 percent of GVO; electrical machinery, 32.4 percent of GVO; metal products, 20.8 percent of GVO; and non-electrical machinery, 16.0 percent. The statistical yearbooks' series, then, are somewhat irregular and often limited in terms of product coverage.

In Table 3.8 we compare various estimated growth indexes for the engineering goods branches. The top row estimate has the smallest product coverage, the second row has a larger coverage, the third row coverage is larger still, and the fourth row coverage is complete. Unfortunately, the third row estimates are based on data for the years 1980–1983 only. Again, WEFA estimates of negative growth are in striking contrast to the estimates of strong, positive growth based on more complete coverage. What is more notable, however, is the direct correlation between the degree of product coverage and the rate of growth. Brundenius/Zimbalist 1, based on twenty-five products, represents almost complete coverage from the Cuban statistical yearbooks, and it estimates significantly lower growth than Brundenius/Zimbalist 2, based on several hundred products, although both estimates use Cuban 1981 wholesale prices. At least for the three industrial branches

TABLE 3.8
Comparison of Estimated Growth Indexes for Engineering Goods
Branches (1980 = 100)[a]

	1980	1981	1982	1983
WEFA[b] (projected using WEFA methodology)	100	123	86	91
Brundenius/Zimbalist 1	100	120	111	127
Brundenius/Zimbalist 2[c]	100	122	138	163
Official Cuban	100	124	139	164

[a]These data refer to three branches: metal products, electrical machinery, and nonelectrical machinery. The WEFA estimates are based on thirteen products and 1973 Guatemalan prices. The Brundenius/Zimbalist 1 estimate is based on twenty-five products and 1981 Cuban prices. The Brundenius/Zimbalist 2 estimate is based on several hundred products and 1981 Cuban prices; it includes only the capital goods (excluding all consumer durables) in these three branches. In value terms it accounts for approximately 37 percent of the production in these three branches according to the official statistics. The official Cuban data are based on all products in these branches and 1981 Cuban prices.
[b]Wharton Econometrics Forecasting Associates.
[c]The third row estimates are taken from C. Brundenius, "The Role of Capital Goods Production in the Economic Development of Cuba," paper presented to the Workshop on Technology Policies for Development, Research Policy Institute, University of Lund, Sweden, May 29-31, 1985.

referred to in Table 3.8, then, the Cubans clearly are not putting an unrepresentative sample of the fastest growing products in the statistical yearbook. Rather, the products in the 1980s yearbooks are, with few exceptions, the same products that appeared in the 1960s yearbooks. Hence, they do not include new products that are often the most dynamic and fastest growing.

In addition to WEFA's troubling treatment of intrabranch weights, WEFA adopts interbranch weights that are highly questionable. Although we do not have the space to discuss this issue in detail, it is important to illustrate the nature of the problem.

WEFA relies heavily on the branch distribution of gross value of output in 1975 to generate its industrial branch weights. The year 1975 is chosen because WEFA believes the branch distribution is strongly affected by the conversion from the gross turnover to the enterprise exit method, and 1975 is the first year for which the enterprise exit method measurements are available. Although this switch is indeed significant, its impact on branch distribution is dwarfed by the impact of turnover taxes, which are included in *precios del productor* (producer or industrial prices) but excluded from *precios de empresa* (enterprise prices). This important distinction between two very different sets of wholesale prices goes unnoticed in the WEFA study. To be sure, the allocation of turnover taxes among branches and sectors accounts, inter alia, for the important inflation of measured output in the commercial sector over time.

In this case, the inclusion of turnover taxes in the series used by WEFA has greatly inflated the value of output of the beverages and tobacco branch. WEFA's weight for this branch is 0.26, or over one-quarter of all industrial output. Viewed differently, the beverages and tobacco branch weight is almost two and a half times the weights given to the second and third largest industrial branches, processed food and chemicals, and more than four times the weight given the sugar industry branch. Such a share for beverages and tobacco is simply out of the realm of possibility.[15] Since the beverages and tobacco branch has a negative growth rate between 1965 and 1980 according to WEFA and a slow growth rate (below 2 percent per annum) from 1974 to 1980, the unrealistically high weight accorded the branch produces a further downward bias in the WEFA growth estimate. Had WEFA recognized the distinction between *precios del productor* and *precios de empresa* in the Cuban MPS methodology and adjusted its interbranch weights accordingly, this bias could have been avoided.

A new independent estimate of Cuban industrial growth, based on constant 1981 Cuban enterprise prices and 1981 Cuban net value-added weights, has been recently published.[16] This estimate tends to confirm the criticisms of the WEFA study and to lend credibility to the official figures suggesting strong industrial growth since 1970 as well as a growth spurt in the early 1980s.

Vanderbilt Conference Paper

In November 1983, Carmelo Mesa-Lago delivered a paper entitled "Cuba's Centrally Planned Economy: An Equity Tradeoff for Growth" to an international conference on models of political and economic change in Latin America at Vanderbilt University. The paper was subsequently published in *Latin American Political Economy: Financial Crisis and Political Change* edited by J. Hartlyn and S. Morley, 1986.

The paper's title suggests its conclusion: that Cuba has sacrificed growth in order to achieve equity. Yet, according to official statistics,

Cuba's real gross social product grew at an average annual rate of 5.7 percent during the 1970s and 7.3 percent during 1981–1985.[17] The rest of Latin America (nineteen countries) experienced stagnation during the first five years of the 1980s.[18]

One aspect of Mesa-Lago's claim, which was reproduced in a *Wall Street Journal* article,[19] is that the Cuban economy is less industrialized now than it was before the Revolution. According to Mesa-Lago, industry as a share of GSP had fallen from 48.2 percent in 1962 to 35.6 percent in 1980. (That industry's share in GDP hovered around 25 percent during the late 1950s is somehow left out of the picture.) Furthermore, according to Mesa-Lago, trade was the only sector whose share was increasing dramatically over this period—from 20.3 percent of GSP in 1962, to 22.0 percent in 1970, and to 34.0 percent in 1980. Were these proportions accurate, they would indeed indicate structural weaknesses in the Cuban economy.

The problem with Mesa-Lago's calculations in this instance is straightforward. Between 1962 and 1968 GSP in Cuban national accounts was calculated in constant prices for all sectors, including trade. After 1970, however, all sectors except trade were calculated in constant prices. That is, Mesa-Lago's findings are purely a result of accounting practices and do not represent a real structural shift in the economy.

One way to bypass this problem would be to consider industry's share in total material product (TMP) over time. TMP excludes trade and hence is given consistently in constant prices. If Mesa-Lago had carried out this exercise he would have discovered that the manufacturing share in TMP increased from 49 percent in 1961 to 52 percent in 1981. Furthermore, if the construction industry is included, total industry increased its share from 64 percent to 78 percent over the same period.

For the first time in the 1984 statistical yearbook the Cubans published estimates for sectoral shares that adjust for the price increases in the trade sector.[20] The results are illustrative of the point we are making: The industrial share in GSP grew from 48.7 percent in 1975 to 54.2 percent in 1984; the share of commerce fell from 22.5 percent in 1975 to 14.7 percent in 1984.

Mesa-Lago's corollary to de-industrialization is that Cuba has failed to break out of its monocultural patterns of dependency on sugar. He supports this contention with two misleading claims. "Another fundamental indicator of the revolutionary failure to diversify is the nation's continuous dependency on sugar which still generates about one-fourth of GSP. According to Table 5, sugar and its by-products accounted for 78 percent of Cuba's total exports in 1958 but rose to 86 percent in 1979" (p. 13).

TABLE 3.9
Structural Changes in the Cuban Economy, 1961-1981

| | Sector Contribution to GDP (%) | | |
	1961	1970	1981
Agriculture	18.2	18.1	12.9
Sugarcane	(7.9)	(9.2)	(4.9)
Other	(10.3)	(8.9)	(8.0)
Industry	31.8	38.4	46.4
Manufacturing	(24.4)	(29.7)	(30.7)
Capital goods	(1.6)	(2.5)	(6.6)
Sugar & derivatives	(4.7)	(4.8)	(3.0)
Construction	(5.2)	(5.7)	(13.0)
Sugarcane & refining	12.6	14.0	7.9

Source: Claes Brundenius, Revolutionary Cuba: The Challenge of Economic Growth with Equality (Boulder: Westview Press, 1984), p. 77.

In Table 3.9 we reproduce part of a table from Brundenius's recent book on Cuban growth, which shows that the share of sugar and its byproducts in estimated GDP fell from 12.6 percent in 1961 to 7.9 percent in 1981.[21] That is, sugar's share in GDP fell by 37.3 percent over these twenty years, a fact hardly consistent with Mesa-Lago's claim of a constant share over time. What of his claim that this share has been one-quarter of GSP? Depending on the year and the estimate, the GDP/GSP ratio varies between approximately 73 and 82 percent, with the ratio rising slightly over time. Giving Mesa-Lago the benefit of the doubt by assuming a GDP/GSP ratio of 0.73 in 1961 and 0.82 in 1981, sugar's share in GSP would be 9.2 percent in 1961 and 6.5 percent in 1981—a far cry from the 25 percent of GSP figure provided by Mesa-Lago.

Mesa-Lago also claims that sugar's share in exports has risen. He compares 1958 with 1979 in his Table 5 and cites as a source an article by Cuban economist José Luis Rodríguez. The curiosities here are manifold. Mesa-Lago's figure for 1958 is simply wrong: The correct figure is 81 percent, not 78 percent. Even 81 percent, however, is unrepresentative of the average sugar share in exports during the last ten years before the Revolution; the share was 84.1 percent. The next problem is his choice of 1979 as an end year. The cited Rodríguez source is a table that has a sugar share figure for 1980 as well as 1979. The 1980 share in this table is 83.6 percent; the 1979 is, as reported by Mesa-Lago, 85.9 percent. Why did Mesa-Lago stop in 1979?

It is also curious, however, that Mesa-Lago chose not to look beyond the article by Rodríguez. Given the November 1983 date of his paper, he surely had access to 1981 and probably 1982 data. The sugar share in exports in these years was 79.1 and 77.1 percent, respectively. In 1983 the share fell further to 73.8 percent. Part of falling share is attributable to the rapid increase in re-exports of Soviet petroleum and does not represent diversification of domestic export production. It is also true, however, that domestic crude oil extraction in Cuba tripled between 1981 and 1984.

Now Mesa-Lago might dismiss this sharp fall in the sugar export share over the last four years, as he did for William LeoGrande's earlier computations, on the grounds that they simply reflect lower world market sugar prices (Mesa-Lago, Vanderbilt paper, pp. 34–35; see also LeoGrande 1979). In fact, however, world market sugar prices were higher for the period 1980–1983 ($.156 per pound on average) than for the 1975–1979 period ($.1149 on average). And despite the fact that sugar prices were 35.9 percent higher during the latter period, the share of sugar in exports was 9.7 percent lower. Thus, when adjusted for prices, the extent of export diversification is even greater than the decrease in nominal shares suggests.

Export diversification is also supported by other evidence. From 1976 to 1980, Cuba introduced 115 new export products, and in 1981 it introduced 17 more. Whereas nonsugar exports equaled 230.5 million pesos in 1978, in 1982 they equaled 640.9 million pesos. Nonsugar exports grew by an additional 27.5 million pesos in 1983 excluding an increase of over 15 million pesos in reexported petroleum. Success in the areas of import substitution and tourism has been even more marked, but this is another story.

In another section of the Vanderbilt paper Mesa-Lago attempts to discuss changes in efficiency in the Cuban economy. He follows the unfortunate practice of discussing trends in labor productivity and capital productivity separately while ignoring joint factor productivity. There are several problems with his discussion, but one stands out. In his treatment of capital productivity Mesa-Lago compares apples and oranges by comparing the Cuban investment ratio as a share of GSP with the investment ratio as a share of GDP in the rest of Latin America. The result is rather astounding: Cuba's average investment ratio over the period 1962–1980 was 13.2 percent, a full ten percentage points below the investment ratio in the rest of Latin America. Other things equal and with similar rates of real GDP growth from 1970 to 1980, this reported lower investment ratio would indicate that capital efficiency was much higher in Cuba than in the rest of Latin America. Mesa-Lago does not deal with this implication of his investment ratio comparisons.

Since Mesa-Lago did not treat joint labor and capital productivity, we shall cautiously present our own preliminary computations. The

TABLE 3.10
Cuban Total Factor Productivity Annual Rates of Change, Stage
Averages (%)

1963-1964	1965-1969	1970-1975	1976-1978	1981
+0.4	-2.2	+7.8	+1.5	+11.4

Note: The capital stock series' construction is described in the
first section of this chapter. Since it is based on gross rather
than net investment data, it probably produces a downward bias in
total factor productivity estimates. The civilian labor force
series is the number of workers as opposed to labor hours.

standard measure is generally called joint or total factor productivity
(TFP). The percentage change in TFP, or $T\dot{F}P$, is a rough indicator of
dynamic efficiency in the economy. $T\dot{F}P$ is equal to the percentage change
in output ($\dot{Q}$, or in this case, $G\dot{S}P$) minus the weighted percentage
change in the inputs:

$$T\dot{F}P = \dot{Q} - (W_K\dot{K} + W_L\dot{L}) \tag{7}$$

where
  W_K is the weight assigned to capital,
  $\dot{K}$ is the percentage change in the capital stock,
  W_L is the weight assigned to labor, and
  $\dot{L}$ is the percent change in the labor force.
No time data on land use are available. The factor weights correspond
to factor shares in national income.

There are no easy ways to estimate factor shares in planned economies,
and aggregate production function estimation under varying elasticity
of substitution assumptions is fraught with problems. Thus, as suggested
by others,[22] we follow the nonelegant method of assuming constant
capital and labor shares of 0.25 and 0.75, respectively. The result,
reproduced in Table 3.10, corresponds closely with other scholars' more
impressionistic accounts of dynamic efficiency in Cuba during different
time periods.

Conclusions

The three papers reviewed in this chapter are riddled with methodological
and theoretical problems. As a result Mesa-Lago and Pérez-López present
a distorted picture of Cuban economic performance. It is our hope that
the foregoing discussion will help to redress these distortions and

contribute to a more dispassionate and rigorous analysis of the Cuban economy.

Notes

1. The November 1982 version we critique here is the "final version" according to the title page of the paper. The paper was subsequently revised to be issued with other CMEA National Income studies as World Bank Working Paper no. 770 in 1985. This 1985 version corrects a few of the errors we allude to. Our initial critique was sent to Mesa-Lago and Pérez-López in November 1984.

2. Although Mesa-Lago and Pérez-López can certainly not be held at fault for yearbooks published after their study, it is interesting to note that the trend toward more complete coverage has continued. Thus, by the 1985 yearbook the macroindicators section contains ninety-six pages, including eleven pages on definitions and methodology. It is also important to observe that the 1985 yearbook was published punctually in October 1986, a shorter lag than for most developed nations.

3. See UN (1971:43–47).

4. Without explanation the authors shift to using net material product (GMP minus depreciation) instead of GMP at a few points. This confusion about the meaning of GMP is also evident in Mesa-Lago's earlier study, *The Economy of Socialist Cuba: A Two Decade-Appraisal* (1981:33), where he erroneously stated that GMP excludes material services (transportation, trade, and communication). Material services are excluded from the concept total material product (TMP), but they are included in GMP.

5. The MLPL estimates of nonmaterial services correspond closely to those in Brundenius (1984:77).

6. Mesa-Lago and Pérez-López, 1985.

7. See Brundenius (1984:61–68); and Banco Nacional de Cuba (1984:23–27).

8. Naturally, many other specifications are also possible. For clarification, sugar output in GSP is valued at a domestically set producer price, not the world market (or Soviet) price. The former does not appear to have been adjusted to reflect the latter, save in the 1981 wholesale price reform.

9. A statistical test of the null hypothesis that $\alpha + \beta = 1$ (first degree homogeneity) reveals that the null cannot be rejected at any reasonable significance level.

10. The figures in parentheses below the coefficients are the t-statistics.

11. Brundenius (1981).

12. A fuller evaluation of the WEFA estimates along with new estimates for industrial growth is provided by Zimbalist (1987).

13. Banco Interamericano de Desarrollo, *Progreso Económico, Social en América Latina, Informe 1982* (Washington, D.C.: 1984); World Bank, *World Development Report 1984* (Washington, D.C.: 1984); J. Wilkie, ed. *Statistical Abstract of Latin America* 23, 1984.

14. This analysis is extended to cover all twenty-one industrial branches in Zimbalist (1987).

64 Claes Brundenius and Andrew Zimbalist

15. According to data received by the authors from the State Statistical Committee, the beverages and tobacco branch accounted for 4.5 percent of industrial net value added in 1981, based on *precios de empresa*.

16. Zimbalist (1987).

17. The rates are calculated from data in Banco Nacional de Cuba, *Informe Económico 1982;* Comité Estatal de Estadísticas (CEE), *Anuario Estadístico de Cuba, 1985;* Banco Nacional de Cuba, *Economic Report 1986.*

18. According to CEPAL (1986:7), real per capita gross domestic product in Latin America (excluding Cuba) actually fell at an average annual rate of 1.7 percent from 1980 to 1985. CEPAL is the Economic Commission for Latin America of the United Nations.

19. Lowenstein (1984:21).

20. These price increases are largely the result of the overwhelming incidence of turnover taxes falling on this sector subsequent to the full nationalization of commerce in 1968, *Anuario Estadístico de Cuba, 1984,* p. 95.

21. Brundenius (1984:77).

22. See the citation and discussion of this literature in Zimbalist and Sherman (1984:188–190). Also see Weitzman (1983).

References

Banco Interamericano de Desarrollo. *Progreso Económico, Social en América Latina, Informe 1982.* Washington, D.C., 1984.

Banco Nacional de Cuba. *Informe Económico.* 1982 and 1984.

Brundenius, Claes. *Economic Growth, Basic Needs and Income Distribution in Revolutionary Cuba.* Lund, Sweden: Research Policy Institute, University of Lund, 1981.

——. *Revolutionary Cuba: The Challenge of Economic Growth with Equity.* Boulder: Westview Press, 1984.

——. "The Role of Capital Goods Production in the Economic Development of Cuba." Paper presented to the Workshop on Technology Policies for Development, Research Policy Institute, University of Lund, Sweden, May 29–31, 1985.

CEPAL. *Revista de la CEPAL 28,* April 1986.

Comité Estatal de Estadísticas. *Anuario Estadístico de Cuba,* 1981 through 1985.

——. *La Economía Cubana,* 1982 and 1983.

Estadística Industrial, 1967. Lima, Peru: 1969.

Halebsky, Sandor, and John Kirk, eds., *Cuba: Twenty-five Years of Revolution, 1959–84.* New York: Praeger, 1985.

LeoGrande, William. "Cuban Dependency: A Comparison of Pre-Revolutionary and Post-Revolutionary International Relations." *Cuban Studies 9,* no. 2 (July 1979):1–28.

Lowenstein, Roger. "Sugar is Cuba's Triumph and Its Failure." *Wall Street Journal,* August 3, 1984.

Martínez, Gilberto Diaz. "El Sistema Empresarial Estatal en Cuba." *Cuba Socialista* 8 (September/November 1983).

Mesa-Lago, Carmelo. *The Economy of Socialist Cuba: A Two-Decade Appraisal.* Albuquerque: University of New Mexico Press, 1981.

———. "Cuba's Centrally Planned Economy: An Equity Tradeoff for Growth." Paper presented to the International Conference on Models of Political and Economic Change in Latin America, Vanderbilt University, Nashville, Tenn., November 1983.

———. "Cuba's Centrally Planned Economy: An Equity Tradeoff for Growth." In J. Hartlyn and Samuel Morley, eds, *Latin American Political Economy: Financial Crisis and Political Change.* Boulder: Westview Press, 1986.

Mesa-Lago, Carmelo, and J. Pérez-López. *Study of Cuba's MPS, Its Conversion to SNA and Estimation of GDP/capita and Growth Rates.* Washington, D.C.: World Bank Working Paper no. 770, 1985.

Pérez-López, Jorge. *Construction of Cuban Activity and Trade Indexes (Final Report of Study to Develop Methodology for Estimating Cuba's GNP).* Washington, D.C.: Wharton Econometric Forecasting Associates, November 1983.

———. "Real Economic Growth in Cuba, 1965–82." Paper presented at LASA meetings, Albuquerque, New Mexico, April 1985.

———. "Real Economic Growth in Cuba, 1965–82." *Journal of Developing Areas* 20 (January 1986):151–172.

Research Team on the Cuban Economy. *The Most Outstanding Aspects of the Cuban Economy, 1959–83.* Havana: University of Havana, Economic Sciences Area, 1984.

United Nations. *Basic Principles of the System of Balances of the National Economy.* Studies in Methods, Series F. no. 17. New York, 1971.

Weitzman, Martin. "Industrial Production." In Abram Bergson and Herbert Levine, eds., *The Soviet Economy Toward the Year 2000.* London: Allen and Unwin, 1983.

Wilkie, James, ed. *Statistical Abstract of Latin America 23,* 1984.

World Bank. *World Development Report 1984.* Washington, D.C., 1984.

Zimbalist, Andrew. "Cuban Economic Planning: Organization and Performance." In Sandor Halebsky and John Kirk, eds., *Cuba: Twenty-five Years of Revolution, 1959–84.* New York: Praeger, 1985.

———. "Cuban Industrial Growth, 1965–1984." *World Development* (January 1987).

Zimbalist, Andrew, and Howard Sherman. *Comparing Economic Systems: A Political-Economic Approach.* New York: Academic Press, 1984.

4

Interpreting Cuban Planning: Between a Rock and a Hard Place

Andrew Zimbalist

Since the creation of the Grupo Central in December 1984, there has been an ongoing and critical reevaluation in Cuba of its system of central planning and economic management. To be sure, self-criticism and impatience with imperfections and deficiencies have characterized the Cuban attitude to the new planning system, the System of Economic Management and Planning (SDPE), since its inception in 1976. Much of this self-criticism has been published in Cuban newspaper accounts, journals, and books. Cubanologists, in turn, have isolated these self-criticisms, at times distorted them, taken them out of context and combined them with testimony from Cuban exiles to produce a misleading analysis of Cuban planning.

Notwithstanding their unscientific marshaling of evidence, the most serious problem with these Cubanologist analyses is their interpretation of the theory and practice of central planning. Their analyses are without proper context; they interpret commonplace planning inefficiencies as cataclysms and misapprehend the underlying dynamics of the system. To situate my own comments on Cuban planning in their proper context and to provide a perspective on the ahistorical approach to this issue represented in recent writings of Carmelo Mesa-Lago and Sergio Roca,[1] I begin this chapter with some background on the nature of central planning and its problems.

Part of this chapter is adapted from Andrew Zimbalist, "Analyzing Cuban Planning: A Response to Roca," in *Cuban Studies* (vol. 17).

The Experience of
Centrally Planned Economies

Dispassionate and serious students of economic systems accept the proposition that both centrally planned and market economies involve trade-offs. It is also accepted that although certain central tendencies inhere to each system there is a significant variety of institutions, policies, and performance results among the planned as well as the market economies. The weaknesses of centrally planned economies help to account for the ongoing experimentation and reform efforts in all the socialist economies. The strengths help to account for their durability.

Among the important advantages of central planning is its ability to maintain full employment with very high labor force participation rates. In part reflecting this, centrally planned economies have also had marked success in the realm of equity. Income distribution figures reveal a strong underlying equality with decile ratios varying between 4 and 7 to 1. Of course, there are perquisites and privileged access to goods and services for the top party leaders, but these are largely, if not entirely, offset by free services such as health and education and heavily subsidized basic goods.

The growth record of the Centrally Planned Economies (CPEs) has been creditable. Central planning seems to offer greater advantages for growth during earlier stages of development and fewer advantages during later stages. During early stages, central planning can put to effective use its ability to quickly mobilize resources for needed projects; to nurture, finance, and protect infant industry; to be a surrogate for the fledgling or nonexistent entrepreneurial class; to coordinate investment projects and reduce uncertainty; to develop human capital and fully employ labor resources. During later stages, the growing complexity of the economy, the approach to the technological frontier in many in-dustries, the poor innovative potential, among other things, seem to encumber the already centralized and overburdened structures of central planning. This is not to say, however, that centrally planned economies are homogeneous either in their structures or in their performance. Some developed CPEs, such as the German Democratic Republic, still have strong growth records, which are superior to those of their capitalist counterparts. Because of different national income accounting systems, different price systems, different currencies, and fixed exchange rates, however, it is an extremely difficult task to measure comparative growth rates and even more difficult to identify comparative living standards.[2] There is still much discussion and disagreement about comparative growth performance.

There is perhaps less disagreement about the nature of the problems engendered by central planning. It would appear to be an uncontestable virtue of the market that its demands for the central collection and processing of information are minimal. Producers and consumers interface directly and communicate through price signals. Eliminate the market, however, and all information must be centrally processed. In an economy like Cuba's there are over one million commodities, thousands of technologies, millions of supply contracts with input specifications and dates, over one million prices to be set, thousands of investment projects, and so on. To balance, let alone efficiently allocate, all of these resources requires comprehensive, accurate, and timely information. This information must then be processed and converted into an operative economic plan.

These informational requirements for a balanced plan are many magnitudes too great to be achieved. Planners, instead, must take shortcuts. The more shortcuts that are taken, however, the greater the margin for error in the plan and the greater the possibility for imbalances. Moreover, since supply contracts among producers and consumer goods production are centrally planned, without direct contact between the seller and buyer, there is always a greater likelihood that what is produced (even if it is produced in the right quantity at the right time) will not be what the consumer wants. If the produced good is unusable and there is nowhere else to obtain the good, then shortages develop. If the good in question happens to be an input to another producing enterprise then that enterprise will not be able to meet its supply contracts to other enterprises. Bottlenecks can thus routinely spread throughout the economy. If the good in question is a consumer good, then the frustrated consumer will learn over time that there is a greater payoff to leaving work early to queue for scarce goods than there is to working harder and earning more income given the insufficient supply of desirable goods.

In the absence of universal altruism, planners must also find a means to motivate producers. This problem has several dimensions. First, since the center cannot possibly know the production technologies, the inventory levels, and the personnel issues at the enterprise level, it must rely on enterprises sharing accurate information on these things in order to plan production. Enterprise managers, however, are rewarded with bonuses or better jobs for meeting the output targets in the central plan. They are judged by the industrial ministry to which they are subordinated, and the ministry is judged according to the industrywide target by the central planning board. At each level the communication is vertical, not horizontal. The effort is to satisfy someone higher up in the planning hierarchy instead of the consumer of product. The easiest way to meet the plan is to overstate need for inputs and to understate output potential. Elicitation schemes to induce accurate information from production units have been devised,[3] but they have foundered.[4]

Second, once the target is set, the problem becomes getting the enterprise to meet its target on time, with the correct output mix and desired quality. But if the enterprise finds some products easier to produce than others or, because of a problematic price system, more profitable than others and it is worried about input shortages, then it is likely to take whatever shortcuts are necessary to meet the most important indicators of the plan. When an enterprise takes shortcuts, such as reducing quality, it is natural for the center to specify new success indicators, such as quality standards. The enterprise counters by finding new shortcuts in a manner perhaps analogous to tax shelter abusers. Eventually, an enterprise may find itself with dozens of success indicators. Under these circumstances, there must obviously be a ranking or prioritization of the indicators. The indicator that inevitably gains top priority is the physical output target. The reason for this is simple: The balance in the national plan is based on this indicator.

Exhortations for greater efficiency and profitability run up against the same constraint. Furthermore, because worker job rights to date have been an inalienable part of the political bargain, enterprises have not been allowed to fail. Hence, being in the red means much less to an executive in a CPE than to an executive in a market economy. The profitability criterion applies at most a weak brake to input hoarding in the face of supply uncertainty. Put differently, financial targets play a distant secondary role to physical targets.[5]

Third, assuming workers' objective functions are more complex than simply wanting to maximize the commonweal, there is the problem of motivating the direct producers. Monetary incentives, however, for reasons that parallel the line of argument just presented, are insufficient at best. Given this, it would seem desirable to give workers a greater voice in enterprise and extra-enterprise decisionmaking. Among other things, if workers were to effectively participate in setting enterprise and national economic goals (as well as in implementing them), it is more likely that they would identify with these goals and be self-motivated to a greater extent.[6] Although only scanty information is available on the degree of worker involvement in management in today's CPEs, the information we have suggests that this involvement, with some unevenness across countries, has been rather limited.[7] Nonetheless, as I have argued elsewhere, the available information is consistent with the observation that the social relations of production in Cuba appear to be both more egalitarian and more participatory than in other CPEs.[8]

The more limited the worker participation, the less will be the progress toward reducing worker alienation. It should be emphasized, however, that the maintenance of full employment along with socialist ideology gives the socialist worker de facto power not present in the typical capitalist factory. This power can be used variously to shirk, to leave work early, to be absent, or, generally, to reduce the intensity of labor. That is, the worker in a CPE appears to possess greater flexibility in identifying the optimal point in his or her work-leisure trade-off.

There does, however, seem to be a new recognition of the economic and political value of worker participation in the socialist economies. Since 1980 in many countries there have been new statutes expanding the scope of worker decisionmaking powers and establishing production brigades, which are subunits of enterprises and state farms. These production brigades are intended (1) to make the decisionmaking process more immediate and relevant to the workers and (2) to connect more directly a worker's pay to his or her effort through brigade-level, in contrast to enterprise-level, incentives. Early indications in Cuba and elsewhere are that the brigades have been successful, particularly in agriculture.

These problems of CPEs denote inefficiency and waste, but they do not signify catastrophe. If they did, the CPEs would not have shown the resilience and durability they have. Put simply, the CPEs as a group have exhibited less efficiency but more equity than the advanced market capitalist economies.

As the possibilities for extensive growth have eroded and growth rates for most CPEs have slowed over the past fifteen years, there has been an ongoing quest to improve the economic mechanisms of planning. The most substantial reforms have occurred in Hungary and China, both of which have been dubbed experiments in market socialism. The reform experience in Hungary is longer and, it appears, more stable and systematic than that in China.

The underlying approach of the 1968–1986 Hungarian reform has been to decentralize (1) by instituting direct material supply contracting between enterprises, (2) by introducing the market mechanism and free or bounded prices wherever feasible, and (3) by allowing private production of goods and services under a watchful eye. In essence, the Hungarian approach recognizes that it is impossible to centrally plan an entire economy and that the more you attempt to control everything, the less control you have over the important parts of the economy. Instead, the Hungarians have retained control of important investments and key industries and gradually allowed more and more economic activity to be regulated by the market. (In this regard, it is interesting to note that at a meeting of the Cuban party leadership in late June

1986 Castro was quoted in the July 4 issue of *Bohemia* as saying: "Por exceso de controles, no tenemos control" [Because we try to control too much, we don't have control].)

This effort has encountered many setbacks and some basic tensions. Trade-offs inherent to the market mechanism have become manifest. For instance, to expect enterprises to make decentralized decisions about production implies reliance upon price signals. Prices must reflect the underlying conditions of supply and demand if they are to promote efficient resource use and market equilibrium. Market pricing, however, opens up the possibility for inflation as well as uncertainty, speculation, and monopoly prices. Further, if the price signals are truly to allocate resources in certain markets, then enterprises producing financial losses must be allowed to fail. This implies job instability and at least short-run unemployment—neither have been acceptable political outcomes to date. On the other side, some enterprises and private small businesses will succeed, generating higher incomes for some and greater inequality— also politically troublesome outcomes.

Moreover, as free markets and private production come to coexist with regulated markets and state production, there is the danger that resources will find their way through semilegal and illegal channels to the private sector. It is also likely that workers will reserve effort from state production for their private production or marketing activities. In short, the existence of a substantial private sector can challenge the predominance of the public sector. Although Cuba has not traveled as far down the path of decentralization as Hungary has, the current (since May 1986) retrenchment and rectification campaign is a response to market-related problems. The Hungarians themselves have proceeded with their reform in starts and stops, including a six-year moratorium beginning in 1972.[9]

This is not to say that mixed economies are impossible. It is rather to acknowledge the complexity of reform efforts and to suggest that such efforts must be, first, carefully planned and prepared and, then, flexibly and gradually administered. The actual process is likely to be fraught with social tensions and political struggles. Thus the preparation for a substantive, decentralizing reform requires not only a modicum of economic balance but also a high degree of political stability and party unity.

Another variant of reform away from central planning began in the early 1950s in Yugoslavia. This reform was prompted as much by political forces as by the economic problems of central planning.[10] Through 1976 the Yugoslavs gradually substituted the market for central planning, until at most a system of indicative planning prevailed. What distinguished the Yugoslav experiment, however, was its system of worker self-management or worker councils in the enterprises, with legal rights for workers to appoint, control, and remove management. By 1976, the Yugoslavs could boast of a good growth record, but they were also experiencing significant economic instability with high unemployment and inflation. Furthermore, the Yugoslav leadership began to see the market as disrupting the socialist fabric of the society, substituting managerialism for worker participation in enterprises, materialism and individualism for collectivism, and so on. The new 1976 constitution sought to replace the market as the coordination mechanism with bottom-up planning. Although the full record is not yet in, it appears that this new system has fallen far short of its goals.

The foregoing sketch of the socialist economic experience suggests that the model of pure central planning is impracticable. The information, coordination, and motivational barriers to this model are insuperable.

The paths to reform are through administrative or market decentralization and/or greater democracy in the management and political spheres. To varying degrees—subject to the prevailing cultural and political constraints—each socialist economy has experimented with one or more of the reform paths.

At the February 1986 Soviet Party Congress, General Secretary Mikhail Gorbachev outlined a long-term strategy for reforming the Soviet economy. He spoke of weakening the power of the ministries, strengthening the power of the enterprises, and reducing the scope of what is centrally planned. This vision is not dissimilar in its economic content to that of the 1960s reform movements in Czechoslovakia and Hungary. As yet, few concrete steps have been taken to suggest that Gorbachev's vision will become reality. The political obstacles to serious reform in the Soviet Union are formidable. Yet there is more open and far-ranging discussion of the need for decentralization to rejuvenate the economy now than at any time since the industrialization debate of the 1920s. Whether or not this debate affects policy in the USSR, it is likely to further legitimate and fuel reform efforts elsewhere in the Soviet bloc.

In part the present debate and reevaluation in Cuba reflect the new political climate within the CMEA. To a greater degree, however, it reflects the political culture of Cuban socialism. Deeply embedded in this culture is a fluidity, an effervescence, a willingness to experiment, an impatience with the torpidity and bureaucratism common to the CPEs. Nonetheless, an understanding of the structures and laws of motion of the CPEs is indispensable to place the Cuban planning experience in its proper context and, hence, to sensibly interpret the present situation. With this background, we can now turn to a specific critique of some Cubanologist writings on the Cuban planning system.

Recent Writings on Cuban Planning

The primary Cubanologist working on Cuban planning is Sergio Roca. He has been involved in a protracted study, based on interviews with exiles, that has produced several articles to date and promises to become a book-length effort. Prior to discussing Roca's work, however, it is of interest to mention a few other studies which, although not based on research on Cuban planning, are prepared to pass strong judgment on the same. One work even purports to know Castro's emotional state, upon which it attributes the failure of Cuban planning to become more efficient: "Humberto Pérez, previous JUCEPLAN president, suggested during the fourth check of the system, the increase of freedom of enterprise and incentive. However, any effort at decentralizing eventually causes the fear of Fidel Castro to lose political power."[11]

Another example of an unfounded judgment is provided by Mesa-Lago, who condemns Cuba's SDPE (post-1976 planning system) as having "excessively centralized control but ineffective coordination" with "appalling" results.[12] Mesa-Lago bases this claim on a Cuban government study[13] that, although openly criticizing the shortcomings of the new system, concludes the opposite, referring to the progress of the SDPE as "completely positive".[14]

Mesa-Lago's interpretation can be explained in part by his failure to appreciate the institutional context (for instance, the inchoate planning apparatus) into which the SDPE was set. It is essential to underscore that the introduction of the SDPE coincides with Cuba's First Five-Year Plan, indicating the prior lack of development of Cuba's planning system. Indeed, many of the problems in implementing the SDPE have had to do with the need to develop an adequate statistical network, a legal system for enforcing contracts, an arbitration system, a management training program, proper financial institutions, a set of reasonably consistent prices, and so on, none of which existed in satisfactory form before 1976.

Mesa-Lago supports his view by selectively presenting the weakest aspects of the SDPE discussed in the government report and omitting mention of its accomplishments. Furthermore, there is cause to challenge the accuracy of Mesa-Lago's reporting on the problem areas. For example, Mesa-Lago reports that "30 percent of the enterprises lacked [quality] controls altogether, and inspections revealed that 90 percent of the products did not meet the quality norms."[15] Yet the Cuban study states "el 90% incumplieron lo establecido en las normas *u otros documentos tecnicos*" (emphasis added).[16] That is, 90 percent did not meet either the quality norms or other technical instructions or procedures. In fact, this sentence follows an enumeration of seven instructions that were to be followed, including the use of precise weighing scales, the use of scientific measurement procedures, the development of special testing laboratories, and so on. In other words, the cited Cuban study refers to a failure of 90 percent of the 507 sampled products to meet any one of the seven instructions—quality norms being just one item on the list. By overlooking the last part of the relevant sentence, Mesa-Lago turns a very understandable tardiness in developing a complete set of technical and scientific procedures into a stinging indictment of Cuban enterprises.

Sergio Roca has already published three articles on Cuban planning and management based on his project. The articles are similar in content but change slightly in emphasis with later versions. I shall concentrate on Roca's most recent publication, "State Enterprises in Cuba Under the New System of Planning and Management (SDPE)," which appeared in *Cuban Studies* in 1986.

At the outset Roca writes that his article is about "the process of economic institutionalization: its extent, depth and nature."[17] Yet nowhere does he inform the reader what he means by the term "economic institutionalization." In his conclusion Roca asserts: "While it is clear that major beneficial changes have occurred since 1975 in the Cuban model of economic planning and management, it is also incontrovertible that the remaining shortcomings . . . make it very difficult to conclude that a fully effective economic system now operates on the island." This actually is a reasonable conclusion, one with which I am in complete agreement. But this is unfortunately rather vague (what country has a "fully effective economic system"?) and does not follow from the thrust of his argument.

Let us turn to Roca's methodology. His primary data base is interviews with twenty-five Cuban exiles resident in the United States. The interviewees held a variety of administrative and managerial jobs in Cuba. They were not selected at random and thus do not constitute a representative sampling of the Cuban exile population. More important, they do not constitute a representative or even reasonable sampling of the population of Cuban administrative, managerial, and planning personnel. There is, rather, every reason to believe that these exiles represent a sample of negatively biased opinions about Cuba and its economy. The anecdotes and interpretations of these individuals are no more reliable a priori than would be a series of interviews about life in the United States with draft dodgers resident in Canada prior to the Carter amnesty. To compound the problem Roca granted his interviewees anonymity, making them unaccountable for whatever claims they made.

Efforts to have Roca release the names responsible for some remarkable quotes (accusations) so far have been unsuccessful.

Roca does not explicitly defend his method; rather he uses the work of Joe Berliner on Soviet managers to explain his approach.[18] However, the two studies are not comparable. First, the Berliner study of 1957 was undertaken at a time when very little was known in the West about the actual operation of enterprises in centrally planned economies. Second, the relationship between Soviet publications and Berliner's interviews with exiles was much closer, more faithful, and systematic than was Roca's. Third, Berliner himself continues to harbor serious doubts about his methods in that study.

Roca comments on his method as follows: "The fact that these informants have emigrated from Cuba does not entitle us to dismiss this group a priori as incapable of providing credible testimony about the conditions of their work experience."[19] Roca's informants are certainly not "incapable" of credible testimony, although maybe they are "unlikely" to provide it in a balanced and reliable fashion. This, however, begs the issue, which is that his sample is not suitable to form the backbone of a study on Cuba's planning and management system.

In his concluding remarks, Roca invokes a puzzle metaphor: "If this research project is likened to a puzzle, then the Cuban materials outline the edges and the interviews fill in the interior space."[20] In my view, Roca is considerably off the mark in making this claim. Roca does indeed use Cuban materials; yet the contours of his argument are not shaped by a balanced use of these materials but by the selective use of only self-critical and negative evaluations. Further, Roca adds at least one point from his interview data that appears nowhere in the Cuban materials: an alleged pervasive "personalismo" of Castro in distorting the rational allocation of resources. Other than this point, (which I shall discuss later in this chapter), Roca adds no new critical analyses of Cuba's planning system. All Roca writes and much more analysis of the deficiencies in the functioning of Cuba's economic mechanisms are available in a plethora of Cuban materials.[21] These materials have the added advantage of providing a historical context and balance in their presentation.[22] In short, Roca's method is not scientific, he does not do what he says he does, and he does not execute his dubious methodology in a rigorous and careful fashion.

I turn now to consider substantive aspects of Roca's argument. Roca repeats the hackneyed claim that the SDPE is "essentially identical to the current Soviet economic model." It is not clear whether Roca refers to the 1965 Soviet reform, to the 1979 reform, or to the Gorbachev reforms, or to parts of all three. In fact, the similarities in form between Soviet and Cuban planning are great, but the content of planning relationships and many details of form are significantly different. Unless one appreciates these differences, it is next to impossible to interpret the dynamics of the Cuban experience. It would, for instance, have been impossible to anticipate the current renewal of the debate on moral versus material incentives or the new restrictions on private market activities on the basis of the Soviet economic model. If anything, Cuban and Soviet economic reforms seem to be moving in contrary directions at the moment.

Shortly after invoking the "essentially identical" argument Roca writes that "profitability was to be established as the key criterion of performance in production centers."[23] This is not true either in Cuba or in the Soviet Union. The key criterion of performance in theory and in practice in both economies is the meeting of the planned output target. This criterion is complemented by indicators of profit, profitability, cost reduction, growth rates, quality standards, and so on. It is not uncommon for Soviet enterprises to be given several dozen performance indicators, each of which impact upon the size of the unit's stimulation and bonus funds. But the key criterion is always the output target (variously expressed) as it has to be if the central plan is to hold together. Any analyst familiar with the logic of central planning or the shortage characteristic endemic to central planned economies knows that financial indicators such as profitability play a secondary role to physical indicators. In this context, Roca's contention about profitability being the key criterion of performance is both factually inaccurate and analytically naive.

There is a general problem in interpreting the citations from Roca's interviews. Frequently Roca does not mention what year or what period the quoted passage is meant to describe, and commonly the context or circumstances of the anecdote are not given. Occasionally, the interviewee appears to have his own story mixed up (perhaps a result of the lack of context). For instance, Roca quotes informant 14 as saying: "I remember that in 1978 and 1979 JUCEPLAN strongly urged central organs and ministries to allow enterprises to generate preliminary figures. This was never done."[24] For both one- and five-year plans preliminary output figures always originate with Juceplan (the central planning board) and then are disaggregated by the ministries before being sent to the enterprises. At this point, the enterprise evaluates the preliminary figures and can make counterproposals along with requests for more inputs. To have the process originate on the bottom may have a democratic ring but in practice would make coordination and balance in the plan impossible (except by monumental coincidence). It is difficult to believe Juceplan ever intended to do this as reported. There are other means to give greater weight to enterprise proposals that are consistent with the logic of central planning.

The time period ambiguity of the interviews and Roca's own faulty understanding of the SDPE at times lead to incorrect statements. Conceding some differences in Soviet and Cuban planning, Roca writes: "Among the differences, the absence in Cuba of material rewards . . . to motivate superior managerial performance stands out."[25] Until the implementation of the SDPE, such rewards did not exist in Cuba. With the SDPE, however, managers share in the distribution of bonus funds roughly in proportion to their salary's share in the total wage bill of the enterprise. That is, contrary to Roca's statement, managers do receive material bonuses based on performance.

Roca cites 1980 statistics illustrating that less than 10 percent of enterprises formed stimulation and bonus funds in that year. He ignores, however, that the funds were first introduced on an experimental basis only in 1979 and that the price reform was not carried out until 1981. It is hardly surprising that so few enterprises benefited from the funds in 1980. By 1985, 52.1 percent of enterprises formed stimulation funds.

Roca's discussion of material incentives points to a serious problem with his entire presentation. He analyzes the "institutionalization" of a post-1976 system on the basis of interviews with individuals who left Cuba in 1980 and whose direct experience with the SDPE often considerably predates that year. It is important to remind the reader that prior to 1976 Cuba did not have a five-year plan and the basic institutions of planning were not in place. The Cubans in most instances had to build the organizations of the SDPE from scratch. Roca (along with Mesa-Lago), then—without acknowledging it or adjusting his interpretation—primarily analyzes initial, not long-term, behavioral problems.

Further, in discussing the application of material incentives Roca does not mention the Cuban *normas* (individual work norms) and seems to confuse them with *primas* (bonuses), which are generally applied to groups. Whereas work norms have had a troubled existence in Cuba, they do apply to over half the work force and have been a major component of material incentives.[26]

Roca devotes seven pages of anecdotes to establish an excessive planning role for the party and Castro. The evidence here is again interpreted out of context and largely consists of dubious informant claims. For example, informant 269 is quoted as saying: "In the case of sugar output targets, Fidel and the Political Bureau made the basic decisions."[27] At a very general level, since the Political Bureau establishes the basic priorities of the plan, this is true. But we do not need eyewitness accounts to tell us what is in the Constitution and well known, nor is it what Roca intends. At a specific level, it is as difficult to accept this simple portrayal of reality as it is hard to believe that an economist at a light-industry enterprise (the job of informant 269) would have access to this information even it were true.

Other anecdotes tell of Castro stepping in to solve particular bottlenecks and allocational problems. These stories are believable, but they hardly establish the fact of regular or pervasive interference or systematic control over the plan by Castro. Nor do they establish that the pattern of Castro-inspired miniplans, common to the 1960s when no effective formal planning apparatus existed, has been recreated. If Castro confronts inefficiencies of the government bureaucracy in his travels about Cuba, it is natural for him to investigate the source of the problem and at times to attempt its resolution. It would probably be difficult to find a chief executive in any country who does not do the same from time to time.

Moreover, given the systemic shortages and torpidity of centrally planned economies it is often necessary for the center to intervene to provide for priority sectors or to cut through the thick bureaucratic morass. Such sporadic intervention, however, is common in centrally planned economies. To be sure, energetic and charismatic leaders, such as Castro and Gorbachev, are likely to be more involved and more visible than others. It is even plausible to contend that Castro's interventions are still too frequent and occasionally damaging. To assert, however, as Roca does that "Fidel exercised a pervasive and detrimental influence at all levels of economic organization and over all functions of economic administration"[28] on the basis of testimony from his informants is unconvincing.

The establishment of the Grupo Central in December 1984 is interpreted by Roca as Castro's Machiavellian plot to assert control over the plan. But why would Castro plot if he already has control as Roca's interviewees claim he did before 1980? The raison d'être of the Grupo Central is too complex for a full analysis here. Suffice it to suggest that the formation of the Grupo Central in part was an effort to weaken ministerialism (both sectorial chauvinism and excessive tutelage over enterprises), in part to facilitate lines of communication and command, in part to deal with the worsening foreign exchange crisis as effectively and expeditiously as possible. Finally, it was an element of a larger effort to reinvigorate the planning apparatus and renovate its personnel.

It is also relevant to mention that according to the Cuban constitution the Council of Ministers is charged with elaborating and overseeing the implementation of the yearly economic plan. Juceplan is part of the council, and roughly 90 percent of the membership of the Grupo Central is from the Council of Ministers.[29]

Conclusion

The principal thrust of my criticism of the literature on Cuban planning has not been that it is too negative or critical of the prevailing situation. I believe this to be true but of secondary importance. Rather, similar to the literature on other aspects of Cuba's political economy, it is characterized by a poverty of conceptualization, theory, and method. To portray accurately the predicament and analyze the dynamics of Cuban planning it is first necessary to understand the planning problematic in its theoretical and experiential dimensions. It is then necessary to situate this problematic in the historically conditioned Cuban reality. The studies under review in this chapter are lacking on all accounts.

Notes

1. Carmelo Mesa-Lago's principal commentary on the SDPE appears in his essay, "The Economy: Caution, Frugality and Resilient Ideology," in J. Domínguez, ed., *Cuba: Internal and International Affairs* (Beverly Hills: Sage, 1982). Sergio Roca's principal essay is "State Enterprises in Cuba Under the New System of Planning and Management (SDPE)," *Cuban Studies/Estudios Cubanos* 16, 1986. An earlier, shortened version of the same essay appeared in *Latin American and Caribbean Contemporary Record* 3 (June 1985).

2. See, for instance, Marer (1985).

3. See, for instance, John Bonin, "On the Design of Managerial Incentive Structures in a Decentralized Planning Environment," *American Economic Review* 66 (September 1976):682–687, and Martin Weitzman, "The New Soviet Incentive Model," *Bell Journal of Economics* 7 (spring 1976):251–257.

4. See Sinan Koont and Andrew Zimbalist, "Incentives and Elicitation Schemes: A Critique and an Extension," in A. Zimbalist, ed., *Comparative Economic Systems: An Assessment of Knowledge, Theory and Method* (Boston: Kluwer-Nijhoff, 1984).

5. For an elaboration of this argument, see Kornai (1980).

6. See Wlodimierz Brus, *The Economics and Politics of Socialism* (London: Routledge and Kegan Paul, 1973), and A. Zimbalist, "Introduction: Reflections on the State of the Art of Comparative Economics," in Zimbalist, ed., *Comparative Economic Systems*, for further discussion of this point.

7. See, for instance, Murray Yanowitch, *Social and Economic Inequality in the Soviet Union* (New York: Sharpe, 1977), ch. 5.

8. See, for instance, A. Zimbalist, "Cuban Economic Planning: Organization and Performance," in S. Halebsky and J. Kirk, eds., *Cuba: Twenty-Five Years of Revolution, 1959–1984* (New York: Praeger, 1985), and A. Zimbalist and S. Eckstein, "Patterns of Cuban Development: The First Twenty-Five Years," *World Development* (January 1987).

9. See, for instance, the discussion of the Hungarian reform in A. Zimbalist and H. Sherman, *Comparing Economic Systems: A Political-Economic Approach* (New York: Academic Press, 1984), ch. 15.

10. For a discussion on the background to the Yugoslav rejection of the Soviet model, see Zimbalist and Sherman, *Comparing Economic Systems*, ch. 16.

11. Staff of Radio José Martí, Office of Research and Policy, *Cuba: Quarterly Situation Report*, May 1986, p. III, 2. The quarterly reports on Cuba by the Radio Martí staff are replete with misleading and inaccurate judgments about the Cuban economy, this quote being only one of many examples.

12. Mesa-Lago, "The Economy," p. 132.

13. Juceplan, *Segunda Plenaria Nacional de Chequeo de la Implantación del SDPE* (Havana: Juceplan, 1981).

14. Ibid., p. 4.

15. Mesa-Lago, "The Economy," 1982, p. 132.

16. Juceplan, *Segunda Plenaria Nacional*, p. 356.

17. Roca, "State Enterprises," p. 156.

18. Joseph Berliner, *Factory and Manager in the USSR* (Cambridge: Harvard University Press, 1957).

19. Roca, "State Enterprises," p. 158.

20. Roca, "State Enterprises," p. 177.

21. In addition to the materials cited by Roca, five particularly useful documents are the following: Humberto Pérez, *Intervención: Clausura de la IV Plenaria Nacional del Chequeo de la Implantación del SDPE* (Havana: Juceplan, May 1985); Fidel Castro, "Main Report to the Third Party Congress," reprinted in *Granma Weekly Review*, February 16, 1986; Arturo Guzman, "Intervención: Clausura del II Evento Científico de la ANEC del Area de Ciencias Económicas de la U.H.," *Economía y Desarrollo* 80, May/June 1984; *Dictámenes de la Cuarta Plenaria Nacional del Chequeo de la Implantación del SPDE* (Havana: Juceplan, 1985); and, José Machado, *Intervención: Clausura del Activo Nacional del Partido acerca de la Rentabilidad de Empresas* (Havana, January 1984). During the first two weeks of July 1986 each of Cuba's fourteen provinces conducted a *Reunión de Empresa*. These began as discussions at the enterprise level and proceeded upward to a provincewide meeting of managers and worker representatives from every enterprise. These meetings were reported upon in great detail in various issues of *Granma* between June 27 and July 18, 1986. They constitute an excellent source of information and critical analysis of the problems of Cuban management and planning. Finally, the *Granma Weekly Review* of December 14, 1986, published a special sixteen-page supplement on (1) the debates at the closing sessions of the Third Party Congress regarding the campaign to "Struggle Against Negative Tendencies" and (2) Castro's final speech. The contents of these documents explore the relationship of incentives, political consciousness, and material conditions to economic performance. Castro identified recent new excesses in the moral/material rewards pendulum and appeared to arrive at a new, more cautious synthesis.

22. I do not mean to suggest that the official documents provide a comprehensive picture or complete analysis of the problems of Cuban planning. In my

view this is far from the case. Rather, I contend that Roca adds neither reliable data nor pertinent analysis to what the Cuban studies provide.

23. Roca, "State Enterprises," p. 160.

24. Ibid., p. 161.

25. Ibid., p. 167.

26. In his 1987 piece, "Planners in Wonderland: Response to Zimbalist" (*Cuban Studies*, Vol. 17), he incorrectly states: "*Normas* are the individual work quotas upon which the (potential) payment of *primas* is based." *Primas*, in fact, are based on other indicators, e.g., quality, material savings, increases in production for export (until mid-1986), and on enterprise plan fulfillment (in special circumstances). Roca goes on to cite an instance where the *prima* is a function of output performance, but he fails to distinguish between individual output performance (according to a *norma*) and enterprise output performance (according to the economic plan). It is the latter to which his example pertains.

27. Ibid., p. 172.

28. Ibid., p. 170.

29. For an interesting analysis of the role of the Grupo Central, see Carlos Rafael Rodríguez, "Discurso de la primera graduación de la Licenciatura de Dirección de la Economía. Acto efectuado el 12 de julio de 1985 en el Instituto Superior de Dirección de la Economía," *Cuba: Economía Planificada* 1, no. 1 (January/March 1986).

References

Berliner, Joseph. *Factory and Manager in the USSR*. Cambridge: Harvard University Press, 1957.

Bonin, John. "On the Design of Managerial Incentive Structures in a Decentralized Planning Environment." *American Economic Review* 66 (September 1976):682–687.

Brus, Wlodimierz. *The Economics and Politics of Socialism*. London: Routledge and Kegan Paul, 1973.

Guzman, Arturo. "Intervención: Clausura del II Evento Científico de la ANEC del Area de Ciencias Económicas de la U.H." *Economía y Desarrollo* 80, May/June 1984.

Juceplan. *Segunda Plenaria Nacional de Chequeo de la Implantación del SDPE*. Havana: Juceplan, 1981.

Kornai, J. *The Economics of Shortage*. Amsterdam: North Holland, 1980.

Koont, Sinan, and Andrew Zimbalist. "Incentives and Elicitation Schemes: A Critique and an Extension." In A. Zimbalist, ed., *Comparative Economic Systems: An Assessment of Knowledge, Theory and Method*. Boston: Kluwer-Nijhoff, 1984.

Machado, José. *Intervención: Clausura del Activo Nacional del Partido acerca de la Rentabilidad de Empresas*. Havana: January 1984.

Marer, Paul. *Dollar GNPs and Growth Rates of the USSR and Eastern Europe*. Baltimore and London: Johns Hopkins University Press for the World Bank, 1985.

Mesa-Lago, Carmelo. "The Economy: Caution, Frugality and Resilient Ideology." In J. Domínguez, ed., *Cuba: Internal and International Affairs*. Beverly Hills: Sage, 1982.

Pérez, Humberto. *Intervención: Clausura de la IV Plenaria Nacional del Chequeo de la Implantación del SDPE*. Havana: Juceplan, May 1985.

———. *Dictámenes Aprobados en la IV Plenaria del Chequeo de la Implantación del SDPE*. Havana: Juceplan, May 1985.

Roca, Sergio. "State Enterprises in Cuba Under the New System of Planning and Management (SDPE)." *Cuban Studies/Estudios Cubanos* 16, 1986.

Rodríguez, Carlos Rafael. "Discurso de la primera graduación de la Licenciatura de Dirección de la Economía. Acto efectuado el 12 de julio de 1985 en el Instituto Superior de Dirección de la Economía." *Cuba: Economía Planificada* 1, no. 1 (January/March 1986).

Staff of Radio José Martí, Office of Research and Policy. *Cuba: Quarterly Situation Report*, May 1986, p. III, 2.

Weitzman, Martin. "The New Soviet Incentive Model." *Bell Journal of Economics* 7 (Spring 1976):251–257.

Yanowitch, Murray. *Social and Economic Inequality in the Soviet Union*. New York: Sharpe, 1977, ch. 5.

———, ed. *Soviet Work Attitudes: The Issue of Participation in Management*. New York: Sharpe, 1979.

Zimbalist, A., ed. *Comparative Economic Systems: An Assessment of Knowledge, Theory and Method*. Boston: Kluwer-Nijhoff, 1984.

———. "Introduction: Reflections on the State of the Art of Comparative Economics." In Zimbalist, ed., *Comparative Economic Systems: An Assessment of Knowledge, Theory and Method*. Boston: Kluwer-Nijhoff, 1984.

———. "Cuban Economic Planning: Organization and Performance." In S. Halebsky and J. Kirk, eds., *Cuba: Twenty-Five Years of Revolution, 1959–1984*. New York: Praeger, 1985.

Zimbalist, A., and H. Sherman, *Comparing Economic Systems: A Political-Economic Approach*. New York: Academic Press, 1984, ch. 15.

Zimbalist, A., and S. Eckstein. "Patterns of Cuban Development: The First Twenty-Five Years." *World Development* (January 1987).

5

Cubanology and the Provision of Basic Needs in the Cuban Revolution

José Luis Rodríguez

The area of social achievement is one to which the study of the Cuban Revolution has increasingly turned. The evolution of criticism in this area has been shaped by, on one side, the improvements Cuba has made in the social sphere since 1959, and on the other, by the ideological debate between Cuban socialists and the country's nonsocialist critics. Whereas a sufficiently generalized recognition of certain social advances existed during the 1970s, by 1980 a campaign was initiated to deny the significance and, in some instances, even the existence of these achievements.

In effect, the arguments that emerged reveal a number of subtle changes between the past decade and the present one, allowing a certain differentiation to be made between these two periods. Hence, the theory positing the possibility of social development without the existence of a real economic base first appears in the 1970s. Most recently, the proponents of this view have attempted—in various arguments—to either refute or reduce the Revolution's achievements in education and public health, among other areas.

Carmelo Mesa-Lago considered five major socioeconomic goals of the Cuban Revolution (growth, diversification, relative external economic independence, full employment, more equal income distribution) in his book *The Economy of Socialist Cuba: A Two-Decade Appraisal*. He indicated that "a major assumption of the book is that not all of these five goals can be pursued at the same time with similar intensity in the short term. The reason is because not all of the goals are mutually reinforcing or compatible; in fact, some of them may conflict."[1] Similarly, Lawrence

Theriot suggested that "the social achievements in Cuba have only been made possible by the Soviet Union's massive economic assistance."[2]

Other authors—who have not dedicated themselves specifically to the study of Cuba—have accepted these conclusions as givens: "The admirable progress made by the Cuban revolution in matters of health and education are byproducts of Soviet aid. Other revolutionary states need to find alternative economic models if they desire to survive and prosper."[3]

In view of these statements it is useful to begin the analysis by stating the conception of development as proposed by the Revolution from its very outset.[4] Poverty is generated not only by a process of social differentiation that engenders wealth at one pole and misery at the other but also by conditions of exploitation, the typical results of capitalism. Under conditions in prerevolutionary Cuba, poverty was merely the social manifestation of underdevelopment: Both conditions are produced by the development process of the capitalist relations of production. It then follows that poverty and underdevelopment could only be overcome by eliminating the social conditions that had created them.

The close relationship between the economic base of underdevelopment and its social effects led the leaders of the Cuban Revolution to seek an integral solution from the very beginning.[5] This simultaneous concern for economic and social problems marks a constant of the Revolution from 1959 to the present time.

Unemployment

It is a widespread opinion of Cubanologists that open unemployment has been converted into underemployment. Carmelo Mesa-Lago contended that "in the 1960s, Cuba transformed most open employment into various types of underemployment, which provoked sharp declines in labor productivity and in turn adversely affected the standard of living of most of the population."[6] He elaborated further on this idea:

This significant feat was accomplished through four means: the exportation of part of the labor force abroad, which opened about 200,000 jobs in Cuba in the 1960s; the removal from the labor market of those below 17 and above 62 years of age through expanding education and social security; the elimination of seasonal unemployment in the countryside through a combination of rural-to-urban migration with overstaffing in state farms, which guarantee jobs throughout the year; and the expansion of employment in social services, the armed forces, and the bureaucracy coupled with overstaffing in industry and subsidies to redundant urban workers, which avoided open unemployment in cities.[7]

First, it is necessary to point out that Mesa-Lago examined the elimination of unemployment by considering only the experience of the 1960s. When presenting his conclusions on unemployment, he virtually extrapolated his conclusions on the 1960s to the entire revolutionary period, thereby creating the impression that the Cuban solution to unemployment has been, at the very least, contradictory.[8] To be sure, certain errors in economic policy were committed during the 1960s that continued to affect employment policy as well and presented, in effect, underemployment situations. However, the Revolution's strong effort in this field during this period cannot be reduced.

According to Mesa-Lago, unemployment appears as if it had been eradicated either by channeling unemployed workers toward other sectors or locations or by giving them superfluous jobs. Mesa-Lago's analysis of the emigration of a portion of the labor force exaggerates its effects and is based on a very questionable assumption about the composition of the Cuban labor force. He assumed that during the years of 1959–1962 emigrants comprised 34 percent of the labor force.[9] Other studies, however, reflect less of an impact in this sense while clearly demonstrating that because of its labor composition, this emigration did not produce the short-run possibility of filling the vacant posts created; instead, owing to the high degree of education they required, it ensured their continued vacancy.[10] In this respect, two Cuban scholars have maintained that the high level of educational attainment of this wave of emigrants "fundamentally expresses the source of their social position in Cuba and the advantageous access they had to education in the pre-revolutionary period, given their urban and class origins."[11]

In other words, the jobs that remained open as a result of emigration were not accessible to a core of the unemployed with very low levels of education. The departure of these people could not have exercised any effect other than to provoke a shortage of a qualified labor force that the remaining population was not in any position to fill in the short term. For example, more than 3,000 doctors, who constituted 50 percent of Cuban resident physicians at that time, departed.

On another count, Mesa-Lago misunderstood labor policy when he interpreted the early social policies of the Revolution as measures to combat unemployment, when these policies were not primarily designed as means for eliminating unemployment but instead as a necessary measure to achieve immediate social justice. This rationale explains the displacement of the young and the elderly from the labor market that occurred as a result of a major extension of education and social security

TABLE 5.1
Changes in Employment Structure, Education, and Social Security
Coverage

	1953	1970
Labor Force (by percentage in age range)		
15-19	46	34
60 and over	40	24
Level of educational coverage in secondary education (percentage of cohort enrolled)	8.7	79.8 (1981)
Percentage of social security coverage in relation to the total of workers (estimate)	50	100

Source: CIEM, A Study of the Eradication of Poverty in Cuba
(Havana: 1983), pp. 19, 23, 76, 107, 124.

coverage and the expansion of employment opportunities in the social
sector. These movements can be clearly inferred from the data in Table
5.1.

Mesa-Lago's hostile and clearly biased treatment of the Revolution is
apparent when he wrote, in reference to the Armed Forces, that "the
demands for internal control, for defense against external aggression,
and for the exportation of the Revolution were satisfied by expanding
employment in the Armed Forces, internal security forces, and the
organizations for the control of the masses."[12] In a subsequent study,
Mesa-Lago returned to the topic to insinuate that Cuba will try to resolve
the employment problems it faces during the present decade by, among
other methods, "the increased involvement in military ventures abroad
(which is difficult due to economic limitations); and the exportation of
the labor surplus abroad (which was obviously done in the spring and
summer of 1980)."[13]

These questions have nothing to do with economic motivations;
instead, they are based on approaches that try to present Cuba as a
fortune-hunting military power that seeks unilateral economic benefits
in its relations with other countries. These arguments illustrate that
certain groups of Cubanologists judge our foreign policy according to
ethical notions that do not correspond in the least to those that actually
govern in Cuba. In this sense, many Cubanologists do not seem to see
that there can be transcending moral motivations for leaving Cuba and
helping other countries preserve their liberty or consolidate their development.

It is essential to emphasize the fact that Cuba had an unemployment rate in 1970 of only 1.3 percent,[14] which would later rise to 3.4 percent in 1981. A 1983 analysis by the Cuban State Statistical Committee concluded that a major component of the 1981 unemployment figure was "frictional unemployment."

> This becomes inevitable when it includes not only people who reach working age at the moment a census is being undertaken and are on the verge of situating themselves but also other people who are in the process of moving from one job to another. Such movement makes it impossible that the unemployment rate—as measured by the United Nations (ONU)—be reduced to zero in the moment of a census investigation. In addition, it must be kept in mind that available jobs do exist for the unemployed in the country's economy, only that in some cases, these jobs do not correspond to the ambitions of those seeking work and in other cases, to the qualifications of the unemployed.[15]

Cuba's labor policy did in fact contribute to the eradication of unemployment, creating more than one million jobs between 1959 and 1982. The average annual growth rate of employment for 1959–1975 was 3.6 percent while the population grew by a rate of 2.1 percent for the same period. This positive relationship was maintained between 1976 and 1982 since the population grew at an annual 0.7 percent during these years while state employment grew at an average of 2.2 percent.[16]

Equality and Rationing

In relation to these demographic patterns, Cubanologist studies have increased in the past few years and have attempted to explain the most recent developments as the "negative effects" incurred by the revolutionary process. For instance, the Cuban population's decreasing fertility of the past few years has been said to "have been influenced in great measure by the poor performance of the Cuban economy."[17]

Also appearing in the sociodemographic field are opinions that try to present racial discrimination as an unresolved problem in Cuba. To this effect Jorge Domínguez wrote that "Cuban blacks and mulattoes are demonstrably poorer; because they are poorer, they are more likely than whites to become sick. This was true before the Revolution, and is still true in the 1970s."[18] Similarly, a demographic analysis of Cubans residing in the United States has been undertaken in recent years. Its goal has been to exalt the supposed superior advantages that the inhabitants of this community enjoy in comparison to those remaining in Cuba.[19]

Other aspects of the Cuban population's standard of living have been the objects of Cubanologist analysis. If we examine their evaluations regarding problems in the distribution of income, prices, and salaries, salient opinions in vital need of scrutiny and clarification emerge. Above all, these views present the reader with a misleading picture of the so-called inequality that still exists in Cuba. In such presentations, equality is interpreted as a synonym of egalitarianism, which introduces a notable distortion concerning the objectives a socialist society pursues.[20] Thus, Cubanologists evaluate as backsliding the natural differences in salaries that are produced in a society—such as Cuba's—that is undergoing the transition from capitalism to socialism and where distribution is fixed according to productivity.

In general, Cubanologists' critical evaluation of the Revolution's price and wage policies does not offer convincing arguments. Their wage estimates are highly questionable, and their conclusions regarding consumer prices and the "black market" lack scientific validity.[21] Similarly, Cubanologist figures referring to consumption after the inception of the rationing system are also unreliable.[22] For instance, in a recent review of Cubanology Nelson Valdés, a sociologist at the University of New Mexico, concluded: "The study already cited, for example, presents only 16 of the 60 products listed in published Cuban statistics. A recent study of the U.S. government on rationing in Cuba treats only 14 products. In general, these studies leave out the products where the most success has been achieved."[23]

The data presented on caloric consumption per capita are similarly trustworthy. One supposedly valid statistic given for the 1951–1958 period[24] has been disputed by solid arguments made by other specialists: "Nevertheless, precisely because these figures are averages, the data concerning prerevolutionary caloric intake and the consumption of certain foods (such as meat) are totally deceptive."[25] It is also affirmed that "although the national average per capita caloric intake has probably declined since 1962, rationing has been instrumental in making food distribution more egalitarian."[26] There was no such decline. The average caloric consumption per capita in 1962 was 2,410 calories, and in 1984 it reached 2,963 calories.[27]

More recently, the nutritional situation of the population has been presented in an even more critical light. The conclusion arrived at is that "the Cuban level of nutrition seems to be better than that of the average third world nation. Nevertheless, it cannot be established that prerevolutionary levels were worse than those that prevail in the 1970s."[28]

In general, for Cubanologists the reasons for and the actual effects of the rationing policy do not appear worthy of examination. It is worthwhile to recall that when the Revolution triumphed, the Cuban economy was not prepared to deal with the increases in demand that were produced. This situation was exacerbated by the growing hostility of the United States—primary supplier to the internal market—and by the consequent necessity to divert resources to the defense of the nation.

In the face of the scarcity that began manifesting itself in 1961, it was decided to avoid the exorbitant rise of prices that would have placed essential articles beyond the means of lower income families and to apply a system of rationing tied to a policy of price freezing, which guaranteed an equitable distribution of available goods. This system would gradually replace itself as the population's income increased. Already in 1983, only around 25 percent of food products and 20 percent of industrial goods available to the public continued to be rationed.

Several studies conducted reveal the results of the policy undertaken by the Revolution to redistribute income. According to these studies, in 1953 the estimated income in wages and salaries for 40 percent of the Cuban population of lower income covered only 13.2 percent of the total income, whereas the top 5 percent of the higher income population received 26.5 percent. In 1978, 40 percent of the lower income population received around 26.1 percent of the total whereas the 5 percent of higher income received only 11 percent.[29]

This redistribution was primarily made possible by the wage policy of the Revolution, which raised the average salary to 186 pesos per month in 1984, making for an average annual increase of 3.5 percent between 1959 and 1984.[30] The population's monetary income grew at an average annual rate of 4.8 percent between 1959 and 1984.[31]

Finally, as a result of the price and supply policy practiced during these years, the following were accomplished:

- Between 1958 and 1980, personal consumption per capita grew at an annual average rate of 2.3 percent, reaching a rate of 7.8 percent between 1980 and 1984.
- Between 1963 and 1980 in many significant cases an annual average increase was produced in the per capita consumption of a set group of basic foods: chicken, 4.2 percent; pork, 14.2 percent; eggs, 4.2 percent; beans, 1.6 percent; potatoes, 2.1 percent; fresh fish, 6.7 percent; milk, 7.5 percent; yogurt, 24.3 percent; cheeses, 5.8 percent.
- Malnutrition was practically eliminated and the population's nutritional levels were raised. In 1984, the daily per capita consumption reached (as already mentioned) 2,963 caloric units while that of protein reached 79.8 grams.[32]

Regarding social security, Mesa-Lago offered a figure of 63 percent for the portion of the work force covered in 1958 (see Table 5.2A). In comparison, official Cuban sources offered a figure 10 percentage points lower. Similarly, the same author emphasized, "around 1976 the average pension was 11 percent greater than in 1959, probably a loss if inflation is taken into account."[33] The growth of the monthly nominal expenditure per pensioner or retiree has in fact been much greater: In 1984 95.4 pesos were spent as compared to 67.2 pesos in 1959, an increase of 42 percent. During these twenty-five years the Cuban state has channeled more than 12 billion pesos to social security, as the number of pensioned persons increased to 800,000.[34]

Cubanologists' use of figures diminishes the social accomplishments of the Revolution. Each area of social policy is seen as self-contained, and in no case is there an assessment of the social policy of the Revolution as part of its general development policy.

Educational Policy

The advancements in education achieved by Cuba after 1959 are attributable, above all, to the conception of integral development. Educational policy has been based on various essential principles. First, education is an inalienable right. Second, education is considered to be the responsibility of the entire society; accordingly, the pedagogic efforts of schools are tied to the concerted actions of the community. As part of the social conditioning that accompanies the educational function, policy is developed to combine work with study so that the educational system may be (and has been) extended to the entire population.

These essential elements of educational policy are ignored by Cubanologists, who turn instead to question isolated data. For example, they cite the 1958 illiteracy rate as 21 percent whereas they dispute the figure offered by Cuban authorities upon concluding the illiteracy campaign in 1961 (3.9 percent)—apparently they base their claims on expert opinion.[35]

Above all, nothing suggests that the illiteracy rate given by the 1953 census—23.6 percent—had fallen to 21 percent in 1958, especially when the evolution of the sociopolitical situation in Cuba during these years is taken into account (see Table 5.2B).[36] Furthermore, there appears to be only one expert who has challenged the figure of 3.9 percent.[37] Other experts conducting careful studies on the matter have not taken this viewpoint.[38]

Nothing is said of the raising of the population's median level of education, which went from two years of primary school in 1953 to a

TABLE 5.2
Selected Indicators of the Development of Basic Social Services in Cuba Between 1959 and 1984

A. Social Security

	1959	1984	1959–1984
Level of coverage in relation to total workers	53% (1958)	100%	—
Number of retired and pensioned persons (000s)	154	800	—
Average annual growth rate			6.8%
State's expenditure on social security (thousand pesos)	10.3	896.7	
Average annual growth rate			19.6%
Monthly spending of social security per retiree or pensioner (in pesos)	67.2	93.4	
Average annual growth rate			1.3%

(continued)

B. Education

	1959	1984	1959–1984
Illiteracy rate	23.6% (1953)	1.9% (1981)[a]	—
Population average of schooling in primary school grades	2.0 (1953)	6.4 (1981)	—
Levels of matriculation in relation to school-age population			
Primary	45.2 (1953)	97.3	—
Secondary	8.7 (1953)	84.4 (1981–82)	—
University	4.0 (1953)	11.1 (1981–82)[b]	—
Structure of matriculation by type of schooling			
Primary	85.8 (1958–59)	45.0	
Secondary	12.1 (1958–59)	43.6	
University	2.1 (1958–59)	7.4	
State spending on education (thousand pesos)	79.4 (1958)	1676.0	
Average growth rate	—	—	12.4%
Education spending per inhabitant (in pesos)	11 (1958)	169	—
Average growth rate	—	—	11.1%

C. Public Health

	1959		1984	1959–1984
Birth rate (per 1,000 inhabitants)	27.3	(1958)	16.6	—
Life expectancy at birth (in years)	61.8	(1955/1960 average)	73.03[c]	—
Infant mortality rate (per 1,000 live births for infants under 12 mo.)	32.5	(1958)	15.0	—
Maternity death rate (per 1,000 live births)	118.2	(1960)	32.0	—
Inhabitants per doctor	1,067	(1958)	500	—
Inhabitants per gastroenterologist	3,510	(1958)	2,000	—
Spending on public health (thousand pesos)	20.6	(1958)	737.0	—
Spending on public health per inhabitant (in pesos)	3.5	(1958)	72.6	—[d]

(continued)

D. Housing

	1959	1984	1959–1984
Total dwellings built	17,089	90,000 (1983)e	1,042,785 (total)
Average growth rate			7.2%
Average number dwellings built per year			43,449.4
Dwellings built per 10,000 inhabitants (annual average)	1.7	9.0	4.3
Total housing			
In poor condition	47.0 (1953)	31.0 (1980)	—
In average condition	40.0 (1953)	47.0 (1980)	—
In good condition and acceptable	13.0 (1953)	22.0 (1980)	—
Housing in rural areas			
In poor condition	74.0 (1953)	20.0 (1980)	—
In average condition	23.0 (1953)	65.0 (1980)	—
In good condition and acceptable	3.0 (1953)	15.0 (1980)	—
Housing with running water	50.5% (1953)	74.1% (1980)	—
Housing with electricity	55.5% (1953)	82.9% (1980)	—

aThis figure represents the population between 15 and 49 years that can neither read nor write.

bThis figure was calculated taking into account the population between 17 and 24 years of age.

cThis figure refers to the life expectancy of infants less than 12 months in 1982.

dFigures estimated by the author, assuming the population's growth rate between 1982 and 1983 for the period 1983/1984.

eThis figure is estimated taking into account the state sector and the annual average of housing built by the private sector between 1981 and 1983.

Sources:

Fidel Castro, Speech on May 17, 1984, Granma, May 19, 1984; Speech on July 15, 1984, Granma, July 17, 1984; Speech on July 26, 1984, Granma, July 28, 1984.

"Social Security in Cuba," Granma Weekly Review, September 14, 1980.

"Study on the existing situation of youths aged 13-16 who broke with the national system of education approved by the National Assembly," Granma, July 21, 1984.

"Let's make the 1984/85 School Year the Best Yet in Quality and Efficiency in the History of the Revolution!" Granma, September 3, 1984.

CEE, Anuario Estadistico de Cuba 1982, pp. 81, 126, 423, 427, 431.

——, Anuario Demografico 1982, p. 61.

——, Comunicado acerca de los resultados definitivos del Censo de Poblacion y Viviendas de 1981, Havana, August 1983.

——, La economia cubana 1983, pp. 5, 6.

——, Boletin Estadistico Mensual de Cuba, no. 6, June 1984, p. 9.

——, Anuario Estadistico de Cuba 1984, pp. 61, 115, 395, 428.

BNC, Informacion estadistica seleccionada de la economia cubana, March 1984, p. 31.

CIEM, Estudio acerca de la erradicacion de la miseria extrema en Cuba, Havana, September 1983, pp. 107, 111, 112, 124, 125, 144, 149, 156, 158, 159.

CEDEM, La poblacion de Cuba, Havana, 1975, pp. 10, 60.

N. Kolesnikov, Cuba: educacion popular y preparacion de los cuadros nacionales 1959/83, Moscow, 1983, p. 243.

MINSAP, Direccion Nacional de Estadisticas.

TABLE 5.3
Average Levels of Education in Rural Areas (% of adult
population)

	1953	1981
Less than 6 years of primary schooling	96.0%	51.9%
6 years or more of primary schooling	4.0	48.1
9 years or more of primary schooling	0.5	13.9

Sources: N. Kolesnikov, Cuba: educacion popular y
preparacion de los cuadros nacionales 1959/83, Moscow,
1983; CEE, Comunicado acerca de los resultados
definitivos del Censo de Población y Vivendas de 1981,
Havana, August 1983.

level of secondary schooling in the 1980s. Nor is anything said of the
increasing enrollment coverage at the various levels of learning, where
primary and secondary schools stand out for having passed from
enrollment levels of 45.2 percent and 8.7 percent of the relevant age
cohorts, respectively, in 1953, to 97.3 percent and 94.4 percent in 1984.
However, the most significant changes, without doubt, have occurred
in the rural areas. It is estimated that before 1959 the number of existing
classrooms was not enough to allow 35 percent of the school-age
population to attend. In addition, there was an illiteracy index of 41.7
percent, and an estimated 44 percent of the population had never
attended school. The transformations effected may be summarized by
looking at the evolution of the median education level in rural areas
(see Table 5.3).[39]

Health

The lack of any study examining the integral social policy developed
by the Revolution is also apparent in Cubanologist analyses of the
Cuban health sector. It thus becomes indispensable to refer to the guiding
principles of this same policy.

First, health in Cuba is conceptualized as a right of all citizens; its
guarantee is a responsibility of the state that offers these services free
to public. Second, public health is conceived integrally. Consequently,
services include medical attention both to the person and to the environment and are directed at the individual, healthy or ill, as a

biopsychosocial entity. Finally, the services offered entail actions of promotional protection, reception, and rehabilitation, which insist on the preventional and educational aspects of health.

Third, the initiatives in the health sector are implemented according to plan through basic health programs as well as through the efforts of multidisciplinary teams. Finally, the tasks for health policy are defined according to their tight interrelationship with the community and mass social organizations—a process that plays a vital role in ensuring the universality of health service coverage.

Abstracting from these basic elements, Cubanologists have selected isolated facts that supposedly substantiate the "poor results" obtained in the health field in Cuba after 1959 (see Table 5.2C). For example, analysis in the area of public health has attempted to use infant mortality rates of the 1960s—among other data—to demonstrate the setbacks supposedly suffered during this period. The conclusions such analysis yields clearly reveal positions that are not objective. For instance, Mesa-Lago wrote:

> Performance in health is less impressive than in education and social security because of the very high standards Cuba enjoyed in 1958 and the significant deterioration suffered in the 1960s and the quality of graduates, and reduction in the supply of medical equipment and medicines. . . . In order to recuperate and in some cases surpass the prerevolutionary health levels lost in the 1960s, it was necessary to increase by eighteenfold the state budget allocation to health, to develop massive vaccinations, and to launch crash programs to graduate medical personnel.[40]

Mesa-Lago accepted pre-1959 statistics uncritically.[41] However, a paper issued by CEPAL affirmed that the 1959 infant mortality rate "could have been greater because the registration was incomplete and did not include numerous births."[42] Brian Pollitt, the English economist, expressed a similar opinion regarding the surveys conducted prior to 1959 about the conditions of rural living.[43] It is difficult to take seriously claims that Cuba had reached high levels of health performance by 1958 only when some 20 percent of deliveries occurred in health institutions, when practically no rural hospitals existed, and when some 36 percent of rural workers suffered from intestinal parasites, 31 percent from malaria, and some 14 percent suffered, or had suffered, from tuberculosis.[44]

A detailed study has been conducted that looks into the factors affecting the quantification of infant mortality rates. The results of this study indicate an improvement in the conditions of public health in Cuba from 1960 to 1968. The more important conclusions of that study were the following:

1. From 1960 to 1968, information on infant mortality has improved considerably. In 1960 there was an underregistration of the deaths of babies less than one day old on the order of 15.8 percent. In 1968, this percentage dropped to 10.3.

2. For the same period, the mortality rate of children aged 28 days to 11 months was reduced by 22 percent. This indicates an important decline in postnatal mortality in the 1980s . . . only the figure for 1969 deviates from the trend. . . . In 1969 a definite increase in infant mortality rate occurred, provoked by the greater incidence of whooping cough, meningitis, diarrhea, and respiratory ailments.[45]

Mesa-Lago presented the death rates for a set of diseases (dysentery, chicken pox, diphtheria, hepatitis, malaria, measles, poliomyelitis, syphilis, tetanus, tuberculosis, and typhus) for the 1958–1977 period and inferred from these data that the state of health deteriorated during this time. According to his figures, only two diseases were eradicated (diphtheria and poliomyelitis) while the mortality rates of only four (malaria, tetanus, tuberculosis, and typhus) decreased slightly, and the rates of the other five (dysentery, chicken pox, hepatitis, measles, and syphilis) rose—some of them to a significant degree.[46] Not surprisingly, for 1958 no data are presented for four of the examined diseases, three of which Mesa-Lago contended underwent an increase—using 1965 figures as a base for dysentery and chicken pox and 1961 base figures for hepatitis. With this simple information, we are supposed to accept the conclusions concerning our health without even having seen any analysis of the evolution of the principal causes of death in these years or of the maternity death rates or of the life expectancy at birth.[47] Mesa-Lago neglected to use the data currently utilized in any international examination of these issues.

Thus, to correct Mesa-Lago's omissions, life expectancy at birth goes from 61.8 years in 1959 to 73 years in 1984; the infant mortality rate passes from between 32.5 and 60 deaths for every 1000 live births in 1959 (depending on the estimate) to 15.0 deaths per thousand in 1984; the maternity death rate for every 100,000 births declines from 118.2 in 1960 to 32.0 in 1984; residents per doctor from 1067 to 500; and infectious diseases such as poliomyelitis and diphtheria were eradicated and typhoid fever, tetanus, and whooping cough were practically eliminated. At the same time, of the ten principal causes of death, enteritis and dysenteric ailments and tuberculosis have disappeared, diseases that respectively constituted the number three, four, and nine killers in 1958.[48]

Housing Policy

The sharpest criticisms appear in the housing sector. For example, Mesa-Lago argued:

Of all social services, housing is the worst in terms of revolutionary performance. . . . My own estimate of the deficit created *under* the Revolution is 700,000. . . . Distribution of housing between urban and rural areas does not seem to have improved significantly. . . . Since the majority of the population probably occupies the same housing that it had in 1960, blacks still live in the worst homes. Perhaps that is why the 1970 population census did not release data on housing distribution by race.[49]

Above all, it has not been Cuban critics but the very leaders of the Revolution that have always objectively evaluated the country's housing situation. Hence, already in 1975 the issue was discussed in the following terms by Fidel Castro:

There is not yet much that the Revolution has been able to accomplish in the area of housing. More than 200 thousand dwellings have been built between 1959 and 1975. The deficit is very large and although the rate of the last few years has multiplied—due especially to the brilliant efforts of the microbrigades—it is still insufficient. In actuality, the need to prioritize economic installations, schools, hospital, and other pressing demands of the nation impedes the allocation of greater resources to the construction of new dwellings. To accomplish that it would be necessary to wait for the first output of the new industries of construction materials presently being built. In effect, the question of housing, by virtue of the magnitude and volume of the problem, is one of the social necessities requiring the most time for our Revolution to solve.[50]

On the other hand, Cubanologist analysis suffers from data deficiencies since it takes into account only the construction of dwellings by the state, not the private construction in these years. According to data compiled by the Ministry of Construction, state-constructed dwellings constituted only around 32 percent of all those built between 1959 and 1984.[51]

This assessment of the pivotal role of private construction is corroborated by more recent figures. In effect, according to an inquiry conducted between 1981 and 1983, 180,000 dwellings for the population were built, 85,785 of which were fabricated by the state, a number roughly equivalent to 47 percent of the total constructed.[52]

It is also important to emphasize that the distribution of housing between urban and rural areas has significantly improved during the years of the Revolution. Hence, in 1953 46 percent of the population lived in rural zones but owned only 39.9 percent of dwellings, whereas in 1981 this proportion was 31.0 percent and 29.9 percent, respectively.[53] It is also necessary to stress that there has been a significant improvement in the quality of rural housing. In effect, the number of dwellings in poor condition was reduced from 74 percent of the total in 1953 to 20 percent in 1980 (see Table 5.3D).

Conclusions

The noteworthy advances achieved by Cuba in the sphere of basic social services that have here been analyzed cannot be contested.[54] Despite this objective record, after 1980 the approach of a group of Cubanologists has changed significantly. During the present decade the tendency to negate the value of the advances achieved in the social arena has become accentuated.

Accordingly, Carmelo Mesa-Lago indicated in a 1983 paper,

> The deterioration of the Cuban economy and the debt obligation has forced a tightening of the belt in the 1980s which threatens some of the social advances accomplished before. This movement began at the end of 1981 when President Castro described the difficult economic situation, promised to fulfill international financial commitments, and announced the need for more restrictions and sacrifices starting with the dramatic increase in consumer prices.

He added:

> Costa Rica equaled or surpassed many of Cuba's achievements in the social sphere . . . and at the same time improved the Cuban record in several economic goals. . . . Costa Rica was able to accomplish all this with a less powerful state and without sacrificing economic and political freedoms of the people.[55]

For his part, Sergio Roca worked in the same direction, as is evident when he wrote in 1983:

> Cuba seems unable to generate substantial and permanent improvement in the quality of consumer goods and in the delivery of public services. . . . Deficiencies in consumer goods make it especially difficult to increase worker productivity. . . . A predictable result of product shortages, service inefficiencies, and bureaucratic paralysis is the growth of illegal and underground transactions.[56]

Last, the U.S. State Department entrusted the consulting firm of Trade and Economic Development Associates with conducting a study of Cuban social and economic accomplishments between 1960 and 1983, comparing Cuba to twenty-one other countries in the Western hemisphere. According to their "impartial" analysis:

The results indicate, contrary to the general impression created by Castro, that history does not favor the Cuban revolution. . . . In almost all the indices, other countries have progressed more than Cuba. What is tragic about this record is that these are in the same areas that are repeatedly referred to when justifying the loss of liberty imposed on the Cuban community by the Castro regime. . . . At the time of the revolution, Cuba had attained a relatively high level of meeting basic needs and could have advanced to the next stage of expansion and economic growth predicted by theory. . . . Instead, the limited achievements, improving the satisfaction of basic needs, have been accompanied by a lack of growth in the Gross National Product.[57]

It may be observed that these propositions are in line with the anticommunist campaign initiated by the Reagan administration. The tactics pursued by this campaign consist in revaluing the prerevolutionary social situation and minimizing the advances achieved after 1959—but also denying improvements previously conceded in areas such as education, health, and social security. Furthermore, other Latin American countries that are supposed to serve as models have been introduced as comparisons.

Perhaps the most novel element in the majority of more recent work is the almost complete lack of academic-scientific language—a trait that characterized the majority of Cubanologists' analysis in the past decade. The methods and language of the 1960s have reappeared.

Finally, it remains to indicate that most of Cubanologist analysis suffers from further deficiencies. In effect, as previously indicated, no analysis of the political situation beginning with 1959 exists. A global evaluation of Cuba's integral strategy after the triumph of the Revolution is missing. Because the interrelationship between the political, economic, and social aspects of the Revolution is not examined, Cubanologists fail to sustain the thesis that social development in Cuba lacks an appropriate economic base.

Notes

1. Mesa-Lago (1981: 2).
2. Theriot (1981: 1). Also see Domínguez (1978).
3. Roett (1983: 133).
4. This point is based on information from a study by the Centro de Investigaciones de la Economía Mundial (CIEM) (1983: 40–43).
5. This integral focus was already being suggested in 1953: "The problem of land, the problem of industrialization, the problem of housing, the problem of unemployment, the problem of education, and the problem of public health: I have here the six concrete points whose solutions should have resolutely

guided our efforts, together with the conquest of public liberties and political democracy" (Castro 1973: 43).

6. Mesa-Lago (1981: 190). See also Mesa-Lago, *The Labor Force, Employment, Unemployment, and Underemployment in Cuba: 1899–1970* (1972).

7. Mesa-Lago (1981: 124).

8. Mesa-Lago (1981: 189, 190).

9. See Mesa-Lago (1972: 41).

10. See Jolly in J. Lowe, ed. (1979: 33).

11. Valdés Paz and Hernández (1983: 7).

12. Mesa-Lago (1972: 55).

13. Mesa-Lago (1981: 191). See also Roca (1980).

14. CEDEM (1976: 189).

15. Comité Estatal Estadística (CEE) (1983: 29).

16. See Castro (1978: 147), and also, CEE, *Anuario Estadístico de Cuba 1982,* pp. 63, 102, 114. Regarding the growth of the population, it should be clarified that—contrary to what certain Cubanologists assume—this comparison maintains its validity. In effect, if the impact of the emigration of antisocial elements in 1980 is not taken into account, the semiannual growth rate would have reached a figure of 1.1 percent, which continues to be less than the growth rate of state employment. These figures were calculated using information from the *Statistical Abstract of the United States 1982–83* (1982: 92).

17. Díaz-Briquets and Pérez (1982: 533). For a scientific interpretation of this problem, see Farnos (1985).

18. Domínguez (1978: 526).

19. See Valdés Paz and Hernández (1983).

20. In this respect, see the interpretations of the differences between minimum and maximum wages, as well as the evaluation of the parallel market in Mesa-Lago (1981: 191–194).

21. See the estimates made for the wages of the military and private farmers in Mesa-Lago (1981: 156), and the source of his data regarding retail prices in the "black market," p. 163.

22. See Roca (1979).

23. Valdés (1983: 37).

24. See Mesa-Lago (1981: 159, 194).

25. See Handelman (1983: 137).

26. Mesa-Lago (1981: 160).

27. CIEM (1983: 97) and CEE, *Anuario Estadístico de Cuba 1984,* p. 96.

28. Gordon (1983, summary).

29. See Brundenius (1981: 142, 151).

30. Calculated with figures from the newspaper, *El Mundo,* November 25, 1960; CIEM (1983: 81), and CEE, ibid., p. 95.

31. CEE (1981: 41), and *Anuario Estadístico de Cuba 1984,* p. 96.

32. See CIEM (1983: 88–100), and CEE, ibid., p. 94.

33. See Mesa-Lago (1981: 195), and *Periódico Granma* (September 14, 1980). Also see CETSS (1983).

34. Except when otherwise indicated, these figures come from Tables 3–6.

35. Mesa-Lago (1981: 164, 195).
36. See CIEM (1983: 22).
37. According to Mesa-Lago, this refers to Richard Jolly.
38. See Lorenzetto and Neys (1974). Also see World Bank (1955 to 1974), as well as Kolesnikov (1983).
39. Data cited by Rodríguez (1985: 25).
40. Mesa-Lago (1981: 195, 196).
41. This refers to Mesa-Lago (1969).
42. CEPAL (1978: 166).
43. This author refers to a study by Lowry (1958) and to la Agrupación Católica Universitaria and to la Universidad Central de las Villas (1959). See also, Pollitt (1967: 50).
44. See Castro (1984). Also see CIEM (1983).
45. This is taken from Alvarez and Sanchez (1972) and from Fernández (1972). Data are cited by CEDEM (1976: 59).
46. Mesa-Lago (1981: 166–168).
47. A similar approach may be noted in Domínguez (1978: 221–224) and in the paper by Roca (1975).
48. See CEE, *Anuario Estadístico de Cuba 1984*, p. 447, and CIEM (1983: 150).
49. Mesa-Lago (1981: 172, 174). A similar approach may be found in the works of Roca (1979) and Acosta and Hardoy (1983).
50. Castro (1984: 74–75).
51. See Ministry of Construction (MICONS) (1982: 30). See also Hamburg (1986).
52. See CEE, *Anuario Estadístico de Cuba 1982*, p. 192, and *La economía Cubana 1983*, p. 6.
53. CIEM (1983: 158).
54. A novel approach to the Revolution's social achievements may be seen in Brundenius (1984, ch. 4).
55. Mesa-Lago (1983a: 28, 31). Similar theses were advanced by Mesa-Lago in the work for the Organization of American States in 1983 (1983b). The same ideas appear later in the paper by the OAS InterAmerican Commission on Human Rights (1983), which was written by several distinguished Cubanologists selected for the occasion.
56. See Roca (1983: 75, 76, 77–78).
57. See the commentary on this work that appears in the article by Domenick Dipasquale (1984). Also in the same line of thought may be seen the book by Thomas, Fauriol, Weiss, eds. (1984, ch. 5), and Eberstadt (1984).

References

Acosta, Maruja, and Jorge Hardoy. *Urban Reform in Revolutionary Cuba.* Antilles Research Program, Occasional Papers, no. 1. New Haven: Yale University, 1983.
Agrupación Católica Universitaria. "Encuesta de trabajadores rurales 1956–57." *Economía y Desarrollo,* no. 12 (July/August 1972).

Alvarez, Luisa, and Carlos Sanchez. "Un aspecto de importancia en el análisis de la mortalidad infantil." *Cubana de Pediatria*, no. 44 (July/December 1972).

Brundenius, Claes. *Economic Growth, Basic Needs, and Income Distribution in Revolutionary Cuba.* Lund: Research Policy Institute, 1981.

————. *Revolutionary Cuba: The Challenge of Economic Growth with Equity.* Boulder: Westview Press, 1984.

Castro, Fidel R. Discurso pronunciado en los Congresos de Pediatria Cubana 1984. Havana: November 11, 1984.

————. *Informe del Comité Central del PCC al Primer Congreso.* Havana: 1978.

————. *La historia me absolverá.* Havana: 1973.

CEDEM. *La población de Cuba.* Havana: 1976.

Centro de Investigaciones de la Economía Mundial (CIEM). *Estudio acerca de la erradicación de la pobreza en Cuba.* (Havana: September 1983.

CEPAL. *Cuba: estilo de desarrollo y políticas sociales.* Mexico City: Siglo XXI, 1980.

CETSS. *24 Años de revolución en la seguridad social cubana.* 1983.

Comité Estatal Estadística (CEE). *Anuario Estadístico de Cuba.* Various editions, Havana.

CEE. *Cuba: Desarrollo económico y social durante el periodo 1958 y 1980.* Havana: December 1981.

————. *Comunicado acerca de los resultados definitivos del Censo de Población y Viviendas de 1981.* Havana: August 1983.

————. *La economía Cubana.* Havana: 1983.

Díaz-Briquets, Sergio, and Lisandro Pérez. "Fertility Decline in Cuba: A Socioeconomic Interpretation." *Population and Development Review* 8, no. 3 (September 1982).

Domínguez, J. *Cuba: Order and Revolution.* Cambridge: Harvard University Press, 1978.

Dipasquale, Domenick. "Análisis refuta alegato cubano de avances sociales y económicos." *Ahora,* Dominican Republic, May 14, 1984.

Eberstadt, N. "Literacy and Health: The Cuban Model." *Wall Street Journal* (December 10, 1984).

Farnos, Alfonso. "La declinación de la fecundidad y sus perspectivas en el contexto de los procesos demográficos en Cuba." Unpublished thesis, CEDEM, Havana, 1985.

Fernández, Carmen. "Tendencias en Cuba de la mortalidad de menores de 1 año durante periodos comprendidos entre 1919 y 1970." *Cubana de Pediatria,* no. 44 (July/December 1972).

Gordon, Antonio M. "The Nutritive of Cubans: Historical Perspective and Nutritional Analysis." *Cuban Studies/Estudios Cubanos* 13, no. 2 (1983).

Handelman, Howard. "Cuban Food Policy and Popular Nutritional Levels." *Cuban Studies/Estudios Cubanos* 11, no. 2 (July 1981); 12, no. 1 (January 1983).

Hamburg, Jill. *Under Construction: Housing Policy in Revolutionary Cuba.* New York: Center for Cuban Studies, 1986.

Jolly, Richard. "Contrasts in Cuban and African Educational Strategies." In J. Lowe, ed., *Education and Nation-Building in the Third World*, World Bank Staff Working Paper no. 317 (January 1979).

Kolesnikov, N. *Cuba: educación popular y preparación de los cuadros nacionales 1959-1982*. Moscow: 1983.

"La seguridad social en Cuba." *Periódico Granma*. Resumen semanal (September 14, 1980).

Lorenzetto, A., and Karel Neys. *Métodos y medios utilizados en Cuba para eliminar el analfabetismo*. Paris: UNESCO, 1974.

Lowry, Nelson. *Rural Cuba*. New York: Octagon, 1970.

Mesa-Lago, Carmelo. "Availability and Reliability of Statistics in Socialist Cuba." *Latin American Research Review* 4, no. 1, 2 (1969).

_____. *The Labor Force, Employment, Unemployment, and Underdevelopment in Cuba: 1899-1970*. Beverly Hills: Sage, 1972.

_____. *The Economy of Socialist Cuba: A Two Year Appraisal*. Albuquerque: University of New Mexico Press, 1981.

_____. "Cuba's Centrally Planned Economy: An Equity Tradeoff for Growth." Paper presented at conference, Vanderbilt University, 1983.

_____. *Los derechos económicos y laborales en Cuba*. Document prepared for the OAS Human Rights Project in Cuba, January 1983.

Ministry of Construction (MICONS). *Informe sobre la erradicación de la miseria extrema en Cuba*. Unpublished work, Havana, 1982.

OAS InterAmerican Commission on Human Rights. *La situación de los derechos humanos en Cuba: Séptimo informe*. Washington, D.C.: 1983.

Pollitt, Brian. "Estudios acerca del nivel de vida en la Cuba pre-revolucionaria: Un análisis crítico." *Teoría y Práctica*, no. 42/43 (November/December 1967).

Rodríguez, J. L. "Los efectos de la Reforma Agraria sobre el campesinado en Cuba." Paper presented to the Mesa Redonda Internacional sobre Formas de Organización y Tenencia en Procesos de Reforma Agraria, Mexico, November 11-15, 1985.

Roett, Riordan. "La política exterior de Cuba y los E.E.U.U." *Nueva Sociedad*, no. 69 (November/December 1983).

Roca, S. "Distributional Effects of the Cuban Revolution: Urban Versus Rural Allocation." Paper presented at the annual meeting of the American Economic Association, Dallas, 1975.

_____. "Housing in Socialist Cuba." Paper presented at the International Conference on Housing Problems, Miami, 1979a.

_____. "Methodological Approaches and Evaluation of Two Decades of Redistribution in Cuba." Adelphi University, December 1979b.

_____. "Aspectos económicos de la presencia de Cuba en Africa." *Cuban Studies/Estudios Cubanos* 19, no. 2 (July 1980).

_____. "Cuba Confronts the 1980s." *Current History* (February 1983).

Theriot, Lawrence. *Cuba Faces the Economic Realities of the 1980s*. Washington, D.C.: Government Printing Office, 1981.

Thomas, H., G. Fauriol, J. C. Weiss, eds. *The Cuban Revolution 25 Years Later*. Boulder: Westview Press, 1984.

Universidad Central de las Villas. *La Educación Rural en las Villas*. 1959.

U.S. Bureau of Census. *Statistical Abstract of the United States 1982–83*. Washington, D.C.: 1982.

Valdés, Nelson P. "The Cuban Economy and Social Developments in the 1980s." Talk delivered at the conference "Cuba in the 1980s," Bonn, May 16, 1983.

Valdés Paz, Juan, and Rafael Hernández. "La estructura de clase de la comunidad cubana en Estados Unidos." *Cuadernos de Nuestra América* 1, no. 1 (July/ December 1983).

World Bank. *Cuba: Economic Change and Education Reform, 1955 to 1974*.

6

Some Thoughts on Vital Statistics and Health Status in Cuba

Sarah Santana

Several recently published works have evaluated the quality of Cuban health and vital statistics and have arrived at varying levels of confidence or mistrust in them (8, 9, 10, 13, 14). The degree to which the figures— even those considered reliable—reflect the true health status of the population, the proportion of the apparent improvement in health conditions that is real and not artifactual, and the appropriateness of the policies that have supposedly produced that improvement have also been recurrent topics of discussion.

In a country like Cuba health status takes on special significance. First, this results because the system and its leaders have made it one measure of the country's political performance. This is similar to the way in which Americans judge the performance of a presidential administration by the improvements in economic indicators such as the unemployment rate, the interest rate, and the consumer price index. Second, because Cuba is enmeshed in international political controversy and for twenty-eight years has been on the receiving end of passive and not-so-passive aggression from external sources, any achievement the country may claim is used by friend and foe to credit or discredit the system. Not surprisingly, then, Cuba itself wants to use the improving health of its population as a legitimate arena for competition with the United States. Only perhaps in areas of human welfare and human resources can an underdeveloped country of 10 million people compete with a world power.

Because health status is so important ideologically and politically, both domestically and internationally, the quality and interpretation of its statistical measures become essential issues to understand. Health and vital statistics are useful only to the degree that they measure the real health status of the population, in absolute or relative terms; reflect changes in health conditions; and enable us to measure or evaluate the effects of deliberate human interventions or changing conditions upon health. In this sense, they are simply tools that must be well honed in order to be used in the decisionmaking about courses of action.

How reliable are the Cuban health data? Are they of high quality, valid, consistent? Do they reflect the real health of the population when compared with other measures? Are they responsive enough to reflect the effects of changing policies? Are they, as some have claimed, tampered with or "fudged" to fit official expectations?

Vital and health statistics are reliable and useful when they offer clarity and uniformity of definitions and virtually universal coverage, are collected and aggregated promptly in a prescribed and standardized manner, and convey information that reflects the true characteristics of the medical or vital event they report, without systematic biases.

Completeness and Coverage

Cuban vital statistics have been evaluated for completeness by foreign and Cuban investigators. In March 1974, Ruth R. Puffer, consultant to the Pan American Health Organization, after reviewing registration procedures, carrying out impromptu and unplanned site visits, hand-tallying birth and death certificates, and comparing these with the delivery rosters in hospitals, concluded that the vital registry was practically complete and recommended that the World Health Organization (WHO) consider Cuba a country with reliable statistics (20). The procedural and supervisory care that has been taken with the registry since then can only have improved the coverage.[1]

Also in 1974, the registry was evaluated by the National Planning Board, which compared it with other independent sources of information about deaths and births, such as the national consumer registry (which issues ration books for each person), the rosters of the Committees for the Defense of the Revolution (block associations), other mass organizations, and cemetery listings (5). At that time the registry was found to have an underregistration of 3.9 percent for deaths of all ages, with the lowest rate among deaths under one year of age.

Another evaluation was carried out in 1980 by the Comité Estatal de Estadísticas. Information on deaths was specifically gathered independent of the registry system. The committee found that 0.5 percent of deaths were not registered (4). The most important condition met by the system in order to provide such high coverage is that birth and death registrations are made in health facilities (as well as civil registries), for which the health personnel bear the primary responsibility. Since over 98 percent of births occur in health facilities (19), as well as a similarly high proportion of deaths, it is the accessibility, high utilization, and coverage of the health care system itself that ensures the completeness of the vital record.

Consistency

The reliability and consistency of the birth and death information have been indirectly confirmed through various means. Hugo Behm of the Centro Latinoamericano de Demografia in Costa Rica and Kenneth Hill of the National Research Council of the United States have used survey data to estimate levels of fertility and mortality and compare them with officially reported statistics (1, 13). Hill, using the same survey data and similar methodology as Behm, found inconsistencies between the survey estimates and the reported infant mortality rate after 1974. Until that time both investigators had found high levels of agreement between the two sets of figures. In the absence of evidence of registry deterioration, Hill believed the reported rates should stand. The discrepancy, he said, may be due to sampling biases that overestimate deaths or to the fact that the estimates assume equal mortality across different mothers' age strata whereas real infant mortality shows large strata differentials. The adjustments for declining fertility made by both Hill and Behm resulted in only a small change in the mortality estimates. However, after adjustments for rapidly decreasing mortality (the Cuban situation), Behm concluded that the survey data are only applicable up to 1974 (including an average of the risks to mothers of all ages), whereas Hill applied the estimates almost to 1979. This may be another reason for the discrepancy Hill observed.

Data from the 1981 census (7)—which employed much improved methodology over the 1970 one, providing larger amounts and better quality of information—have been published in great detail (including age breakdowns by single-year categories, and not, as Eberstadt (10) mistakenly claimed, in groupings so large that analysis is impossible). This will permit new comparisons with the current vital record.

When health and vital statistics are of good quality and reflect true health status they generally fit a pattern that relates morbidity, mortality, and fertility rates. There is generally internal consistency from year to year in the mortality and morbidity rates published in Cuba. The few anomalies or unexpected figures have logical explanations, based on the particular conditions and circumstances of the country at that time and the definitions of the morbidity data collected.

The progressive continuum from morbidity to mortality without medical intervention does not always hold true once treatment intervenes, lowering mortality risks without necessarily affecting morbidity. There may then surface an apparent distortion in the data showing relatively high levels of some types of morbidity with relatively low levels of mortality.[2] Certain mortality rates (such as infant and child mortality) can be specifically targeted and lowered without greatly improving the quality of life of the people involved. In some cases these strategies only postpone death a short time. In other cases they enable the child to live through a vulnerable period but may not improve living conditions or nutritional status, for example. In fact, low mortality, implying longer life expectancy, can raise morbidity levels. If death is averted, the person has a greater chance of being included in morbidity statistics. This is the case with morbidity from chronic diseases.

Of course, very high morbidity of diseases like diphtheria and pertussis with high case fatality rates, or lethal disease combinations (diarrhea and malnutrition, for example), inevitably spell higher mortality rates, even in the presence of medical care. But this is not at all the Cuban case.

Morbidity in Cuba is reported by continuous data and by specially collected survey data. Forty-four diseases are obligatorily reported. Some others like acute diarrheal and respiratory infections are reported as numbers of encounters with physicians for that diagnosis. There are leprosy and cancer registries and registries of patients regularly followed for chronic diseases (diabetes, hypertension, and asthma). Some statistics gathered for planning purposes also provide indices of disease activity: hospital discharges by diagnosis category, work-related morbidity, and ambulatory encounters by diagnosis.

The quality of morbidity data is not as high as that for mortality data in all diseases. Those diagnoses for which there exists a control or immunization program have very good data and low rates of under-registration. Leprosy, tuberculosis, polio, diphtheria, pertussis, tetanus, and so on all show fairly complete reports. The new program of family medicine, by which family physicians are placed in the community, will greatly improve the morbidity information.

The apparently rising morbidity from certain diseases has led some to partially doubt health improvements or declining mortality (10, 17). Morbidity data are, in fact, perfectly consistent with both improving health status and mortality reductions.

The supposed "uncoupling" of morbidity and mortality statistics in Cuba is false. The few diseases with rising incidence are unrelated to infant mortality, such as syphillis, imported malaria, and hepatitis. The

TABLE 6.1
Measles Morbidity and Immunizations, Cuba

Year	Rate per 100,000	Immunizations
1965	118.8	--
1970	104.2	--
1975	113.4	123,983
1980	38.9	167,176
1982	239.0	303,463
1983	33.3	242,952
1984	34.2	229,163
1985	28.6	335,377

Source: MINSAP, Salud Pública en Cifras, 1985.

one exception is meningococcal infections, which are on the rise almost all over the world.

Morbidity from acute diarrheal and respiratory infections in Cuba is reported as the number of physician visits caused by that particular diagnosis. It is more a measure of health care utilization than of true morbidity because it does not reflect episodes, cases, or patients. The same illness episode of similar severity could be represented by one or more encounters, depending on medical availability. Similarly, hospital admissions per 100 population increased as hospital availability and capacity expanded, from 10.6 admissions in 1968 to 16.0 in 1985 (19), without a concomitant increase in mortality. This is a universal phenomenon and does not mean there have not been diarrheal or respiratory infection outbreaks, only that general incidence is not necessarily on the rise and negatively affecting mortality.

Measles has not been an important cause of death in Cuba, since acute malnutrition is not present. Measles incidence increased in 1982, after several years of decreases, because of low immunization levels. After these levels were raised again, incidence continued to decrease (see Table 6.1). The low mortality from this disease (as well as for chicken pox) placed it in a low priority for immunization programs. The increase in malaria incidence up to 1985 has been entirely the result of imported cases.

It is precisely these diseases, with the accompanying data that clarify the behavior of the incidence rates, that confirm the cogency and internal consistency of the Cuban data. The number of measles cases increased after low immunization levels. Venereal disease rates increased dramatically after the inception of new case-finding programs (as well as some real increases). And so it goes. Patterns like these are observed even in such developed and sophisticated health areas as New York City, where at certain periods the incidence of measles or hepatitis or venereal diseases increased as infant mortality decreased (3).

The fact that Cuba regularly publishes both positive and negative statistics about the health of its population is indicative of the veracity of its figures. Health statistics in Cuba are used as real planning tools (although some authors would encourage even wider use of them) (21) and for evaluation of programs. Hence, they form the main mechanism by which health authorities are held accountable for their programs and actions. It is to everyone's interest then to keep them as reliable as possible.

The evolution of the mortality structure in Cuba is consistent with its general socioeconomic development. In 1959 Cuba's infant mortality rate hovered between 50 and 70, although officially set at 34.7 (1, 14). Recorded mortality increased until 1962 when it began to decline very slowly (mostly holding steady) until 1968 when it rose slightly and then very sharply in 1969. The peak mortality in the late 1960s has been interpreted as reflecting a real deterioration of health conditions. It seems more likely that registration steadily improved, although real mortality decreased (see Table 6.2). The figure for 1969 reflects a single-year peak of real deterioration in the rate, attributable mainly to increases in cause-specific mortality from whooping cough, meningitis, and acute diarrheal and respiratory infections (26).

Calculating the percentage of change in the infant mortality rate by using 1969 as the base year is not good methodology. The decrease should be measured from 1970 on. Although the percentage reduction is therefore smaller, it is a fairer assessment of the time trend.

The causes for the upturn in mortality in 1969 have never been very clear. A series of epidemics, for whatever reasons, may have converged on the country that year. The increased pertussis rate could be an indication of immunization failures. The point is that the health system, contrary to what happened in later years, was not yet well enough equipped to respond to an emergency situation in time. This response capability would have depended on adequate surveillance (which would have detected the beginning of the increase the previous year) and the ability to mobilize resources once the problems were detected. One result of this year's experience was the renewal and more vigorous application of an improved infant mortality reduction and surveillance program from 1969 on. At any rate, this was a single-year occurrence, and because the rate returned to its previous low levels the following

TABLE 6.2
Infant Mortality, Cuba

Year	Rate per 1,000 Live Births
1959	34.7
1960	37.3
1961	39.0
1962	41.7
1963	38.1
1964	37.8
1965	37.8
1966	37.2
1967	36.4
1968	38.2
1969	46.7
1970	38.7
1975	27.5
1980	19.6
1985	16.5 (provisional)

Sources: 1959-1968: Hugo Behm, <u>Cuba: La
Mortalidad Infantíl Según Variables
Socioeconómicas Regiones, 1974</u>; 1969-1985:
MINSAP, Salud Pública en Cifras, 1985.

year, the 1969 rise could not possibly have reflected entrenched adverse conditions.

Since then the infant mortality rate has steadily declined, and rates for age categories above fifteen have been reduced slightly or remained level. Although the cause- and age-specific mortality rates of many diseases have decreased, the reductions in fertility and increased life expectancy have caused a consequent increase in the proportions of the population in older age categories. This has kept the crude death rate hovering around 6 per 100,000.

As evidence of real improvements in mortality, the percentage of deaths to persons older than fifty years increased from 60.8 percent in 1960 to 78.2 percent in 1985, a change of 29 percent, whereas the general population over sixty-five years old increased by 66 percent from 4.8 percent in 1960 to 8.0 percent in 1985. Cuba now faces the problems of an aging urban population whose main problems are chronic and degenerative diseases.

Evaluation of the System
of Health and Vital Statistics

Few if any authors writing outside Cuba (perhaps with the exception of Ruth Puffer) have included in their evaluations of Cuban data the actual system of collection and aggregation of the information. The Cuban statistical system meets most of the conditions and requirements generally considered necessary to achieve a complete reliable register and produce valid, trustworthy data:

- Citizens find it necessary, desirable, easy, and free of charge to register births and deaths.
- Registration takes place largely in health facilities, and health staff members, not relatives, are primarily responsible for it.
- Items in birth and death certificates include socioeconomic and biologic information as recommended by WHO.
- A large proportion of deaths are confirmed by autopsy, in some age categories (under one year of age, for instance) over 50 percent. This contributes to the validity of the information.
- The WHO definitions of live birth and fetal death have been in use since 1965 and are uniformly applied through the country.
- The data are differentiated by residence, occurrence, and registration.
- Death certificates are signed by physicians, and deaths occurring outside health facilities are submitted for certification to the forensic medicine department.
- There are training programs for hospital workers, as well as for municipal and provincial registrars, medical students, physicians, and statistical technicians.
- Work is continuously supervised, and periodic surveys examining the quality of the certificates are carried out.
- Sufficient resources are allocated for review, confirmation, and correction of the information as it is collected.
- The staff is sufficient.
- The system and documents were designed and are handled jointly by the two agencies whose purposes they serve, the Ministries of Justice and of Public Health.
- There is one unified statistical system that provides health data on all facilities and agencies, thus avoiding the pitfalls of multiple discrepant publications.
- There is central control of the system at the national level.
- Penalties are applied for failing to report vital events.

• The main user (Ministry of Public Health) processes and publishes the information.

All these features have been recommended by international committees for the development of efficient statistical systems (24, 27).

Oversight of all statistical information in Cuba is the responsibility of the Comité Estatal de Estadísticas, which carries out its own independent tabulations of death certificates. The two agencies involved must agree on the figures before they are declared the official statistics for that year.

The Ministry of Public Health publishes data promptly, usually within the first four months of the year following the one to which the figures correspond. Statistics are classified as provisional or preliminary for approximately one to two years, until definitive figures for each municipality and province are agreed to.[3] For example, for data published in 1986, the provisional category applied only to 1985 figures.

Conclusions

Although comparisons across international boundaries can be helpful, they should be undertaken only if one can examine in depth the statistical structure and quality of the information of the countries compared. Spain, for example, has a very low infant mortality rate of 10 (23), but it is one of the few countries that still excludes from its register deaths under certain birthweights and younger than twenty-four hours of age. Costa Rica has a crude death rate lower than Cuba's (23) but also has a much higher fertility rate and a much younger age distribution, so that unless standardized, the lower death rate can be misleading. Mexico, as late as 1977, listed the majority of deaths in some states without physician certification and did not have a clear definition of live births and fetal deaths (24). In 1977 in Jamaica up to 33 percent of deaths went unreported in some parishes (24).

It would take more time and space than that available to examine Cuba's statistical profile side by side with that of countries of comparable development levels and populations. One can generally assert, however, that Cuba's statistical system is as complete as any and that the data it produces are a reasonably accurate reflection of the real health status of its people. In spite of its relatively low gross national product (GNP) per capita (23), its health status is one of the highest among underdeveloped countries.

The issue of whether or not Cuba would have achieved its present health levels without a revolutionary regime is a false one. The fact is that Cuba's government is socialist and that health is one of the explicit measurements it uses to evaluate its own performance. The issue, then, is only how well Cuba is doing and if there are sufficient data of good enough quality to make that judgment.

Notes

1. The author has been working in Cuba with birth and death registration in a collaborative research project about diarrheal mortality in the postneonatal period. The project is being sponsored by Columbia University and the Ministry of Public Health. The zealousness and strict adherence to guidelines that are observed throughout the country in the gathering, processing, and reporting of the vital data are impressive. Although results from the research are not yet available, in the course of these four years of work no inconsistencies or misleading reports have been observed, and occasional errors have been few and usually promptly detected and corrected by the system's own routine supervision mechanisms.

2. The opposite—low morbidity with high mortality—rarely happens, since morbidity must precede mortality, though mortality need not follow morbidity, with the exception of deaths from accidents, suicide, homicide, and so on.

3. N. Eberstadt (9, 10) erroneously asserted that infant mortality rates have been treated as provisional since 1972, citing changes in the rate for the Isle of Youth for the year 1973 as an example of arbitrary "fudging." Andrew Zimbalist (25) published a correction of this statement, showing that the changed rate was a calculation or printing error and that the raw data from which it was calculated were available for review alongside the rate. The absolute number of deaths had in fact been adjusted, but upward, by six additional deaths.

References

1. Behm, Hugo. *Cuba—La Mortalidad Infantíl Según Variables Socioeconómicas Regiones, 1974.* San José, Costa Rica: Centro Latinoamericano de Demografia, 1980.
2. Benjamin, Medea, et al. *No Free Lunch—Food and Revolution in Cuba Today.* San Francisco: Institute for Food and Development Policy, 1984.
3. City of New York. *Annual Summary of Vital Statistics,* 1980, 1981, 1982, 1983, 1984. New York: Department of Health.
4. Comité Estatal de Estadísticas y Ministerio de Salud Publica. *Investigación sobre la Integridad del Registro de Defunciones en Cuba.* 1980 (unpublished).
5. Comité Estatal de Estadísticas (CEE). *Evaluación en 1974 de los Registros de Defunciones.* Havana: CEE, 1980.

6. Comité Estatal de Estadísticas. *Informe sobre el comportamiento de algunos indicadores de la natalidad y la fecundidad entre 1959-1983.* Havana: Editorial Ciencias Medicas, 1984.
7. Comité Estatal de Estadísticas. *Censo de Población y Vivienda, 1981.* Vols. 1–15. Havana: CEE, 1984.
8. Diaz-Briquets, Sergio. "How to Figure Out Cuba—Development, Ideology and Mortality." *Caribbean Review* 15, no. 2 (spring 1986):8.
9. Eberstadt, N. "Literacy and Health: The Cuban Model." *Wall Street Journal,* December 10, 1984.
10. Eberstadt, N. "Did Fidel Fudge the Figures?" *Caribbean Review* 15, no. 2 (spring 1986):5.
11. Espinel Blanco, J. *Sistema de Información Estadístico de Defunciones, Defunciones Perinatales y Nacimientos de Cuba.* Havana: IDS, 1981.
12. Gutierrez Muniz, J. A. *La Economía Cubana y la Atención Infantil—Aspectos Básicos, 1959-1983.* Havana: Editorial de Ciencias Medicas, 1984.
13. Hill, Kenneth. "An Evaluation of Cuban Demographic Statistics, 1938–80." In P. E. Hollerbach and Sergio Diaz-Briquets, eds., *Fertility Determinants in Cuba.* Washington, D.C.: National Academy Press, 1983.
14. Hollerbach, Paula E., and Sergio Diaz-Briquets. *Fertility Determinants in Cuba.* Washington, D.C.: National Academy Press, 1983.
15. Juceplan, Direccion de Estadísticas de Población y Censos. *Las Estadísticas Demográficas Cubanas.* Havana: Editorial Cincias Sociales, 1975.
16. Last, John M., ed. *Maxcy-Roseneau Public Health and Preventive Medicine.* 11th edition. New York: Appleton-Century-Crofts, 1980.
17. Mesa-Lago, Carmelo. *The Economy of Socialist Cuba.* Albuquerque: University of New Mexico Press, 1981.
18. Ministerio de Salud Publica de Cuba. *Informe Anual, 1980, 1983.* Havana: MINSAP, 1984.
19. Ministerio de Salud Publica de Cuba. *Salud Pública en Cifras—Resumen Estadístico, 1985.* Havana: MINSAP, 1986.
20. Puffer, Ruth R. *Información Acerca de la Calidad y Cobertura de las Estadísticas Vitales y sobre Investigaciones de Mortalidad Perinatal e Infantil en Cuba.* Organización Panamericana de la Salud, AMRO, 3513, 1974.
21. Rios Massabot, Eneida N. *Estado Actual de los Sistemas de Información de la Morbilidad en Cuba.* Havana: IDS, 1981.
22. Rios Massabot, N. Eneida. "Information Systems for Vital Statistics in Cuba." In A. Fernandez Perez de Talens et al., eds., *Health Informatics in Developing Countries.* Amsterdam: Elsevier–North Holland, 1983.
23. UNICEF. *The State of the World's Children.* New York: Oxford University Press, 1986.
24. World Health Organization (WHO) and Office of International Statistics, National Center for Health Statistics (NCHS). *Vital Registration Systems in 5 Developing Countries: Honduras, Mexico, Philippines, Thailand and Jamaica.* Hyattsville, Md.: USDHS, Pub. no. (PHS) 81-1353, Series 2, no. 79, 1980.

25. Zimbalist, Andrew. "Twisting Statistics to Attack Cuba." *Cubatimes* (January/February 1985).

26. López Fernández, C. "Tendencies en Cuba de la mortalidad en menores de un año durante los períodos comprendidos entre 1910 y 1970." *Revista Cubana de Pediatría* 44 (July/December 1972).

27. Puffer, R. R., and C. V. Serrano. "Datos Básicos sobre nacimientos y defunciones esenciales para la planificación de salud y las estadísticas demográficas." *Boletín de la Oficina Sanitaria Panamericana*, March 1974.

7

On the Problem of Studying Women in Cuba

Carollee Bengelsdorf

The Cuban Communist party began its most important statement to date on the issue of women with the simplest of conclusions: "In practice," it said, "the full equality of women does not yet exist."[1] Yet the very simplicity of that phrasing both masks and underlines the enormous complexity of the issue. And it is a complexity that observers in the West—feminist and otherwise—have not yet come to grips with, even in the most schematic terms. Indeed, the literature produced thus far about women in the Cuban Revolution has been extraordinarily limited. It has tended to cover, again and again, the same terrain in rather summary fashion, with variations that predictably play themselves out. There is, first, the body of literature produced by the academic "Havana watchers."[2] The subject of women occupies only a minor role in their work: Their overriding concern centers upon watching the peregrinations of what they term the "elites" of the Revolution, and by their own definition "elites" virtually excludes women. When they do consider the subject of women, their discussion and conclusions are misplaced and misleading.

Second, there is the body of feminist work that tends to look at the Cuban experience only to dismiss it as yet another example of the fact that socialism does not liberate women.[3] The inability of Western feminists and Cuban women leaders to communicate is notorious and, by all appearances, very much a two-way street. Thus, for instance, Vilma Espin, the head of the Federation of Cuban Women, still regularly replies to questions concerning her impressions of the Western women's movement by saying, "We're feminine, not feminist." And Western feminists' inability to deal with the specifics of the Cuban situation is perhaps nowhere more clearly captured than in the reaction of a recent delegation of U.S. women to Cuba to the Cuban painting "The Rape of the Mulattas," a canvas that speaks to the reality of a colonial, slaveholding society: "In the U.S.," said one member of the delegation, "we carry whistles."

And finally, some observers define themselves as socialist feminists; as women sympathetic to both socialist and feminist theory and practice, who believe that some fusion, some union of the two is possible. A series of articles has been produced by socialist feminists on the subject of women during the twenty-five years of the Cuban Revolution: Each tends by and large to be simply a rewrite of its predecessor.[4]

These three approaches have, strange as it may seem, a great deal in common. Above all, each of them has been unable, or at least has failed thus far, to get at the complexity of the issues surrounding the situation of Cuban women. Thus, for instance, whatever its particular perspective, every article written on the subject seems to treat the issue of women's changing or unchanging position in revolutionary Cuba as if it were on a continuum—a process that began in 1959 and has proceeded apace since that time, a process that can therefore be stopped at any given point and measured in its totality. Yet no serious student of the Cuban Revolution would dream of treating the economy, or political structures, or the position of workers, along this same continuum. And for good reason: It would be impossible to understand changes in political structures from the 1960s to the 1970s, or in workplace organizations, without understanding the fundamental alterations or swings in the Cuban leadership's concept of how socialism and communism are to be achieved. These changes in political and economic organization must be located within the abandonment of the 1960s idea that the Cubans could find their own path to communism, using, as Fidel Castro phrased it, consciousness to create wealth, and not wealth to create consciousness.[5] This notion that socialism and communism could be achieved simultaneously was rejected by Cuban leaders in 1970: In its place, they substituted the more orthodox conception that the passage to communism is achieved through stages, that Cuba was in the initial stage of the transition to socialism, and that institutions, structures, and value formation must correspond to this reality. The effects of this far-reaching revision upon political and economic structures have been documented, however inadequately. Yet in concrete ways, these fundamental changes must have had an equally dramatic effect on the position of women within Cuban society: The available literature, however, gives no indication of the nature of these effects.

We can, perhaps, see more clearly what this means by examining briefly the patterns of change in two areas that vitally concern women, areas central to any assessment of their position within a given society: the family and women's entry into the labor force.

With regard to the family, the continuum approach tells us that, for better or worse, the Revolution has had a fairly consistent attitude and has pursued a consistent policy. In fact, this is not so: The transition from the 1960s to the 1970s generally is mirrored by a definitive and fundamental change in the Revolution's attitude and policy toward the family. In the 1960s, the family as an institution was in a very real sense ignored: This approach is perhaps best captured by Ché Guevara, who, while serving as minister of industries in the early 1960s, was asked by an interviewer if the Revolution was actively making policy against the family. His response was all revealing: not so much against the family, he replied, as without taking it into consideration. This was a period of enormous collective activity and movement. Perhaps the scope of this activity is best exemplified by the 1961 Literacy Campaign, in which over 100,000 young people, some only twelve or thirteen years old, went off to the countryside to live with, work with, and teach illiterate peasants. Of this 100,000, some 55,000 were young girls, many of whom went in active defiance of middle-class parents who had rigid and traditional ideas about the proper realm of activities for their daughters.[6]

It was a period in which plans were being laid for a school system that would essentially provide a sphere for education separate from the family. The schools in the countryside, boarding schools where children live, study and work, were projected to be established not simply at the junior high school level (where indeed they were eventually instituted) but throughout the educational structure. And it was a period in which families were being physically torn apart: There could hardly have been a family on the island that did not have some relative among the people who left Cuba in the first five years of the Revolution.

This dynamic alone required and reinforced the insistence by the leadership that the Revolution itself be the central focus of concern, the central institution, that its survival and its development be the chief priority. Inherent in this notion was the idea that the Revolution would replace the family as the primary, if not the only, agency of socialization. Children would be brought up in the Revolution: They would imbibe it in their every contact; they would be steeped in it in their schools and their activities; they would learn from the example of revolutionary leaders. Revolutionary society itself, defined both as institutions and as a general atmosphere, would take over the entire process of socialization and education: The role of parents was to be of secondary, if any, importance. Again, Ché Guevara best captured this vision: In a letter he wrote to Castro upon his departure to become a revolutionary guerrilla in the Andes of Bolivia, he declared, "I leave my children and wife nothing material, and I am not ashamed. I am glad it is so. I ask nothing for them, as the state will give them enough with which to live and be educated."[7]

With the transition to the more orthodox view of socialist construction in the early 1970s, a different and far more conservative and traditional view of the family clearly emerged, for reasons directly related to changes in the situation of the Revolution and the process of institutionalization that it initiated in the 1970s.[8]

At some level, this shift was simply a recognition of reality: Given the enormity of the change that the Revolution initiated, and the inevitable chaos that ensued upon this change, the family provided a sense of refuge and respite, an anchor. Indeed, people never considered abandoning it. Moreover, with the 1970s and the emergence of a new generation born into the Revolution and not therefore formed or informed by prerevolutionary reality, a youth problem—though not on a major scale—began to emerge. This problem was accentuated by the reintroduction in the early 1970s of material incentives and with it, the growth in availability of goods and the usefulness of money. The Cuban leadership identified one source of youthful delinquency as precisely those forces operating to dilute the role of the family. The state—the Revolution— could not handle by itself the entire education and socialization of children: The family had to take on a central, if not the central, role in this process. This was the cause of the emergence, in the 1970s in Cuba, of the concept of the socialist family and the enormous prominence and importance the family has assumed. At this point the Revolution began to articulate a conscious policy with relation to the family. The 1975 Family Code, which put forth a new set of norms for family life in Cuba, cannot be understood outside this context.

In the case of women's entry into the work force, we have an excellent example in one recent, massive study on Cuba, of the manner in which adherence to a continuum results in misleading—indeed false—conclusions. Jorge Domínguez, one of the deans of the Havana watchers, in his study, *Cuba: Order and Revolution*, interpreted women's entry into the work force after 1959 as follows: "A modernization hypothesis is sufficient to explain the trends in the incorporation of Cuban women into the paid workforce. Indeed, it is difficult to perceive any effects of the advent of the revolution on women's employment, since the rate of incorporation is fairly steady."[9]

Yet, if we break down this rate of incorporation, as Lourdes Casal did in her article, "Revolution and Conciencia: Women in Cuba,"[10] if we attempt to understand it within the historical and socioeconomic context in which it took place, such a conclusion would simply be impossible. Thus, for instance, if we examine the early years of the Revolution, what is most remarkable is that there was not a drastic decline in the number of women working: It is remarkable on a number of levels. First, the Revolution immediately undertook an enormous project of reeducating women who had been forced, in the years prior to 1959, to work in degrading and subservient occupations. These efforts at reeducation touched, in particular, the large numbers of domestic servants (30 percent, or more than one of every four women in the labor force, worked as domestics before the Revolution),[11] and prostitutes. Second, the general and widespread expansion of educational opportunities, at all levels and in all areas, certainly affected women who might otherwise have entered the work force directly. And finally, the redistributive policies of the government and its guarantees of basic needs must have acted as a disincentive, a pull out of the labor force for many women who formerly worked as a matter of survival.

The disincentive to work could only have been underscored by the dramatic decline in the availability of goods that began in the early years of the Revolution and reached a climax during the years of "simultaneous construction of socialism and communism," when a U.S.-led blockade and a 31 percent investment ratio combined to virtually wipe clean the shelves of every store on the island.[12] The fact that there was little to buy made money increasingly abundant and increasingly superfluous as the 1960s proceeded. Clearly, given these incentives to withdraw from the paid labor force, the fact that the 1960s saw a steady, if gradual, overall increase in the number of women working indicates that something was indeed having an effect on incorporating women into the work force—and it would not be amiss to suggest that this something was probably the Revolution. Yet, no account of all this can be taken if we consider only the figures on the rate of entry into the work force.

Nor do the figures alone—all that the continuum model takes into account—give insight into the significance of the patterns in women working in the 1970s and 1980s. Institutionalization has seen the end of labor shortages and even some unemployment (estimated at about 80,000 by Castro at the June 1978 meeting of the National Assembly of Popular Power). This is exactly the situation in which the Havana watchers and certain scholars who defined themselves as feminists[13] predicted that the Revolution would stop fooling around with women and end its efforts to recruit them into the paid labor force. And yet, this has not happened. In 1975, women represented 25.3 percent of the paid work force.[14] By 1980 this figure stood at 32.4 percent, and at present, it is 37.3 percent.[15] Again, this is significant on a number of levels. First, it gives evidence that the leadership is indeed committed to the goal of incorporating women into the work force and not merely to make up for scarce labor. Second, again we have a clear reflection of the change the Revolution underwent in the 1970s: We can assume that women's continued entry into the work force after 1970 reflects, at least in part, Cuba's return to a more traditional path to socialism in which money again had value and goods were available for purchase.

The tendency to measure the changes in women's position after the Revolution along a continuum has, of course, something to do with the availability of evidence and with the fact that much of the material that is available—including official Cuban government statements—assumes this same continuity. It has something also to do with the failure of observers to understand revolution as a process and, more than this, to understand that that process does not mean a straight line and cannot, in fact, be frozen at any given stage. The experience of women in Cuba cannot be selectively extracted without taking into account tendencies, directions, and contradictions—that is, without locating this experience within the whole. This is both cause and result of the fact that work about Cuban women tends so overwhelmingly to be descriptive; that only occasionally does it attempt to address theory and almost never to redress it.[16] This is true even of the socialist feminists' writing about Cuban women, for whom such theoretical considerations should be a key concern. The point is not to use the Cuban experience to measure or dismiss socialist theory vis-à-vis women but rather to examine that theory in the light of what we know about that experience, of what we see as tendencies common to all the societies of actually existing socialism.

What is true—particularly for socialist feminists—is that the Cuban experience with relation to women is problematic. A part of this experience is specific to Cuba: It derives from inherited traditions and ways of doing things; a part of it is the legacy of underdevelopment and the unbroken constancy of external threat. But much of the situation is demonstrated not simply by Cuba but by all existing socialist countries, developed and underdeveloped. This widespread nature would seem to indicate that its roots are not simply in practice but in socialist theory itself, as it relates to women. For in fact certain structural barriers that this theory predicted would disappear in the transition to socialism remain and have even been fortified.

In Cuba, all this must be considered—indeed can only be understood—within the context of the enormous changes and transformations that the Revolution has wrought upon the lives of women, changes aimed directly at removing the structural base of women's inequality. In general, and for all Cubans, the transition to socialism, with the consequent elimination of private property and redistribution of the surplus, has meant recognition and action upon basic human rights: the right to be literate and to be educated; the right to free and full health care; the right to a means of subsistence. For women, all this has also meant a release from economic subservience, from inescapable bondage to males as the sole means of survival for themselves and their children. This release is starkly reflected in the divorce rate, which, in the first ten years of the Revolution, jumped to 5 times its size in 1959.[17]

Moreover, the Revolution has evolved policies that relate specifically to women. The first of these policies can be understood as the recognition, from the very beginning of the Revolution, of the depth of the problem concerning women. This recognition was embodied in the creation of the Federation of Cuban Women (FMC). Of the socialist revolutions of more than a decade's duration, only Cuba's has maintained an unbroken commitment to a mass organization of women (albeit—and this is critical—set up by, and an agency of, the revolutionary leadership). Moreover, the Revolution has initiated changes in the legal system that essentially dismantle, on a formal level, the structures of discrimination. The 1976 Cuban constitution, in Article 45, establishes the equal rights of men and women in the economy, in political and social fields, and explicitly extends this equality to the realm of the family. In this way, the constitution reaffirms the 1975 Family Code, which, in six articles, spells out the equality of rights and duties of men and women within matrimony, extending to considerations of material and emotional support and to the sharing of household duties. The Maternity Code, enacted in 1973, places Cuba among the world's most advanced countries with regard to maternity rights: It extends to women eighteen weeks of paid maternity leave and a year's unpaid leave.[18]

In another realm, by stretching the limits imposed by a still underdeveloped economy, the Revolution has moved in limited arenas toward the socialization of domestic labor, at least for women who work: The most visible expressions of this movement are workers' cafeterias, laundry services, boarding schools in the countryside, and the provision of day care. Further, various experiments have been carried out, with equally varying degrees of success, to facilitate women's entry into, and continuance in, the paid labor force: special shopping hours for women workers in stores; the ineffective *plan jaba* (shopping bag plan), which gave women workers priority in food marketing; and where possible, varying work hours.[19] All these measures are particularly impressive given the more or less continuous economic difficulties that have plagued the Revolution during the course of its twenty-seven years.

Yet, although all of these measures represent a wide-ranging attempt to remove the structural barriers barring women's equality and their ability to develop to their full potential, in one area such structural barriers remain firmly in place and relatively pervasive. They center around and are rooted in a continuing sexual division of labor: This factor must be seen as the key perpetuator of inequality between men and women in Cuba. The effects of this continuing sexual division of labor can be seen in the type of work in the public sector in which women are primarily engaged. There are exceptions inconceivable in prerevolutionary Cuba—exceptions that include the increasing number of women working in construction, for instance (44,017 members of the work force in construction are now women),[20] or more recently a woman ship's captain. Although these exceptions receive a good deal of attention in the Cuban media, nonetheless, they remain exceptions.

The overwhelming majority of women work in areas in which women have traditionally worked—in Cuba as elsewhere. Thus, Cuban women generally dominate textile and plastics manufacture and light industry, including tobacco, a key industry for the Cuban economy and an area in which the importance of a woman's "lighter," more "delicate" touch has always been highly regarded. Further, women are disproportionately employed in the areas of education, public health, and services in general, again reflecting traditional worldwide patterns in the sexual division of labor. Moreover, in employment areas in Cuba where household tasks have been collectivized, to whatever degree—areas such as daycare, laundry services, or collective cafeterias, that is, in the social projections of traditional privatized women's work—women carry out these tasks in the public sphere. Thus, the very collectivization of women's work serves to reinforce the sexual division of labor. The basic lines of this feminization of job categories form a pattern not only in Cuba but in all the countries of actually existing socialism.

The sexual division of labor is the crucial underpinning to the systematic and serious underrepresentation of women in leadership positions in the major political institutions of the country, including not only the governmental structures and the party but also the youth organization of the party (UJC) and even the leadership of the mass organizations. The party is, of course, the directing body of the Revolution: Underrepresentation of women here means that men overwhelmingly chart the nature of revolutionary initiatives and the direction of the Revolution itself. Entrance into the ranks of the party passes through the workplace: Workers choose candidates for party membership from among their ranks. Thus, the fact that women compose 37.3 percent of the work force places immediate structural limitations upon the numbers of women who might be eligible for party membership. Actual female party membership in 1975 constituted only 13.23 percent of total membership.[21] In 1980, after a concerted drive to increase female representation in the party to make it equal to the percentage of women in the work force, this figure was increased to 18.9 percent.[22] In the leadership structures of the party, the number of women decreases dramatically: In 1975, women held only 2.9 percent of leadership positions at the base municipal level, only 6.3 percent of the provincial level, 4 percent at the regional level, and 5.5 percent at the national level.[23]

The campaign to increase female representation in party leadership ranks has apparently had more success at the national level—where the Central Committee, which emerged from the 1986 Party Congress, includes 20 women out of 146 members (about 13.8 percent)—than it has at municipal or provincial level.[24] Nonetheless, at the highest pinnacle of the party structure, women remain virtually absent: The newly appointed fourteen-member Politburo includes one woman (Vilma Espin). Two women serve as alternate members. The Secretariat of the party is entirely male.[25] This same pattern occurs in Popular Power, the new governmental structure set up on a nationwide basis in 1976. After four national elections, in the 1984 assemblies the total number of women delegates at the base (municipal) level stood at 11.5 percent.[26] Again, if one looks to the summit of this structure, the pattern remains the same: At the national level of Popular Power, women make up 22.6 percent of the total number of deputies;[27] only two women serve on the Council of Ministers, and these women head ministries that encompass the traditional female work categories—education and light industry.[28]

Perhaps the most telling evidence of the holding power of the sexual division of labor is that these same patterns, even if proportionately less severe, are reproduced within the Communist Youth Organization (UJC), which is made up of those between the ages of eighteen and twenty-seven. That is, the pattern reproduces itself even among those born into the Revolution and formed within its structures. In 1975, total female membership stood at 29 percent; only 10 percent of the total leadership of the UJC in that year was female.[29] And even in the neighborhood organizations, the Committees in Defense of the Revolution, where women (who constitute 50 percent of the membership) seem to play a much more active role, they make up only 19 percent of the leadership at the national level.[30] Only in the ranks of the trade union leadership do women fill positions proportional to or in excess of their representation in the concerned population at the base level: By 1984, 45.8 percent of all trade union officials in the workplace itself was female.[31] This proportion may well be another reflection or result of the conscious and concerted effort made by the Revolution with relation to women and work in the productive sector.

The underrepresentation of women in leadership positions in the political structures of Cuban society is given a concrete, explicit form in the economy. In 1976, despite opposition expressed by the Federation of Cuban Women at its second congress in 1974, the State Committee on Work and Social Security (CETSS) issued a list of some 300 employment areas from which women were to be excluded.[32] This list has been gradually whittled down to about twenty-five occupations. Moreover, women already working in any restricted occupation were not summarily dismissed from their jobs. Nonetheless, the list gives the force of law to a systematized division of labor. Though some of the categories seem to make no sense except as expressions of age-old prejudices and fears about women (such as prohibitions on women working under water or on construction of buildings of more than five stories), by and large the classification is based on possible dangers inherent in a given job for future childbearing. The list operates on the assumption that all women want to be mothers. (This belief in a woman's destiny and need is raised almost to the level of ideology in daycare centers, where all those who work directly with children are female. Cubans explain, if asked, that young children require mother's or substitute mother's love.)[33]

This belief rests at the heart of the sexual division of labor. In its turn, it critically underpins the continuation (despite the Family Code) of a double burden for women in Cuba. And this double burden makes it so difficult, for instance, for women to gain access into the party because such access requires not simply their presence in the work force but the kind of active participation in the workplace that might distinguish individual women as potential candidates. For women, who are chiefly responsible for both home and children, such active and time-consuming participation is often simply impossible. This is nowhere more starkly captured than in a survey done by the party after the 1974 Popular Power election in Matanzas, which served as a forerunner to the establishment of Popular Power on a national scale. In that election, only 7 percent of those nominated and only 3 percent of those elected as base level delegates were female.[34] When women were asked whether, if nominated, they would have agreed to run, some 54.3 percent said no, overwhelmingly because of domestic obligations.[35] And, similarly, in a party survey of 211 workplaces, 85.7 percent of the women asked said that domestic obligations inhibited greater participation on their part.[36]

The leadership of the Revolution is aware of the numerical dimensions of the problem and has, particularly over the last twelve years, launched a frontal attack at least on its overt manifestations. The campaign initiated and carried out by the leadership to correct continuing numerical inequities is reflected in its policies and policy statements. It is reflected in the results of the drive to increase female representation in political leadership structures. Thus, for instance, the jump in female party membership from 13 percent in 1975 to 18.9 percent in 1980, or perhaps more significantly, the 11 percentage point increase (to 40 percent) of women members of the UJC.[37] It is reflected in the fact that, within the governmental structure, the numbers of women deputies to the national assembly have been three times as many proportionately as the numbers of women delegates to the base level municipal assembly.[38] This represents an exact reversal of the pattern held consistently true in Eastern Europe and the Soviet Union[39] and must reflect the fact that the selection of candidates for national assembly deputies is strongly influenced by upper level party structures and that, at its upper levels, the party is pushing women's representation. This same tendency underlines the increase in the proportion of women who now serve as members of the Central Committee of the party itself.

Nor is the problem tangential to wider public consciousness: The ferment, reaction, and discussion that surrounded a recent Cuban film, *Portrait of Teresa*, which dealt with the double burden of women and with double sexual standards, give clear evidence of this. Moreover, in the long term, the fact that women constitute 50 percent of all those presently engaged in advanced scientific or technological studies and 42 percent of the student population in fields such as economics suggests that, at a minimum, the educational foundation for women's participation in high-level decisionmaking is being laid.[40]

But it is both necessary and critical to note that certain key aspects of the ideological underpinnings of the sexual division of labor remain almost unchallenged, above all the notions surrounding the female as mother and the absolute primacy of biological functions. The most visible evidence of this is, of course, the existence of the job listing, whether adhered to or not, even in the aftermath of the Family Code (which is commonly understood as a radical challenge to the inherited family structure) and the terms of the discussion that seem always to surround this listing. This discussion inevitably centers around the need to protect the "female reproductive organs," without, seemingly, any conception that a woman might choose not to be a mother. Indeed, it is reasserted in the constitution itself, which states simply that women should be "given jobs in keeping with their physical makeup."[41]

The question that has to be addressed is, of course, that of the sources of the sexual division of labor. Its seeds are embedded and embodied very clearly in the family and in concepts of sexuality—not simply in the heritage of classical Marxist thinking (or lack of it) on these issues but in the specific historical reality of the family and of sexuality in Cuban colonial/slave society, in postcolonial Cuba, and in revolutionary Cuba. This is one critical direction that future work by feminists about the experience of Cuban women must take.[42] I pick up only one strand of this historical/theoretical web: the legacy of Marxist thought concerning the family and the manner in which the Cuban experience speaks to and underlines its critical inadequacies.

The heritage of Marxist thinking about the family is, at the least, confused, contradictory, and fragmented. According to it (largely as it is distilled by Friedrich Engels), capitalism, though not the original generator of a sexual division of labor, acts in practice to aggravate sexually based exploitation. The development of capitalism first generates the critical split between the private and the public spheres, privatizing the family, creating in its wake, Engels's "millions of tiny (and isolated) workshops." Thus, though capitalism itself generates the preconditions, within the public sphere, of its own destruction, both by developing the means of production and by concentrating workers in larger and larger workplaces, thereby enabling a transformation of the social relations of production, no such concentration or the transformation of consciousness it allows happens in the private sphere.[43] Rather, the family has been atomized and stripped of all productive activity not specifically and directly tied to the replacement of labor power—that is, to reproduction. This atomization of the family serves political as well as economic functions. Among its effects, it guarantees, by isolating her, the ideological backwardness of the woman remaining in the household.

The legacy of Marxism with regard to the future of the family under socialism is rooted in this analysis and is at best ambiguous. It alternately seems to point to the elimination of the family (as its most radical implication) or, at a minimum, the elimination of the most regressive aspects of the family. It takes as a given that only with the disappearance of the regressive content of the family can the oppression and exploitation of women disappear. Much of this content centers around the economic functions of the family: The idea is that socialism, by undermining and eventually freeing the household of its economic content and of its role in economic exploitation, will free women for full development.

Clearly, the progression of history has spelled the error of this formulation. In Cuba specifically, the family has been largely freed of its function in the cycle of economic exploitation. And there has indeed been an enormous increase in the number of women engaged in activities outside the home, that is, outside the atomizing unit which, according to Marxist theory, had guaranteed their stunted growth. Yet certain key features of the old sexual division of labor remain both in the public sphere and in the home. And they have proved enormously difficult to root out exactly because these roots are embedded so deeply in the private sphere—in the family and in sexuality.

This, perhaps, leads us to some hypotheses about why Cuba has been so much more successful in getting rid of the structural and nonstructural bases of racism than it has in ridding itself of the bases of sexual discrimination and oppression. Racial questions tend to be rooted and played out in the public sphere, and exactly the public sphere—the civil society—has been transformed by the Revolution. The privatization of the family, part and parcel of Cuba's heritage as a capitalist—albeit in a distorted form—country, inhibits such transformation. Almost by definition, intervention in the private sphere is taboo. Thus, for instance, if we compare Cuba to China, a country that largely skipped the capitalist stage, we must be struck by the much more active, more direct intervention into family matters for better or for worse that has been carried out by the Chinese.[44] In Cuba, even in the 1970s and 1980s, when the institution of the family has been invested with far greater importance, the farthest the Revolution has dared to push in directing this institution is the Family Code, which with regard to male-female behavior is not so much a legal code as a set of norms designed to influence this behavior.

All of this stands merely as a suggestion of possible interpretations, a suggestion, again, reinforced by the fact that the perpetuation of a fundamental sexual division of labor remains a feature common to all socialist countries, developed as well as underdeveloped. It points us toward a thorough reexamination of theory and a revision of it that takes cognizance of the realities of actually existing socialist societies.

During the two and one-half decades since the Revolution took power Cuba as a whole has always been seen in the West in extreme terms: It has tended to be described either as heaven, hell, or paradise lost. Many people, including many women, especially in the 1960s, saw it as the first: the place where all the problems that plagued societies would be solved overnight. In hindsight this view seems ridiculous from the outset, given the indisputable and unchanging fact that it is a tiny, underdeveloped island. In the 1970s as the women's movement began to move in different directions, many of these same people began to see Cuba as a kind of paradise lost, an interpretation reinforced by Cuba's return to a more traditional route to socialism. And at the same time, many people, both exiles and otherwise, saw it, from the Revolution's beginnings up to the present, as the equivalent of hell on earth. One of the curious features about these three extreme interpretations is that issues related to women have been used and focused upon by people attempting to prove each of them.

It is perhaps most clear, given all this, that what is needed in the study of women in Cuba is a framework. This framework must be rooted both in theoretical considerations and in a practical understanding of the daily reality of being a woman in Cuba. It must be capable of taking into account both the fundamental transformations of this reality that have occurred and are occurring and, at the same time, the fundamental problems that remain.

Notes

1. "Sobre el Pleno Ejercicio de la Igualdad de la Mujer," in Departamento de Orientación Revolucionaria, *Tesis y Resoluciones: Primer Congreso Del Partido Communista de Cuba* (Havana: 1976), p. 563. This document is available in English translation in Elizabeth Stone, ed., *Women and the Cuban Revolution* (New York: Pathfinder Press, 1981).

2. Among the deans of the academic Havana watchers only one, Jorge Domínguez, in his work, *Cuba: Order and Revolution* (Cambridge: Belknapp Press, 1978), has given any consideration to the situation of women. For the fullest discussion and critique of Domínguez's treatment of the subject see Lourdes Casal, "Revolution and Conciencia: Women in Cuba," in Carol Berkin and Clara Lovett, eds., *Women, War and Revolution* (New York: Holmes and Meier, 1980).

3. In this regard, see especially Susan Kaufman Purcell, "Modernizing Women for a Modern Society: The Cuban Case," in Ann Pescatello, ed., *Female and Male in Latin America* (Pittsburgh: University of Pittsburgh Press, 1973).

4. An extensive body of articles and one or two books have been written by a variety of women over a fifteen-year span, including: Elizabeth Sutherland, *The Youngest Revolution* (New York: Dial Press, 1969); Linda Gordon, "Speculations on Women's Liberation in Cuba," in *Women: A Journal of Liberation* (1970); Chris Camarano, "On Cuban Women," in *Science and Society* 35, no. 1 (1971); Margaret Randall, *Cuban Women Now* (Toronto: Women's Press, 1974), and *Woman in Cuba: Twenty Years Later* (New York: Smyrna Press, 1981); Joan Berman, "Women in Cuba" in *Women, A Journal of Liberation*, summer 1975; Carollee Bengelsdorf and Alice Hageman, "Emerging from Underdevelopment: Women and Work in Cuba," in Zillah Eisenstein, ed., *Capitalist Patriarchy and the Case for Socialist Feminism* (New York: Monthly Review, 1977); Marjorie King, "Cuba's Attack on Women's Second Shift, 1974–1976," in *Latin American Perspectives*, issues 12 and 13, 5, nos. 1 and 2 (winter/spring 1977); Cynthia Cockburn, "Women and the Family in Cuba," in John Griffiths and Peter Griffiths, eds., *Cuba: The Second Decade* (London: Writers and Readers, 1979); Inger Holt-Seeland, *Women of Cuba* (Westport, Conn.: Lawrence Hill, 1982). Casal's "Revolution and Consciencia" is perhaps the best single work among these generally repetitive essays.

There have been a few efforts to directly engage the Cuban experience in a discussion of issues related to the difficult discourse between Marxism and feminism. See, in particular, Marifeli Perez-Stable, "The Emancipation of Cuban Women," paper presented at the Institute of Cuban Studies Conference on Women and Change in Cuba, Boston University, May 6–7, 1977; and Nicola Murray, "Women and the Cuban Revolution, Parts 1 & 2," in *Feminist Review* nos. 2 and 3 (1979). Murray is particularly courageous in attempting to confront the Cuban situation as a feminist and a socialist, although her sources of information are not entirely reliable. Furthermore, several articles have appeared recently that attempt to arrive at a framework of analysis by including Cuba within a comparative examination of the experience of women in various socialist societies. See, in particular, Elizabeth Croll, "Women in Rural Production and Reproduction in the Soviet Union, China, Cuba and Tanzania: Socialist Development Experiences" and "Case Studies," *Signs* 7, no. 2 (winter 1981); and Maxine Molyneaux, "Socialist Societies Old & New: Progress Towards Women's Emancipation," *Feminist Review* 8 (summer 1981).

5. See Fidel Castro, "Creating Wealth With Political Awareness, Not Creating Political Awareness With Money or Wealth," in Martin Kenner and James Petras, eds., *Fidel Castro Speaks* (New York: Grove Press, 1969).

6. Richard Jolly, "Education," in Dudley Seers et al., eds., *Cuba: The Economic and Social Revolution* (Chapel Hill: University of North Carolina Press, 1964), p. 200.

7. Ernesto "Ché" Guevara, "Letter to Fidel," in Rolando Bonachea and Nelson Valdes, eds., *Ché: The Selected Works of Ernesto Guevara* (Cambridge: MIT Press, 1969), p. 423.

8. This involved practically every structure that had functioned and/or misfunctioned during the 1960s. It encompassed the reorganization of the work process (including the introduction of norms, a return to material as opposed to moral incentives, and a drastic decline in reliance upon voluntary labor); the reinvigoration of the trade unions, together with the remainder of the mass organizations; the reorganization of the legal and juridical structure culminating in 1975 in the passage of an entirely new constitution; the reorganization of the party structure and the search for a more collective form of leadership; the restructuring of the organization of the state itself through the introduction, on an experimental basis in 1974 and on a national basis in 1976, of the system of Popular Power; and finally, a reemphasis upon the family as the major agency of socialization within the Revolution, as captured in the 1975 passage of the Family Code.

9. Domínguez, *Cuba*, pp. 498–499.

10. See Casal, "Revolution and Conciencia," pp. 189–191.

11. Ibid., p. 188.

12. Bertram Silverman, ed., *Man and Socialism in Cuba: The Great Debate* (New York: Atheneum, 1973), p. 30. Silverman cites the figure of 31 percent for the year 1968.

13. Purcell, "Modernizing Women."

14. "Sobre el Pleno Ejercicio de la Igualdad de la Mujer," p. 580.

15. Fidel Castro, "Main Report to the Third Congress of the Communist Party of Cuba," *Granma Weekly Review*, February 10, 1986, p. 12. The past two years have witnessed a slight decline in the percentage of women in the work force as a whole, from a high of 38.9 percent in 1984. See Vilma Espin, "Report to the Fifteenth Congress of the Cuban Trade Confederation," *Granma*, February 2, 1984, p. 3.

16. The work of Isabel Larguia and John Demoulin constitutes perhaps the sole exception to this rule. See, in English translation, Larguia and Demoulin,

"Toward a Science of Women's Liberation," in *NACLA's Latin American and Empire Report* 6, no. 10 (December 1972), "The Economic Basis of the Status of Women," in Ruby Rohrlich-Leavitt, ed., *Women Cross-Culturally: Change and Challenge* (The Hague: Mouton 1975), and "Aspects of the Condition of Women's Labour," in *NACLA's Latin American and Empire Report* 9, no. 6 (September 1975).

17. J. Hernandez et al., *Estudio Sobre el Divorcio* (Havana: Centro de Informacion Científica y Técnica, 1973).

18. The Maternity Code and excerpts from the Family Code are available in English translation in Elizabeth Stone, ed., *Women and the Cuban Revolution* (New York: Pathfinder Press, 1981). The entire Family Code (in translation) is printed in the Center for Cuban Studies *Newsletter* 2, no. 4.

19. The issue of work hour adjustments remains disputed terrain. Women in individual workcenters proposed that the Fifteenth Congress of the Cuban Trade Confederation (the CTC) consider the idea of extending weekday working hours and thereby eliminating the need to work on Saturdays (the regular Cuban work week includes one Saturday morning in two). These proposals had largely to do with concerns about children who are generally unsupervised on Saturday mornings. The leadership has thus far rejected proposals for an across-the-board national solution such as this. In an interview on the eve of the 1984 National CTC Congress, Roberto Veiga, general secretary of the organization, cited two reasons for the rejection of this specific proposal. First, he argued, the fact that women are concentrated in the service areas of the economy (see page 11) makes national elimination of Saturday working hours unfeasible. And second, such a change of policy, he argued, would have to be extended to all workers— men included—and would therefore constitute a luxury for a small underdeveloped economy. Veiga employed a somewhat rhetorical flourish in dismissing the appeal for revision of work hours as an attempt to gain more leisure time. The difficulties that confront women workers, he declared, "cannot be resolved by working less . . . (but) only by working more" (*XV Congress de la C.T.C.: Memorias* [Havana: Editorial de Ciencias Sociales, 1984], pp. 102–104). When the FMC convened its fourth congress the following year, discussions focused upon basically the same issues, this time in the context of keeping daycare facilities and schools open on Saturday morning (see *Granma*, March 7, 1985). One problem with such a solution is that daycare facilities remain limited: As of December 1983, there were some 835 daycare centers nationwide, servicing 89,900 mothers, or 8.2 percent of all working mothers.

Also hotly argued at the FMC Congress was the rule that only female relatives are allowed to give constant attendance (on a twenty-four hour basis) to a sick person in hospital—and in the case of a child, only the mother. Obviously, an alteration here would ease demands on working women's time (see *Granma*, March 7, 1985).

20. *Granma*, March 7, 1985. This represents an increase of women workers in construction from 1982, when women constituted 11.5 percent of the construction work force.

21. "Sobre el Pleno Ejercicio de la Igualdad de la Mujer," p. 585.

22. Fidel Castro, "Speech to the Closing Session of the Third Congress of the Federation of Cuban Women," in *Granma Weekly Review*, March 16, 1980, p. 3.

23. "Sobre el Pleno Ejercicio de la Igualdad de la Mujer," p. 585. These figures were compiled before the new administrative reorganization—which eliminates the regional level, rationalizes the size of the municipalities, and expands the number of provinces from six to fourteen—went into effect.

24. Castro, "Report to the Third Congress of the Communist Party of Cuba," p. 12.

25. See *Granma Weekly Review*, February 10, 1986, pp. 23–24.

26. *Granma*, April 24, 1984, p. 1. The percentage of women elected to the municipal-level assemblies in the three prior elections (1976, 1979, and 1981) fluctuated slightly, downward and then upward. Thus, in 1976, 8 percent of those elected were women; in 1979, the figure decreased to 7.2 percent; in 1981, it rose to 7.8 percent (Comisión Electoral Nacional, *Información Estadística del Proceso Electoral 1981* [Havana: 1982], pp. 13, 14). The 4 percent increase to 11.5 percent is then significant but clearly hardly an indication of equality nor even a confirmation of an upward trend.

27. Ibid., p. 16.

28. Cited in Casal, "Revolution and Conciencia," p. 196.

29. "Sobre el Pleno Ejercicio de la Igualdad de la Mujer," p. 585.

30. Ibid., p. 585.

31. Vilma Espin, "Report to Fifteenth Congress of the C.T.C.," in XV Congresso de la C.T.C., p. 3. On the other hand, according to Espin, in the higher reaches of the trade union structure the pattern observed in the party and in the popular power structures reverses itself: The percentage of women in leadership positions declines considerably at higher levels of the CTC. Thus, at the next level (the municipal level) the percentage of female professionals is 15.9 percent; at the provincial level, it is 14.7 percent.

32. *Granma*, June 1, 1976.

33. There is, however, some indication that this option is beginning to be challenged. Thus, for instance, Osmany Cienfuegos, representing the leadership on the occasion of International Women's Day in 1983, spoke of the need for more "enfermeros" and "enfermeras," or nurses, in the daycare centers. His explicit use of the male form, "enfermeros," implies the beginning of a fundamental change in the practice of employing women exclusively to work on a daily and direct basis with children in daycare centers.

34. See Fidel Castro, July 26, 1974, in Matanzas, *Granma Weekly Review*, August 4, 1974.

35. "Sobre el Pleno Ejercicio de la Igualdad de la Mujer," p. 584.

36. Ibid., p. 586.

37. Castro, "Speech to the Closing of the Third Congress of the Federation of Cuban Women," p. 3.

38. See "Sobre la Constitucion del Poder Popular" (Havana: n.d.), and *Información Estadística del Proceso Electoral 1981*.

39. See Barbara Wolfe Jancar, *Women Under Communism* (Baltimore: Johns Hopkins University Press, 1978), in particular ch. 5.

40. See Casal, "Revolution and Conciencia," p. 192.

41. *Constitution of the Republic of Cuba* (1976), Chapter V, Article 43. The constitution is published in English translation by the Center for Cuban Studies.

42. Some background work has been done already in this direction, specifically, Vera Martinez Alier's *Marriage, Class and Colour in Nineteenth Century Cuba* (Cambridge: Cambridge University Press, 1972); Maria de la Torre Mulhare's *Sexual Ideology in Pre-Castro Cuba*, unpublished PhD thesis, University of Pittsburgh, 1969; Julianne Burton's excellent discussion of *Portrait of Teresa* in *Social Text*, no. 4 (fall 1981); Alan Young's work on *Gays Under the Cuban Revolution* (San Francisco: Grey Fox Press, 1981); and the Lourdes Arguelles/ B. Ruby Rich study of "Homosexuality, Homophobia and Revolution: Notes Toward an Understanding of the Cuban Lesbian and Gay Male Experience," parts I and II, in *Signs* (summer 1984 and autumn 1985).

43. The discussion that follows owes a great deal to the work of Isabel Larguia and John Demoulin. See note 16.

44. See, in particular, Kay Ann Johnson, *Women, Family and Peasant Revolution in China* (Chicago: Chicago University Press, 1983). We are not here by any means advocating greater state intervention into the family as a solution. The results of recent Chinese policy attempting to regulate the number of children women are allowed to bear is only the most recent of a long list of such manipulations of women's bodies and lives by certain actually existing socialist states.

8

The "Sovietization of Cuba Thesis" Revisited

Frank T. Fitzgerald

The Sovietization of Cuba thesis has informed the analyses of many Cuba scholars, as well as the political statements of cold war ideologues. In its ideal-typical form, this thesis claims that revolutionary Cuba's political and economic relationship with the Soviet bloc has become equivalent, both in character and in consequence, to prerevolutionary Cuba's dependence on the United States, and that, as a result, revolutionary Cuba has been forced to institute a Soviet-style system domestically and to serve as a Soviet proxy internationally. Cold war ideologues frequently state this thesis more fully and baldly than Cuba scholars. But, as Carollee Bengelsdorf has pointed out, the Sovietization thesis is "pervasive," characterizing "both scholarly and popular understanding of Cuba."[1]

Opponents of the Revolution raised the spector of Sovietization almost from the beginning, but such warnings subsided in the late 1960s as the Cuban Revolution began to chart a defiantly independent course. Internationally, the Cubans vociferously criticized the moderate coalition politics of the orthodox Communist parties and promoted armed struggle and guerrilla warfare, especially in Latin America. Domestically, the Cubans veered from the orthodox Soviet view of socialism and communism as sequential stages of societal evolution and claimed to be constructing both simultaneously. But with the capture and murder of Ché Guevara in Bolivia in 1967, and with the failure of the economy to produce the 10 million tons of sugar targeted for 1970, this "Cuban heresy" came to a halt.

As the Cubans again changed course after 1970, both Cuba scholars and cold war ideologues began to detect renewed movement toward

Sovietization. Perhaps the most influential statement of the Sovietization of Cuba thesis in this period came from Carmelo Mesa-Lago, whose *Cuba in the 1970s* "set the general tone of . . . scholarly appraisals of Cuba"[2] for the next several years. According to Mesa-Lago, after 1970 revolutionary Cuba's dependence on the Soviet bloc reached "a point of no return" and became analogous to prerevolutionary Cuba's dependence on the United States.[3] Mesa-Lago cited the resultant Soviet influence as a "steady variable" to explain what he viewed as a new "Soviet die" into which Cuban society was being molded and a new "Soviet imprint" that was being imposed on Cuban foreign policy.[4] But Mesa-Lago, along with most other Cuba scholars, never went so far as to claim that Cuba had simply become a proxy for the Soviets internationally. Cold war ideologues have made this claim, but Cuba scholars generally have not.[5]

The basic outlines of Mesa-Lago's argument have been supported by a host of subsequent scholarly works on Cuba. Perhaps the most influential work has been Jorge Domínguez's *Cuba: Order and Revolution*,[6] which focused on the multiple political and economic organizational changes of the later 1970s that the Cubans and others refer to as the institutionalization of the Revolution. Whereas the Cubans have viewed this institutionalization as a process of decentralization of political and economic participation, Domínguez viewed it as a process of increasing bureaucratization and centralization of power. In this process, according to Domínguez, the Cuban leadership increased its autonomy relative to the rest of Cuban society and acted as a collaborative "elite," intent upon casting Cuba increasingly in a Soviet mold. For Domínguez, then, institutionalization signified little more than the practical working out of the process of Sovietization posited by Mesa-Lago.

In this chapter, I will analyze the various claims of the Sovietization of Cuba thesis. In the first section I will examine the character and some of the consequences of post-1970 Cuba's economic relationship to the Soviet bloc. In the second section I will examine whether the notion of Sovietization adequately explains Cuba's domestic course after 1970. And, in the third section, I will examine whether post-1970 Cuba serves as a Soviet proxy internationally.

Cuban-Soviet Economic Relationship
After 1970

In the post-1970 period, the Cuban economy has clearly become more closely integrated with the socialist world. In July 1972, the Council for Mutual Economic Assistance (CMEA, the Soviet common market) granted

Cuba the full membership status that the country had requested shortly before. At the same time, the Cubans promised to stabilize their sugar deliveries to the Soviet bloc; in return, the Cubans were to receive CMEA assistance in developing their nickel, sugar bagasse, and other industries. In January 1973, Fidel Castro announced a far-reaching set of new Soviet-Cuban economic agreements, which rescheduled Cuba's Soviet debt, granted new credits for Cuban development projects, and set new commodity agreements for sugar and nickel. Beginning with Cuba's first five-year plan of 1976–1980, Cuba's economic plans were coordinated with those of other CMEA countries, and the price of Cuban sugar exports to the Soviet Union was indexed to the prices of Cuban imports, especially petroleum, from that country.

A great deal of controversy has surrounded the question of the actual size of the Soviet subsidy to the Cuban economy contained in the agreements, especially the indexing agreement. The CIA, for example, has estimated that this subsidy ranged around $2.5 billion per year from 1976 to 1982; others have argued that it has been much less significant.[7] Whatever the case, however, it is perhaps worth noting that even the Sovietization theorists do not seriously argue that the Soviets have been draining Cuba of economic surplus.[8] For it is clear that the Soviets have been adding to the available Cuban surplus. Thus, virtually everyone is forced to agree that the Soviet-Cuban economic relationship is in this way different than the type of relationship traditionally associated with the concept of dependency.[9]

It is worth noting that, from the Cuban viewpoint, international economic integration is a necessity in the contemporary world. As then–foreign minister Carlos Rafael Rodriguez stated in 1972: "Without integration there is no development. This is an era of great communities, both capitalist and socialist."[10] And as Fidel Castro reiterated two years later: "A small, isolated Latin American country can do absolutely nothing. . . . [I]n the future only large communities will be in a position to face the great problems of humanity."[11] It would be hard to gainsay this argument. With its poor resource base, its limited internal market incapable of sustaining modern high-technology industries, its reliance on export markets, and its need for imports, an isolated Cuba would certainly lack viability in the contemporary world economy.

Yet, this does not mean that the Cubans seek integration solely with the Soviet bloc. As Castro took care to emphasize in announcing the Cuban-Soviet economic agreements of 1973: "We are Latin Americans. . . . [I]n the future we should integrate ourselves with Latin America."[12] Moreover, almost a decade later, the Cubans were, as usual, broadening the point by emphasizing, in their report to the Seventh Summit Conference of the Non-Aligned Countries, the need for greater coop-

TABLE 8.1
Cuban Trade with Capitalist and Socialist Economies, 1970-1984
(in millions of current pesos)

Year	Capitalist Economies Value	Capitalist Economies Percent	Socialist Economies Value	Socialist Economies Percent	Total
1970	678.0	28.7	1683.0	71.3	2361.0
1971	714.2	40.8	1034.5	59.2	1748.7
1972	624.0	31.8	1336.7	68.2	1960.7
1973	835.9	32.0	1779.7	68.0	2615.6
1974	1826.6	40.9	2635.9	59.1	4462.5
1975	2457.9	40.5	3607.4	59.5	6065.3
1976	1917.8	32.7	3954.2	67.3	5872.0
1977	1596.1	25.0	4783.9	75.0	6380.0
1978	1249.0	17.8	5764.9	82.2	7013.9
1979	1249.9	17.4	5936.9	82.6	7186.8
1980	2186.2	25.7	6325.8	74.6	8512.0
1981	2044.4	21.9	7293.4	78.1	9337.8
1982	1388.4	13.3	9088.3	86.7	10476.7
1983	1583.4	13.5	10157.0	86.5	11740.4
1984	1718.2	13.6	10951.1	86.4	12669.3

Source: Author's computations based on data presented in Richard Turits, "Trade, Debt, and the Cuban Economy," World Development (January 1987), table II.

eration among all Third World economies.[13] Clearly, in the minds of the Cuban leaders, economic integration with the Soviet bloc has not closed off their hope for integration with the Third World, of which they consider themselves a part.

On the other hand, as shown in Table 8.1, since the early 1970s Cuba's trade has become increasingly concentrated with socialist economies. Between 1971 and 1975, Cuba's trade with socialist economies averaged 65.2 percent, and between 1976 and 1980, the years of the country's first five-year plan, it averaged 73.3 percent. And this percentage hovered between 86 and 87 percent from 1982 through 1984. Yet, closer examination reveals that this move toward trade with socialist economies did not develop in a strictly linear fashion. In fact, in 1974 and 1975 Cuba's trade with the socialist economies actually dropped to around 59 percent, while its trade with the capitalist economies actually increased to about 41 percent. Of course, from that time forward, except for the 1980–1981 reversal, the percentage of Cuban trade with the socialist economies did steadily rise (see Table 8.1).

What explains this particular pattern of trade partner concentration? The most likely answer is that, in the mid-1970s and 1980–1981 when the world market price for sugar was unusually high, Cuba diverted its sugar exports to the world market in order to accumulate hard currency;

and that, after the mid-1970s when the world market price for sugar plummeted and the price of manufactured goods that Cuba would like to have purchased on the world market rose dramatically, the Cubans moved defensively to reconcentrate their trade with the socialist world. In addition, in the late 1970s and the 1980s, the anti-Cuban hostility of U.S. governments grew perceptibly, and the Cubans needed to defend themselves against real and possible economic pressures emanating from this powerful imperium. In other words, it is the "push" of the capitalist world market and of the policies of its major power as much as the "pull" of the socialist world that accounts for the geographical pattern of Cuban trade.

This fact is often overlooked by the Sovietization theorists, who are apt to compare prerevolutionary Cuba's trade dependency on capitalist economies with revolutionary Cuba's trade relationship with socialist economies but who forget that, of necessity, Cuba remains ensconced in the world capitalist market, at least partially.[14] The best the Cubans can hope for, given the character of their economy, is to diversify their international economic relationships. And, as I have pointed out, the pattern of Cuba's trade suggests that it is not totally "locked into" trade concentration with the socialist world. For when it is economically propitious, revolutionary Cuba seems to move easily toward diversifying its trade relations between both the socialist and the capitalist worlds. Certainly, prerevolutionary Cuba never had such flexibility.[15]

It also seems that, unlike its prerevolutionary relationship to the United States, Cuba's relationship with the Soviet bloc has helped rather than hindered the Cubans in diversifying their economy and the product composition of their exports. For example, CMEA has aided Cuba in modernizing and expanding its nickel industry. Production of nickel, moreover, is seen as only the first phase of CMEA involvement. In the long-term CMEA design, Cuba is not simply to become a more diversified exporter of primary commodities but is to develop the capacity to convert nickel and other mineral resources into intermediate and final products.[16] With such CMEA help, Cuba has since the mid-1970s successfully shifted the emphasis of its development from agriculture to industry. In the 1971–1975 period, agriculture took 29 percent of all investments, while industry took only 21 percent. But in the 1976–1980 period, agriculture's percentage dropped to 19, while industry's rose to 35.[17] From 1970 to 1980, overall industrial production grew by 80 percent, while agricultural production grew merely 27 percent.[18] As shown in Table 8.2, this shift toward industry has been reflected in a lessening of Cuba's dependence on sugar exports, especially in the 1980s. If, as planned, Cuba continues to emphasize industrial development, this pattern should hold firm.

TABLE 8.2
Cuban Reliance on Sugar Exports by Value, Selected Years
1976-1983

Year	Sugar as Percent of Exports	Year	Sugar as Percent of Exports
1976	88	1981	79
1979	84	1982	77
1980	86	1983	74

Source: Claes Brundenius and Andrew Zimbalist, "Recent Studies on Cuban Economic Growth: A Review," Comparative Economic Studies (April 1985).

The Cuban economy continues to suffer from a variety of problems that cannot be examined here.[19] But, since the early 1970s, its overall performance has been impressive. According to the estimates of Claes Brundenius, for example, the annual growth rate in gross domestic product averaged 7.8 percent for the ten-year period from 1972–1981, while the per capita rate averaged 6.5 percent over the same period.[20] Moreover, between 1970 and 1981, per capita daily caloric intake rose from 2,565 to 2,892. Between 1975 and 1980, life expectancy at birth rose from seventy to seventy-three years. And between 1975 and 1984, infant mortality dropped from twenty-seven deaths per thousand live births to fifteen.[21]

These and other successes can, in part, be attributed to Soviet and CMEA aid. But they must also be seen as stemming from the fact that the Cubans now exercise direct control over their economy. Development choices are now in the hands of a political leadership committed to growth with equity and no longer in the hands of domestic or foreign private capitalists committed only to their own wealth. These choices are doubtless conditioned by what the Soviets are willing to give, but there is no evidence to suggest that the Soviets simply dictate economic or other types of policies to the Cubans. Rather, the Soviet-Cuban relationship seems to be characterized by negotiated give and take.

Of course, as Carmelo Mesa-Lago has pointed out,

The USSR has the capacity to cut the supply to the island of virtually all oil, most capital and intermediate goods, and probably all weaponry. Additionally, loss of Soviet markets would mean an end to their buying about half of Cuban sugar at three times the price of the market as well as purchase of substantial amounts of nickel also at a subsidized price. The USSR could also exert powerful influence over such COMECON countries as the GDR, Czechoslovakia, and Bulgaria, which are particularly the key ones in trade with Cuba, to stop economic relations with Cuba.[22]

But it is equally true that this worst case scenario is highly unlikely. It must be noted that the Soviets have made a deep political commitment to Cuba and that Cuba is for the Soviets a showcase of the benefits of socialism, especially of Soviet-allied socialism, in Third World countries. Any move by the Soviets to unduly pressure or to abandon the Cubans would, therefore, have severe negative political consequences for the Soviets throughout the Third World and beyond. By pulling the plug on Cuba, the Soviets would also isolate themselves. And this isolation would doubtless prove harder to overcome than the capitalist encirclement that the Soviets have been chipping away at for decades. It is inconceivable that the Soviets would welcome such a turn of events, and this alone supports the Cubans with considerable leverage in their negotiations with the Soviets.

Talk of Cuban dependence on the Soviets has its point. But two things must be kept clear. First, dependence here does not signify that the Soviets can dictate to the Cubans or even influence the Cubans when the latter have reason to be unreceptive. Second, dependence here does not signify that revolutionary Cuba's relationship to the Soviet Union is comparable to prerevolutionary Cuba's relationship to the United States. As I have shown, Cuba's dependence on the Soviet Union has a very different character and very different consequences.

Domestic Sovietization of Cuba?

According to Mesa-Lago, since 1970 Soviet-style institutions and practices have been imposed on Cuban society, and the Cuban system has been thoroughly "Sovietized." As he put it: "The uniqueness of the Cuban revolution . . . has gradually dulled and the more conventional features of socialism 'a la Eastern Europe' appear increasingly stronger on the island."[23] Among these features, Mesa-Lago counted the return to material incentives and wage differentials to spur productivity and the imposition of economic and political institutions that on a small scale replicate Soviet institutions. These latter, he claimed, are characterized by "central controls, dogmatism, administrative and bureaucratic features, and limited mass participation resembling the Soviet system."[24] All of these changes, moreover, have been brought about by a Cuban "elite," increasingly dependent on the Soviet bloc and, therefore, increasingly responsive to "Soviet pressure."

Several aspects of this argument are notable. First, the Sovietization thesis assumes rather than demonstrates the existence of Soviet pressure.

Mesa-Lago and his followers would doubtless object to this being pointed out on the grounds that Soviet pressure is hidden from view because scholars lack access to the negotiations that take place between Cuban and Soviet officials. This is certainly true. But there is reason to believe that the Cubans maintain considerable leverage in their dealings with the Soviets and that the Cuban-Soviet relationship is, consequently, one of negotiated give and take. At the very least, this would seem the more reasonable hypothesis.

Second, the Sovietization thesis views the changes of the post-1970 period as nothing more—or less—than an elite imposition. Sovietization theorists operate with an elite/mass conception of Cuban society, in which an omnipotent and politically relevant elite can and does freely impose its will on an impotent and politically irrelevant mass. In other words, the behaviors of workers, peasants, and other groups in Cuban society are here discounted as irrelevant to either the causes of the post-1970 changes or the ongoing operation of the institutions that these changes have put into place. This wildly distorts what we know about Cuban reality.

It is clear, for example, that the post-1970 changes were precipitated by the political-economic crisis of 1970. This crisis had many facets and cannot be discussed in detail here.[25] But, at base, it was a crisis of confidence in the policies being pursued by the revolutionary leadership. The population expressed its discontent in a variety of direct ways, such as complaints about poorly organized work, lack of sufficient consumer goods, and lack of channels through which to register criticisms. But mostly, the population evinced its discontent indirectly by increasingly not cooperating with official policies. As a result, productivity plummeted and absenteeism soared. In 1969, for example, Leo Huberman and Paul Sweezy estimated that the agricultural labor force was utilized at about 50 percent of practicable capacity[26] and that the rate of absenteeism among permanent farm workers in Camaguey province never fell below 35 percent.[27] The supposedly omnipotent elite proved not so omnipotent after all and had to find ways to recuperate mass cooperation.

Interestingly enough, the leading Sovietization theorists do not dispute this. But what they empirically admit they never allow to affect their overall theoretical understanding of how the Cuban system operates. Jorge Domínguez, for example, went so far as to speak of the "strike of 1970." And, although this characterization overstates the political and organizational cohesion of those involved, it does lead Domínguez to accurately point out that "this protest is important because it shows that the power of the central leadership in Cuba has its limits."[28] Yet, with this much said, Domínguez quickly reverted to his elite/mass conception and never discussed the bases or extent of popular leverage in revolutionary Cuba.

It must be kept in mind that the Cuban system is socialist, which means that it guarantees something very close to full employment. In this respect the Cuban and other socialist systems are qualitatively different from capitalist systems, which typically reproduce a surfeit of labor that functions to keep workers disciplined and subservient. This difference between capitalist and socialist systems is, moreover, not simply economic but profoundly political. In socialist systems, what Max Weber once called "the whip of hunger" no longer operates with full force, and productive effort must be elicited from workers through different means.

Basically, the revolutionary leadership in such a situation has two types of choices. It can opt either for coercion—a short-run solution that always entails long-run problems—or for some combination of political exhortation, mass participation, and consumer goods. Although, like all socialist leaderships, Cuba's has combined both of these types of choices, it seems to me that the latter type of choice has predominated, especially since 1970.[29] But the real point here is that the very fact that socialist leaderships cannot resort to unemployment to back up their attempts to elicit productive effort gives workers considerable political leverage, which they typically express by their level of cooperation or noncooperation with economic goals, policies, and so on.

In other words, crises such as occurred in Cuba in 1970 are an ever-present danger in socialist systems, and, to avoid such crises, socialist leaderships normally seek to elicit productive effort voluntarily, that is, on conditions to which workers consent.[30] This in part explains the peculiar institutional structure of socialist societies, which put great emphasis on mechanisms of mass participation. Those who scoff that such mechanisms allow only ritualistic participation have to be asked why so much time and energy, and so many resources are typically spent on mere window dressing. Surely such mechanisms signal the need of socialist leaderships to elicit cooperation from labor that is no longer threatened by the "whip of hunger." Here is one basis of popular leverage that Sovietization theorists with their elite/mass conception entirely miss, and, because they miss this, they mistakenly judge many of the post-1970 changes in Cuba simply as moves in the direction of greater elite control of a politically irrelevant mass.

Third, the Sovietization thesis is ahistorical, in that it suggests that the post-1970 changes in Cuba have effectively obliterated the unique features of pre-1970 Cuban socialism. Certainly, there are discontinuities between pre- and post-1970 Cuba, but there are also important continuities. Take, for example, Mesa-Lago's suggestion that after 1970 the

Cubans simply jettisoned moral incentives and turned to material ones.[31] This view overlooks the fact that material incentives were in force in the pre-1970 period and that moral incentives have remained in force in the post-1970 period. As I have fully explained elsewhere,[32] after 1970 the Cubans altered the mix of their incentive system and attempted to link material incentives to productivity, but, contrary to Mesa-Lago, they retained, though sometimes in different form, moral incentives as an important part of their overall system. This is just one continuity that Sovietization theorists typically miss.

Fourth, the Sovietization thesis presumes that Soviet institutions have been the demiurge of change in post-1970 Cuba. It is true that since 1970 the Cubans have borrowed many institutional forms from the Soviet system. But it is unsound to simply assume, as the Sovietization theorists typically do, that these forms operate in Cuba precisely as they do, or, more correctly, precisely as the Sovietization theorists assume they do, in the Soviet context. At best, what the Sovietization theorists have established is an analogy between Soviet and Cuban institutional forms. But they have failed to seriously address the much more important question of whether these forms encompass an analogous content in the Soviet Union and Cuba.[33]

A focus on content shows that the introduction of Soviet institutional forms in post-1970 Cuba has served not to muzzle the popular discontent of the late 1960s but, as Carollee Bengelsdorf has stated, to "define the space for its expression."[34] Among other things, after 1970 the Cuban leaders put elected assemblies, partly modeled on Soviet forms, in charge of state administration at the national, provincial, and municipal levels. They opened up avenues, again partly modeled on Soviet forms, for greater and more stable worker participation in work centers and in the national economic arena. And they revitalized their not-always-so-Soviet mass organizations. Thus, contrary to the Sovietization thesis, the direction of change in post-1970 Cuba has been toward greater bottom-up expression, not toward greater top-down control.

This is not to suggest that the Cubans have created a perfect socialist democracy or anything near it. Elements of authoritarianism persist in present-day Cuba. And, although some of these stem from the character of some of the Soviet institutional forms introduced after 1970, many are a legacy of some of the—very Cuban—"heretical" forms and practices of the late 1960s. As then–minister of planning Humberto Pérez commented in the late 1970s, those "who work in the distinct state organizations . . . are impregnated with the *old* [i.e., pre-1970] *centralizing and in many cases bureaucratic habits*" (emphasis added).[35] Although the explanation of the origin and persistence of these "habits" cannot be presented here,[36] it is interesting to note that those who view the dynamic of present Cuban reality primarily in terms of the imposition of Soviet forms thereby overlook the need for such an explanation. Somewhat ironically, then, the Sovietization theorists not only fail to adequately comprehend the movement in post-1970 Cuba toward greater popular expression and participation, which they typically deemphasize, but also fail to correctly understand many of the remaining elements of authoritarianism, which they often strain to highlight.

Cuba as an International Soviet Proxy?

U.S. Senator Daniel Patrick Moynihan has called the Cubans the "Gurkhas of the Russian Empire,"[37] while the less poetic Reagan administration has simply dubbed them Soviet proxies.[38] Cuba scholars, on the other hand, have to varying degrees generally distanced themselves from such outbursts. As H. Michael Erisman correctly pointed out, Cuba scholars typically view the proxy thesis as a simplistic and ultimately misleading explanation of Cuban foreign policy. Instead, they tend to view Cuban foreign policy as partly an outgrowth of Cuban interests and its post-1970 closeness to the foreign policy of the Soviet Union as an outgrowth of a "convergence of interests."[39]

Although the notion of convergence more adequately captures the relationship between many of the foreign policy positions and actions of the Cubans and the Soviets, it would be wrong to suppose that Cuban and Soviet foreign policies never diverge. For example, less than two years after gaining Soviet backing for their military venture in Angola, to defend the new Popular Movement for the Liberation of Angola (MPLA) government against an invasion from South Africa, the Cubans came into conflict with the Soviets in that country. In May 1977, a faction of the MPLA plotted a coup to topple Angolan President Agostinho Neto, whom it considered insufficiently pro-Soviet. Although it is unclear whether the Soviets were directly involved in this plot, they reportedly knew of it and failed to warn Neto. The Cubans, on the other hand, clearly supported Neto. When the plotters moved, Cuban troops joined MPLA forces to defeat them. Although these events did not involve a direct confrontation between the Cubans and the Soviets, as Nelson Valdés has pointed out, "the pro-Soviet line within the MPLA was defeated by Agostinho Neto with the complete backing of Cuba."[40]

Cuban and Soviet policies also partially diverged in Ethiopia, where the Cubans and Soviets cooperated: The Cubans supplied troops and the Soviets supplied logistical support and officers to repulse a Somalian invasion of the Ogaden in late 1977 and early 1978. Once the Somalian invasion was defeated, the Ethiopian government, with Soviet backing, turned its full attention to fighting against the Eritrean insurgency, which had been going on since 1962 and which the Cubans had historically supported. At this time, both the Ethiopians and the Soviets reportedly petitioned Havana to lend the estimated 16,000 to 17,000 troops it then had in the country to the anti-Eritrean campaign. The Cubans, however, refused, maintaining that, unlike the Somalian invasion, the issue of Eritrea was an internal affair that should be resolved politically, not militarily.[41]

Both of these examples are notable because the Cuban interventions in Angola and Ethiopia at the time lent steam to proponents of the proxy thesis. Yet, closer examination shows that in neither case did the Cubans simply play a proxy role. In fact, it was most likely the Cubans who pulled the Soviets into Angola rather than the other way around.[42] And, although in both the Angolan and the Ethiopian cases Cuban and Soviet policies converged in some respects, they clearly diverged in others.

Still, it is sometimes suggested that, although Cuban and Soviet foreign policies have not always been identical, Cuba's overall subordination to the Soviets is evidenced by the fact that since the late 1960s the Cubans have refrained from publicly criticizing even the most controversial Soviet international initiatives. In fact, the Cubans publicly supported the Soviet invasions of Czechoslovakia in 1968 and of Afghanistan in 1979. Outright condemnation of either of these invasions would probably have angered the Soviets and created untold problems for the Cubans. But in both of these instances, the Cubans were not simply playing the role of well-behaved subordinates.

Fidel Castro's speech supporting the Czechoslovakian invasion, for example, was, as Jacques Levesque correctly stated, "more provocative than conciliatory."[43] In it, Castro blamed the Czechoslovakian crisis on the domestic political and economic policies, which were being pursued at the time in Eastern Europe and in the Soviet Union itself. In essence, Castro argued that the Soviets had brought the crisis and therefore the need for an invasion on themselves. Moreover, in this same speech, Castro charged the Soviets with being soft on imperialism. Noting that the Soviets had justified their invasion by declaring that they would allow no one to "tear away a link in the community of socialist states," Castro asked: "Will they [the Soviet leaders] send in Warsaw pact divisions to Cuba if the Yankee imperialists attack our country, or even threaten to attack, if our country requests it?"[44] Rather than simply subordinating Cuba to Soviet policy, Castro was clearly attempting to parlay Cuban support for the Czechoslovakian invasion into stauncher Soviet protection for Cuba against U.S. imperialism.

Although the Cubans supported the revolution in Afghanistan from its inception, they were clearly embarrassed by the subsequent Soviet invasion of that country. Probably fearful of straying too far from the Soviet fold, the Cubans voted against the UN resolution that condemned the Soviet invasion, but they neither applauded this Soviet action nor questioned the right of the United Nations to take a stand on it, as did some other Soviet allies. Moreover, the Cubans made their displeasure widely known and proceeded to seek a political solution that would lead to a Soviet withdrawal.[45] But, perhaps most dramatic of all, the Cubans, who before the invasion had argued forcefully for the idea of a natural alliance between the Soviets and the Third World at the Sixth Summit Conference of the Non-Aligned Movement in 1979, after the invasion presented the Seventh Summit Conference of 1983 with a document that charged both the developed capitalist and the socialist countries with wasting the world's resources on military expenditures.[46] Although the need for friendly relations with the Soviets in this instance limited what the Cubans felt they could do, they did not simply subordinate themselves to the Soviets. Rather, they did everything possible within those limits to distance themselves from the Soviet actions.

The Afghanistan embarrassment clearly scarred the Cubans, but it did not stop them from pursuing what Erisman calls their globalist foreign policy, which, although it partly relies on Soviet support, stems from the Cubans themselves. Although the Cubans have not entered into any more joint military ventures with the Soviets since Afghanistan, they have continued to assert leadership in Third World affairs, as witnessed by Castro's outspoken call for the cancellation of the Latin American and Third World external debt.[47] Paradoxically, Cuba's unwillingness to fully break with the Soviets over Afghanistan can be seen not only as a signet of partial subordination but also as part of a strategy for increasing Cuban autonomy over the long term. The Cubans need Soviet support, but they also attempt to use that support to enhance their independence. As Erisman put it:

> The Cubans' Soviet connection gave them a greater sense of security by alleviating their fears about their country's economic and military vulnerability to U.S. hostility and by providing a larger resource capability to wield influence in world affairs. As such, Havana's dependency on the USSR served to promote both subjective and objective conditions conducive to vigorous Cuban internationalism. By parlaying its close ties with Moscow into global activism, Havana hoped to eventually nurture a power base in the Third World sufficient to protect its interests irrespective of its relations with any superpower and to allow it to deal with other states on the basis of relative equality, thereby fulfilling the old nationalist dream of an autonomous Cuba.[48]

Clearly, neither Cuba's international behavior nor its long-term goals are those of a proxy.

Conclusions

In sum, close examination reveals that the Sovietization of Cuba thesis involves a host of gross overstatements. First, the Sovietization thesis fails to fully see that the Cuban-Soviet economic relationship is qualitatively different in both its character and its consequences from pre-revolutionary Cuba's relationship to the United States and from the type of relationships usually associated with the concept of dependence. Second, the Sovietization thesis fails to move beyond formal analogies to explain the dynamics of the Cuban revolutionary process. And, third, the Sovietization thesis fails to adequately account for Cuba's international behavior and for its long-term foreign policy goals.

By the nature of the subject, a chapter of this sort, though it can hint at positive interpretations of Cuban reality, must concern itself mostly with negative conclusions. Yet, given the pervasiveness of the Sovietization thesis, negative conclusions can here serve a positive function. Perhaps they will move Cuba scholars to jettison the Sovietization approach and to replace it with new approaches, which may bring greater understanding of Cuba's still dynamic and in many ways unique socialist experiment.[49]

Notes

1. Carollee Bengelsdorf, *Between Vision and Reality: Democracy in Socialist Theory and Practice*, PhD dissertation, Massachusetts Institute of Technology, Cambridge, 1985, p. 157. For an early critique of the Sovietization thesis, see Frank T. Fitzgerald, "A Critique of the 'Sovietization of Cuba' Thesis," *Science and Society* 42 (spring 1978):1–32.

2. Max Azicri, "The Institutionalization of the Cuban Revolution: A Review of the Literature," *Cuban Studies/Estudios Cubanos* 9 (July 1979):66.

3. Carmelo Mesa-Lago, *Cuba in the 1970s* (Albuquerque: University of New Mexico Press, 1974), p. 17.

4. Ibid., p. 106.

5. For a representative collection of scholarly analyses of Cuban foreign policy, see Cole Blasier and Carmelo Mesa-Lago, eds., *Cuba in the World* (Pittsburgh: University of Pittsburgh Press, 1979). And for a typical example of the proxy thesis, see U.S. Department of State and U.S. Department of Defense, *The Soviet-Cuban Connection in Central America and the Caribbean* (Washington, D.C.: March 1985).

6. Jorge Domínguez, *Cuba: Order and Revolution* (Cambridge: Harvard University Press, 1978).

7. For example, Richard Turits, "Trade, Debt, and the Cuban Economy," *World Development* (January 1987). With some logic, the Cubans reject the notion that this indexing arrangement constitutes a "subsidy." For this notion assumes that the commodity prices reign on the capitalist market constitute the gauge of equal exchange relationships in the world. But the Cubans, along with such organizations as the Non-Aligned movement, view the capitalist world market as a realm of unequal exchange and, therefore, demand from the developed capitalist countries a new international economic order to correct this imbalance. In this view, what the indexing arrangement ensures the Cubans is not a subsidy but equality, such as the Third World, thus far without effect, has been demanding from the developed capitalist world. See, Fidel Castro, "Speech to the U.N. General Assembly, New York, October 12, 1979," in H. Michael Erisman, *Cuba's International Relations* (Boulder, Colo.: Westview Press, 1985), pp. 108–109; and Fidel Castro, "Latin America's Debt Must Be Canceled," in Michael Taber, ed., *Fidel Castro Speeches: War and Crisis in the Americas* (New York: Pathfinder Press, 1985), pp. 222–223.

8. The only possible exception to my knowledge is Robert A. Packenham, "Capitalist vs. Socialist Dependency," *Journal of Interamerican Studies and World Affairs* 28 (spring 1986):59–92; also reprinted in Jan F. Triska, ed., *Dominant Powers and Subordinate States* (Durham, N.C.: Duke University Press, 1986), pp. 310–341. Packenham claimed, with no serious evidence and without defining his term, that Cuban and Soviet leaders are "exploiting" the Cuban people.

9. See, for example, Andre Gunder Frank, "Mechanisms of Imperialism," *Latin America: Underdevelopment or Revolution* (New York: Monthly Review Press, 1969), pp. 162–174. For an overview of the dependency concept and its place within the development literature, see Frank T. Fitzgerald, "Sociologies of Development," in Bruce McFarlane and Peter Limqueco, eds., *Neo-Marxist Theories of Development* (New York: St. Martin's Press; and London: Croom and Helm, 1982), pp. 12–28.

10. Cited in Fitzgerald, "A Critique," p. 15.

11. Cited in ibid.

12. Cited in ibid., p. 16.

13. Fidel Castro, *The World Economic and Social Crisis* (Havana: Council of State, 1983), esp. ch. 9. In the mid-1980s, the Cubans were again emphasizing the need for Latin American integration, presumably including Cuba. See Fidel Castro, "Speech to the Meeting on the Foreign Debt of Latin America and the Caribbean" (Havana: Editora Politica, 1985), pp. 34 and 52.

14. On this point, see Susan Eckstein, "Capitalist Constraints on Cuban Socialist Development," Working Paper no. 6 (Washington: Wilson Center, March 1978).

15. Turits, in "Trade, Debt," demonstrates another aspect of Cuban flexibility, namely, the country's ability to build down its debt with the capitalist world without resorting to the usual austerity measures, something no other Latin American country has been able to accomplish.

16. Jose Peraza Chapeau, *EL CAME y la Integración Económica Socialista* (Havana: Editorial de Ciencias Sociales, 1979), pp. 66–70.

17. Claes Brundenius and Andrew Zimbalist, "Recent Studies on Cuban Economic Growth: A Review," *Comparative Economic Studies* (April 1985).

18. Gonzalo M. Rodriguez Mesa, "El Desarrollo Industrial de Cuba y la Maduración de Inversiones," *Economía y Desarrollo*, 68 (May-June 1982):127.

19. For a useful summary of these problems, see Turits, "Trade, Debt."

20. Author's computations based on data presented in Claes Brundenius, *Revolutionary Cuba: The Challenge of Growth with Equity* (Boulder, Colo.: Westview Press, 1984), p. 40.

21. Dated cited in Frank T. Fitzgerald, "Politics and Social Structure in Revolutionary Cuba: From the Demise of the Old Middle Class to the Rise of the New Professionals," PhD dissertation, State University of New York, Binghamton, 1985, pp. 452–453; and Fidel Castro, "Speech to the Meeting," p. 45.

22. Carmelo Mesa-Lago, *The Economy of Socialist Cuba: A Two-Decade Appraisal* (Albuquerque: University of New Mexico Press, 1981), p. 187.

23. Mesa-Lago, *Cuba in the 1970s*, p. x.

24. Ibid., p. 115.

25. For extended discussions, see Fitzgerald, "A Critique," pp. 4–13; and Fitzgerald, *Politics and Social Structure*, ch. IV.

26. Leo Huberman and Paul Sweezy, *Socialism in Cuba* (New York: Monthly Review Press, 1969), p. 143.

27. Ibid.

28. Domínguez, *Cuba*, p. 276.

29. Much evidence for this claim is presented in Bengelsdorf, *Between Vision and Reality*; Fitzgerald, "Politics and Social Structure"; Linda Fuller, *The Politics of Workers' Control in Cuba, 1959–1983*, PhD dissertation, University of California, Berkeley, 1985; and Marifeli Perez-Stable, *Politics and Conciencia in Revolutionary Cuba, 1959–1984*, PhD dissertation, State University of New York, Stony Brook, 1985.

30. This is not to say that socialist leaderships must simply accept workers' attitudes and refrain from attempting to manufacture the consent they require. The massive discussions, which took place throughout 1986, of the draft program of the Third Congress of the Communist Party of Cuba are a case in point. Through these discussions, the Cuban leadership clearly hoped to rally worker support for certain economic goals and practices.

31. Mesa-Lago, *Cuba in the 1970s*, p. x.

32. Fitzgerald, "A Critique."

33. For an excellent discussion of the distinction between Soviet forms and Cuban content in the area of economic planning, see Andrew Zimbalist, "Cuban Economic Planning: Organization and Performance," in Sandor Halebsky and John M. Kirk, eds., *Cuba: Twenty-five Years of Revolution, 1959–1984* (New York: Praeger, 1985), pp. 213–230.

34. Bengelsdorf, *Between Vision and Reality*, p. 260.

35. Humberto Perez, *Sobre las Dificultades Objetivas de la Revolucion: Lo Que el Pueblo Debe Saber* (Havana: Editora Politica, 1979), p. 15.

36. For extended discussions, see Fitzgerald, *Politics and Social Structure*, chs. X and XI; and James Petras and Frank T. Fitzgerald, "On the Transition to Socialism in Latin America," *Latin American Perspectives* (forthcoming).

37. Cited in Erisman, *Cuba's International Relations*, p. 3.

38. For a representative statement by the Reagan administration, see U.S. Department of State and U.S. Department of Defense, *The Soviet-Cuban Connection*.

39. Erisman, *Cuba's International Relations*, pp. 3–7.

40. Cited in ibid., pp. 4–5.

41. Ibid., p. 5. For an excellent discussion of the Ethiopian/Eritrean situation and the Soviet and Cuban roles, see Bereket Habte Selassie, *Conflict and Intervention in the Horn of Africa* (New York: Monthly Review Press, 1980).

42. Jacques Levesque, *The USSR and the Cuban Revolution* (New York: Praeger, 1978), pp. 186–187.

43. Ibid., p. 151.

44. Cited in ibid.

45. See Erisman, *Cuba's International Relations*, pp. 127–131.

46. Castro, *The World Economic*, p. 20. For a thorough analysis of the debate over the "natural alliance" thesis, see A. W. Singham and Shirley Hume, *Non-Alignment in an Age of Alignments* (Westport, Conn.: Lawrence Hill, 1986).

47. Castro, "Speech to the Meeting."

48. Erisman, *Cuba's International Relations*, p. 92.

49. Although the question of what these new and better approaches might be is beyond the scope of this chapter, I will simply indicate that I think one of the more promising approaches is that of interest group analysis—focusing on intermediate groups and their relationships to both the revolutionary leadership and the masses—such as I have attempted in Fitzgerald, *Politics and Social Structure*.

9

Why Cuban Internationalism?

Susan Eckstein

Why does resource-poor Cuba have extensive overseas commitments? Is the aid provided at the behest of the Soviet Union, as many Americans believe, or because of a genuine commitment to global socialist solidarity, as the Cuban government and Communist party assert? After briefly describing Cuba's internationalist programs—above all its relatively unknown civilian component—the two opposing explanations of Cuba's overseas activities will be discussed. Neither explanation will be shown to be satisfactory. In addition, domestic considerations—including economic experiences—will be shown to account for certain of the overseas activities. The roots of Cuban internationalism have shifted somewhat over the years, as political and economic conditions have changed. Paradoxically, civilian aid programs that are publicly legitimated in terms of "proletarian internationalism" since the late 1970s have been designed to help address Cuba's economic relations with Western countries. Ideological differences between the Soviet and Western blocs conceal important economic ties.

Cuban Overseas Activities

Unlike prerevolutionary Cuba and most Third World countries today, Castro's Cuba offers extensive military and civilian assistance to Third World countries. Even when the Revolution had not yet been consolidated and the United States threatened to undermine the new regime, Cuba did not confine its energies to the island. Militarily, it initially aided national liberation and guerrilla movements; it subsequently also helped protect "progressive" governments in power. The civilian programs have involved social and economic assistance.

Military Component

In the 1960s the United States persuaded Latin American governments, with the exception of Mexico, to break diplomatic relations with Cuba. Cuba, in turn, trained and assisted guerrilla movements in the region. Among the groups it trained and armed were the Frente Sandinista de Liberación Nacional (FSLN), but the group, like most other guerrilla movements at the time, was of limited significance; it involved fewer than fifty Nicaraguans. Since none of the Cuban supported movements gained substantial followings, after Ché Guevara was captured and murdered in Bolivia in 1967 Castroites reversed their policy and reduced their material aid to guerrillas.

In the 1960s Cuba focused on Latin America, but it concomitantly laid the foundation for its African military assistance program. Cuba provided Algeria, shortly after it attained independence, with some arms and troops when it was attacked by Morocco. It also supported national liberation movements and progressive governments in Angola, Guinea-Bissau, Mozambique, and Congo-Brazzaville.

During Castro's second decade of rule Cuba's African commitments surged. The island established advisory and training missions in Sierra Leone, Equatorial Guinea, and Somalia, and it sent large numbers of combat troops to Angola and Ethiopia. By 1978 Cuba had some 38,000 to 40,000 military cadre in Africa, up from about 750 to 1,000 in the mid-1960s (Erisman 1985:75; LeoGrande 1980:30). The military aid, however, has been heavily concentrated in Angola and Ethiopia.

The Angolan mission has had the greatest impact. It helped the Popular Movement for the Liberation of Angola (MPLA) there consolidate power and subsequently fend off foreign-backed rebel groups. As of 1985 some 30,000 Cuban troops were still there. Since the Angolan government has only about 110,000 troops, Cuba weighs heavily in the African country's defense system. Castro has said that Cuba would reduce its military presence there when Pretoria both grants independence to Namibia and ceases to support Angolan rebels (Unita).

In Ethiopia Cuba's military presence has always been less decisive. At its peak in the late 1970s, some 10,500 Cubans were stationed there. However, by the mid-1980s the mission was one-third that size (EIU February 1984:8); by then it was, according to Castro, largely symbolic, involving only a few well-equipped units with combat capabilities (Elliot and Dymally 1986:179). Cuban assistance helped the Ethiopian government win the Ogaden war with neighboring Somalia, but Cuba refused to be drawn into Addis Ababa's domestic problems with Eritrean rebels. Castro cut back the military mission there when a new Somalian attack appeared unlikely.

During most of the 1970s Cuba's military involvements in Latin America were, by contrast, insignificant. Cuba instead improved government-to-government relations, which became possible early in the decade when progressive governments came to power in such countries as Peru, Chile, and Argentina. Yet Castro did not resume efforts to export revolution when the populist governments fell. Instead, the resurgence of repressive regimes in the region resulted in official recognition of Latin America's limited revolutionary potential. Castro noted in his main report to the Communist party's First Congress in 1975 that "Latin America is not yet on the eve of the kind of overall changes that lead, as happened in Cuba, to sudden socialist transformations" (Erisman 1985:87). The only Latin American government toward which Cuba then had any ideological affinity was Michael Manley's democratic socialist regime in Jamaica.

Cuba's basis for hemispheric pessimism proved, however, to be ill-founded by the end of the decade. Socialist governments gained power in Nicaragua and Grenada, Guyana established a left-leaning government, and the El Salvadorian rebel movement became a serious political force. As a consequence, at the twenty-fifth anniversary of the island's revolution in 1984, Castro expressed a new-found optimism. He asserted that revolution in Latin America was inevitable without Cuba's instigation: "Cuba cannot export revolution. Neither can the USA prevent it" (EIU February 1984:7).

As revolutionary movements gained force in the region Castro made limited military assistance available. In 1978 Cuba provided insurgents in Nicaragua with training, advice, and military equipment, but Cuba contributed less than some other Latin American countries. After the Sandinista victory in 1979, Havana's military assistance picked up. However, the aid paled in comparison to Angola's and Ethiopia's. The Reagan administration claimed that Cuba had some 3,000 military personnel in Nicaragua in early 1984 and about 800 two years later (*Boston Globe* July 1, 1984:10; May 24, 1986:4). According to Castro, though, Cuban military advisers in Nicaragua numbered about 200 in 1983 (EIU August 22, 1983:9). The Cubans helped train Sandinistas in weaponry use and national security.

Also in 1979, Maurice Bishop's socialist New Jewel movement assumed power in Grenada. Cuba was no more instrumental in the turn of events there than in Nicaragua, and it supplied Bishop, once in power, with only limited light arms and a few dozen security advisers.

Havana has trained and armed leftist guerrillas battling the El Salvadorian government. However, the Reagan administration has also grossly exaggerated Cuba's assistance here, and Cuban weaponry appears to have been reduced to a bare minimum after the failure of the "final offensive" in January 1981 (Erisman 1985:141). Havana has strongly endorsed the diplomatic efforts of the Contadora group (composed of Mexico, Panama, Venezuela, and Colombia) to reduce Central American tension.

Cuba's military presence in the rest of the Third World has been modest. Nonetheless, Havana has sent small contingents to Southeast Asian countries and more substantial ones to some Middle Eastern countries. In particular, Cuba sent combat units to Syria in 1973, and advisory and training missions to South Yemen and Lebanon.

Civilian Component

The island's civilian assistance program expanded substantially in the 1970s, along with the military program. Construction constitutes the principal civilian component. Cuba offers materials, organizational and planning advice, building cadre, and topographic surveys. The overseas construction program began modestly in the early 1970s, when island workers built six hospitals in Peru following an earthquake. The program expanded in 1974–1975 with the building of a hospital, highway, hotel, several poultry complexes, and thirteen milking barns in North Vietnam. At the close of the Vietnam war Cuba sent an additional 900 workers to help in national reconstruction. Construction assistance grew rapidly in the later 1970s to the point that some 7,900 Cubans, involving 3 percent of the island's construction labor force, worked on overseas assignments. Between 1978 and 1979 alone the number of construction workers abroad more than doubled, with Angola and Ethiopia receiving especially large contingents. Cubans have built housing in Angola and a cement plant and road in Ethiopia. Meanwhile, in Laos, Guinea, and Tanzania Cuban brigades have built roads, airports, schools, and other facilities.

In the early 1980s the program's expansion tapered off, government plans notwithstanding. As of 1983 the number of construction workers overseas was no higher than in 1979, even though the government had hoped to involve some 25,000 workers in overseas construction assignments. Cuba's principal new construction projects at the time were in the Middle East—in South Yemen, Algeria, Iraq, and Libya—and in Nicaragua and Grenada. By the end of 1985, 35,000 Cuban workers had helped build projects in some twenty Asian, African, and Latin American countries.

From the U.S. vantage point, Cuba's most controversial construction program involved airport building assistance in Grenada. The program, according to Maurice Bishop (Marcus and Taber 1983:125), involved some 250 Cubans. Cuba had agreed to build the $50 million new airport and absorb half the cost (Erisman 1985:90). The Reagan administration claimed that the airport was to be used for military purposes, a rationale for the U.S. invasion. However, Bishop had always claimed that the airport was intended to help develop island tourism, and the English firm that supplied and installed the electrical and technical equipment for the airport confirmed the Grenadian leader's stated purpose.

The island's second and third largest civilian assistance programs are educational and medical. In 1979, at least 2,300 Cuba teachers were abroad; the following year some 3,500 were, the equivalent of 2 percent of the island's stock of teachers (calculated from *GWR* November 16, 1980:4). Since the Sandinista victory Nicaragua has received the largest contingent of teachers: By 1983 some 20,900 Cuban teachers were working there (*GWR* February 13, 1983:3). Cubans helped in the Sandinista's initial mass literacy campaign (modeled, in part, on Cuba's) and afterward in government efforts to expand formal schooling. Cuba's foreign educational assistance program also involves educating foreign students on the country's Isle of Pines. In 1980, 9,000 foreign students were there; five years later some 22,000 scholarship students from more than eighty countries were there (*GWR* November 30, 1980:3; Castro 1985:129). Foreign students can receive training in medicine and engineering as well as other technical fields.

Along with construction and education assistance, Cuba developed a medical assistance program. The number of medical cadre abroad rose from 700 in 1977 to some 2,000 three years later (Roca 1980:58; *GWR* September 21, 1980:2). The 1980 overseas program employed between 7 and 13 percent of the island's stock of doctors (estimated from *GWR* August 3, 1980:3 and September 21, 1980:2), as well as dentists, nurses, technicians, and support personnel. By 1983 health missions involved an additional thousand cadre in twenty-six countries on three continents. Its program in Nicaragua involved some 600 health personnel and in Iraq nearly 400 cadre (*GWR* August 17, 1986:10). Smaller health contingents have been sent to Jamaica under Michael Manley, to Guyana under Forbes Burnham, to Grenada under Maurice Bishop, and to Peru under Alain García (to assist in earthquake relief in Cuzco in 1986) (*GWR* May 11, 1986:5; Maingot 1983:20).

Cuba's overseas economic programs, in turn, include specialists in agriculture, sugar cultivation and refining, mining, fishing, transportation, cattle raising, irrigation, industry, economic and physical planning, and management. The island sends specialists abroad who help train local personnel. Cuba has sent, for example, technicians to Vietnam to train local persons in hotel and restaurant management and to Guinea-Bissau, the Republic of Equatorial Guinea, and Somalia to provide training in economics, education, and public health. Castro agreed in October 1978 to send hundreds of economic specialists to Ethiopia and two years later to send 700 technicians to Mozambique (Roca 1980:60). In 1980 Cuba also sent to the People's Republic of the Congo livestock and dairy industry aid, to Ethiopia 200 specimens of its best breed of cattle, to Angola internationalists to help reconstruct the sugar industry and get other industries into operation, and to South Yemen technicians and specialists in livestock, poultry farming, mining, fishing, tobacco growing, education and sports, maritime transport, and port and shipyard work (*GWR* November 16, 1980:12; November 23, 1980:8; December 21, 1980:12). Cuba expanded its civilian assistance to Ethiopia—involving agriculture, sugar industry, and trade assistance, plus public health and educational aid—in the mid-1980s while contracting its military mission. Castro agreed to provide the civilian assistance when the Reagan administration halted all economic aid to the African government. The United States terminated its aid program in the impoverished country when the Ethiopian government criticized the United States' South African policy (*GWR* July 20, 1986:9).

Civilian assistance has dominated Cuba's overseas programs in Latin America, with Nicaragua receiving the largest civilian mission. In 1982 Cuba pledged to provide $130 million worth of agricultural and industrial machinery and construction equipment, as well as 3,800 technicians, doctors, and teachers, and food and medicine to the Sandinistas. In 1982 approximately 1,200 Nicaraguans also went to Cuba for technical training. As in Ethiopia, in Nicaragua Cuba's civilian assistance increased as its military presence declined. Some 6,000 civilian aides were reportedly in the Central American country in 1985 (EIU February 1985:16; May 1985:9). Ambitious as Cuba's Nicaraguan program has been, Castro has been a restraining force there. Castro has urged Managua to adopt moderate policies. Specifically, Castro has advised the Nicaraguans to avoid alienating the private sector at home and the United States abroad.

In Grenada there were slightly under 800 Cubans when the U.S. invasion brought Castro's aid program there to an abrupt halt. Cubans assisted the New Jewel movement in a literacy campaign, the fishing industry, and road construction, as well as in the building of the airport and health care provisioning. Although the Grenadian program was not Cuba's largest, Havana had a major presence there. Cuba provided one-fifth of all Bishop's foreign aid, more than any other single country (Erisman 1985:146). According to Castro (in Bishop 1983:326), the airport project alone involved $60 million worth of materials and labor, the equivalent of $500 per inhabitant.

Cuba also assisted the Burnham government in Guyana. It offered to train technicians there in health and education and to provide technology for the sugar industry. Its Guyanese aid program included, in addition, shipments of cattle to build up the local beef and dairy industry (EIU February 1985:9).

All told, the civilian program entails fewer Cubans than the military program, but more countries receive civilian than military assistance. In 1979 Cuba had some 14,000 economic and technical aid personnel overseas, and the following year the government announced that it had civilian missions in thirty-seven countries on three continents (*GWR* November 30, 1980: supplement, p. 3). Africa has received the largest civilian as well as military contingents, but civilian and military aid are not always extended hand in hand. The mix of civilian and military assistance varies considerably by region. Until the 1980s Cuba offered almost exclusively civilian aid to Latin America, military aid to the Middle East, and a combination of the two to Africa and Indochina. In the 1980s the civilian component became more important, and the military component less important in Africa, whereas military aid to sympathetic governments in Nicaragua and Grenada and to rebels in El Salvador picked up. However, the Central American military missions remain much smaller than the civilian missions and much smaller than the military missions sent to Angola and Ethiopia. Moreover, Cuba has never sent troops to regional allies.

In sum, Cuba has offered foreign assistance ever since Castro came to power. Nonetheless, the nature and scope of the assistance changed considerably in the latter 1970s. The program became much larger and began to include civilian assistance. Also, the military component in some countries came to include troops on a significant scale for the first time. Finally, aid programs became directed primarily toward established governments, not, as in the 1960s, toward guerrilla and national liberation movements. Aid tended to be given cautiously, to movements with strong political bases. In 1985 Castro even informed Western sources that Cuba would withdraw its military support to the Nicaraguan and Angolan governments as part of global peace settlements in Central America and southern Africa (EIU May 1985:8).

Why has Cuba offered such extensive foreign aid when other Third World countries have not? Does Havana assume the foreign commitments at the behest of Moscow? If the programs are Cuba's own doing, what prompts the government to divert scarce resources to internationalist activities: a moral or ideological commitment to "proletarian internationalism," pragmatic geopolitical and material interests, or a personal obsession on Castro's part to be a world power? Scholars and political commentators have offered such diverse interpretations; the validity of the contesting interpretations will be evaluated, in turn, in the following sections.

Cuba as a Soviet Surrogate

According to the surrogate thesis, Havana operates as a Soviet mercenary; it is a superpower puppet, engaging in foreign ventures at the behest of the superpower. This view of Cuban overseas involvements was widely voiced, especially by the U.S. government and U.S. media, in the mid-1970s, when the island's overseas aid programs expanded dramatically and came to include troops.

U.S. officials and the press have depicted Cuba as a helpless pawn of Soviet imperialist interests and as a willing Soviet collaborator. U.S. Senator Daniel Moynihan, for example, has referred to the Fidelistas as nothing more than the "Gurkhas of the Russian Empire," stirring up trouble on Moscow's behalf and functioning as a vehicle for indirect Soviet subversion and eventual domination of targeted developing countries (cited in Erisman 1985:3).

Though it is impossible to determine, on the basis of available information, the precise nature of Cuban-Soviet relations, if Cuba is a Soviet surrogate it should not extend aid to countries with which the USSR has hostile relations. Also, there should be evidence of Cuban-Soviet overseas coordination, and Cuban overseas involvements should vary with ups and downs in Cuban-Soviet relations. Moreover, if Cuba operates primarily as a Soviet puppet, the Cubans should have no major reason of their own for promoting internationalism. The evidence summarized in the following suggests that the Soviet Union disapproved of Cuba's overseas activities in the 1960s. Since the 1970s the two countries have more typically advanced complementary and coordinated military assistance programs, but Cuba has had its own reasons for the programs and it occasionally has pressured a reluctant Soviet Union to extend aid. Moreover, the island's civilian programs appear rarely to be coordinated with the superpower.

That certain Cuban and Soviet overseas military activities are closely coordinated is, however, undeniable. There is, in particular, evidence of Cuban-Soviet collaboration in Somalia, Ethiopia, Angola, Syria, and Indochina. Most Cuban-Soviet involvements in these countries have been complementary. Especially in the larger overseas programs the support of both countries has been crucial. The Soviets have provided equipment and financing while the Cubans have provided personnel. Cuban troops would have been much less effective without Soviet material. The Cuban government itself admits close international collaboration with the Soviets. It even claims that the alliance is a permanent element of its international policy.

Though Cubans acknowledge collaboration with the Soviet Union in some of their internationalist ventures, they argue that they have assumed the commitments on their own. In speaking of the military support Cuba lent the Angolan MPLA, for example, Castro (1985:121, 173) noted: "Cuba alone bears the responsibility for taking that decision. The U.S.S.R. had always helped the peoples of the Portuguese colonies in their struggle for independence . . . but it never requested that a single Cuban be sent to that country. . . . A decision of that nature could only be made by our party." Castro added that Cuba sent troops to Angola in 1975 to help the newly independent country stave off a South African invasion. "That aggression is what motivated us to send troops . . . to fight the South Africans." The South Africans attacked some training centers where a few dozen Cuban instructors had been.

Merely because Castro publicly claims that Havana makes its own foreign policy is not in itself, of course, adequate evidence of decision-making autonomy. Castro may have reason to convey the impression that his government is not subservient to the superpower. Yet most U.S. studies—including studies by such agencies as the Center for Naval Analysis, which does classified research—conclude that Cuba has not merely acted at the behest of the superpower, even when the two have collaborated (see, for example, LeoGrande 1980; Durch 1977; Domínguez 1978; Blasier 1979:40; Blasier 1980:40; González 1980:43–48; Adams 1981:109–112). Such studies note that Cuba has had a consistent foreign policy since Castro first came to power and that it has aided revolutionary movements without Soviet backing. It is widely believed that if the Soviets had their way, Cuba would not have engaged in guerrilla activities in the 1960s, especially in the Western hemisphere. The Soviets even had diplomatic, trade and credit relations with governments that Cas-troites tried to subvert. The Soviet Union then advocated "peaceful coexistence" and détente; it tacitly recognized the Western hemisphere as the U.S. sphere of influence. In Bolivia, for example, the Soviet-dominated Communist party refused to assist Ché Guevara. Cuban internationalism in the 1960s actually caused tension between the two countries.

Wayne Smith (1985:338), the head of the U.S. Interest Section in Cuba under President Jimmy Carter, went so far as to argue that in the 1960s Cuba's policy of exporting revolution was more a byproduct of U.S. than Soviet policy. He noted that Castro proposed, in an interview with Richard Eder of the *New York Times* in 1964, to withhold material support from Latin American revolutionaries if the United States would cease its own hostile actions against Cuba. In Castro's major annual July 26 speech later that year he repeated the proposal. With his overture to the United States rebuffed, Castro returned with a vengeance to the export of revolution as a policy and to armed struggle as a tactic. To the Soviets this smacked of "infantile adventurism." Some analyses that acknowledge that Cuban internationalism initially occurred despite the Soviet Union argued that since the 1970s it occurs because of the Soviet Union. Juan M. del Aguila (1984:111), for instance, claimed that after the first decade of Castro's rule "the politics of clientelism replaced Havana's freewheeling zealousness of the 1960s." He argued that the Soviet invasion of Czechoslovakia was a turning point in Cuban-Soviet relations. It was followed by a political reconciliation, with Castro moderating his proguerrilla line and the Soviet Union rewarding him with increased economic assistance.

Other studies show, however, that even in the 1970s Cuban overseas involvements were not always at the behest of the superpower. William LeoGrande (1982:172) and William Durch (1977:46–47), for example, showed that Cuba initiated the commitment of massive combat troops in Angola. In 1974 Cuba extended aid to Angola when the USSR pulled out and gave the then MPLA leader, Agostino Neto, a "chilling reception" in Moscow. The Soviets resumed their aid to Angola only after the Cuban military buildup had begun. Moreover, in May 1977 a faction within the MPLA, which felt that Neto was not sufficiently pro-Soviet, organized a coup to topple him. Though there is no strong evidence that the Kremlin was directly involved in the plot, the Soviets reportedly knew of the maneuver beforehand but did not warn Neto. Havana, by contrast, stood firmly behind Neto and helped put down the uprising (Erisman 1985:4). Although Cuba's aid to Colonel Mengistu Haile Mariam in Ethiopia, in its struggle with Somalia over the Ogaden, appears to have been more closely coordinated with Moscow from the onset, Erisman (1985:73) noted that even in Ethiopia Havana resisted Soviet pressure to commit Cuban units to crush the Eritrean rebels.

Jorge Domínguez (1983:100), in turn, presented evidence countering the Soviet surrogate thesis in the Western hemisphere. He noted that Cuba formulated its own foreign policy toward Central America, with the Soviet Union more a follower than a leader. Cuba, for instance, took the lead in establishing close relations with Bishop's New Jewel movement in Grenada, subsequently persuading the Soviet Union to extend aid as well.

Ironically, at the same time that Cuba was portrayed as a Soviet puppet in the United States, Castro captured the leadership of the Nonaligned movement's 1979 summit conference. Castro served as the organization's chairperson until 1983. Cuba's active internationalist role—especially against racist South Africa in Angola—was widely hailed in the less-developed world. Cuban internationalism therefore strengthened the island's standing among self-proclaimed nonaligned Third World countries, countries that deliberately maintained a degree of autonomy from both the Western and Soviet blocs.

The attitude of the Nonaligned movement toward Cuba changed only after Havana refused to criticize the Soviet invasion of Afghanistan. Erisman (1985:132) argued that Cuba's close identification with the Soviet Union there restricted its internationalist military assistance options because of widespread Third World hostility to the Soviet attack on the Afghani "popular" movement. He posited, in essence, that Cuba was penalized for policies not of its making and that the very alliance that purportedly accounted for Cuban internationalism was there a constraining force. Erisman believed that the foreclosing of military options gave Cuba little choice but to make the development, or civilian, component the mainstay of its Third World globalism in the 1980s.

Erisman's contention cannot, however, be substantiated. The cutback in Cuba's military assistance program in the 1980s is largely the result of the withdrawal of its forces from Ethiopia. Since the Ethiopian government has maintained close ties with the Soviet Union at the same time that Cuban troops have pulled out, the retrenchment cannot be attributed to Ethiopian anti-Cuban sentiment grounded in the island's close association with the superpower. Rather, the retrenchment results from a declining need for the forces, once Ethiopian government tensions with Eritrea and Somalia subsided, and from government difficulty in absorbing the cost of the $6 million a year aid program (*New York Times* January 25, 1984:2; *Boston Globe* March 13, 1984:6). Cuba contracted its smaller Western hemisphere missions, in turn, in the 1980s, in response to U.S. pressure; it did not do so because of Third World condemnation of its ties to the Soviet Union.

Signs of some foreign policy friction between Cuba and the Soviet Union in the 1980s further challenge the validity of the Soviet surrogate thesis. Articles in the Western press (see EIU February 1984:8; February 4, 1986:9) claim evidence of divisions between Moscow and Havana over strategy in Africa and Central America. First came claims of disagreement over the attitude to adopt toward the Grenadians responsible for overthrowing Maurice Bishop (prior to the U.S. invasion). Then Moscow is alleged to have been angered by Cuba's decision to reduce its troop strength in Ethiopia and its offer to withdraw from Angola. In late 1985 Western diplomats in Havana also believed they detected significant areas of disagreement between Cuba and the Soviet Union concerning Central America, an area of paramount importance to Cuba but not to Moscow. Such appraisals of Cuban-Soviet relations may be accurate, but they do not explain why Cuba continues to coordinate certain of its overseas involvements with Moscow and why Cuba continues to offer extensive foreign assistance when relations with the superpower are tense. Recognition of such friction while Cuban overseas involvements continue full force suggests that Cuba has its own reasons for its extensive overseas involvements.

Proponents of the Soviet surrogate thesis presume that Cuba carries out the superpower's global ambitions because it is economically dependent on Moscow. Yet Cuba was at its peak economic dependence on the superpower for trade in the late 1960s, when the foreign policy of the two countries most diverged—when Cuba tried to foment revolution and the Soviet Union emphasized détente. Indeed, Cuba expanded its overseas commitments—both military and civilian—only after its economic relations with the West improved. In 1974 Western countries accounted for 41 percent of Cuba's trade, up from a low of 17 percent in 1962 (Eckstein 1980:264). Moreover, in the mid-1980s, when Western media and Western diplomatic circles recognized signs of Cuban-Soviet foreign policy friction, Cuba was once again heavily dependent on the Soviet Union for trade. Trade with market economies (as a percent of total trade) by then had dropped to levels of the late 1960s.

None of the Soviet surrogate discussions focus on Cuba's civilian assistance program. Since there is little evidence that Cuba coordinates its education, construction, medicine, and technical assistance programs with the superpower, either the military and civilian components of Cuba's foreign aid program have different roots, or Cuba in general does not extend aid at the behest of the superpower. Since Cuba contracts civilian programs and many military programs at its own initiative, it would appear that Cuba has not "gone international" primarily at the behest of the Soviet Union.

However, Soviet bloc dynamics could induce client states to "go international," even when not specifically demanded by Moscow. In serving Soviet interests Cuba undoubtedly increases its worth to the Council for Mutual Economic Assistance (COMECON) superpower and in so doing increases the probability of continued Soviet economic and military subsidies. However, since no other Soviet bloc Third World country is as actively involved internationally as Cuba, COMECON membership cannot in itself account for Cuba's massive overseas commitments. Moreover (as I will argue in the next section) Cuba promotes internationalism, especially the civilian component, to address certain *Soviet bloc deficiencies*. The Soviet's inability to meet all Cuba's needs, and not merely the big Soviet stick, inclines Cuba to extend assistance to other Third World countries.

In sum, the Cuban government has not expanded its overseas activities simply at the behest of the USSR. Generally, though, Cuban and Soviet foreign interests have converged, and in large military ventures the two countries have coordinated their involvements. Cuban internationalism has strengthened the Soviet Union's global hegemonic position, but the island has (as will be discussed) its own reasons for offering foreign assistance. Until Cuban-U.S. relations improve, the island will benefit from involvements that strengthen the Soviet's as well as its own positions in the international arena.

Ideological Bases for Cuba's
Overseas Involvements

The Cuban government can and has justified most of its aid programs, including missions coordinated with the Soviet Union, on moral grounds. It has appealed to anti-imperialist, anticolonial, anti-Zionist, Marxist-Leninist proletarian, racial, and revolutionary sentiments in promoting internationalism; it has even grounded the foreign commitments in nationalism. The government has drawn on such themes to mobilize the populace and foster a global vision domestically and to account for and legitimate overseas involvements. Though certain of the moral appeals are comparable to the Soviet Union's, others are distinctively Cuban.

If the island primarily supports overseas activities for moral and ideological reasons, Cuba should receive no regular and significant quid pro quo for its assistance, and it should limit its aid to ideologically sympathetic countries. Any material gains from its involvement should be minor, and they should not be anticipated when contracting to provide the aid. Above all, the island should be willing to risk receiving no economic payoffs.

The government promoted international solidarity before officially becoming a Marxist-Leninist state. It undoubtedly was prompted, in part, by revolutionary zeal, having just challenged successfully U.S. hemispheric hegemony. Del Aguila (1984:103, 126), for example, traced Havana's foreign policy to revolutionary messianism and revolutionary romanticism. During the 1960s Castro pressed upon Cubans that "the duty of every revolutionary is to make the revolution."

Castro has drawn on nationalist as well as revolutionary motifs to foster anti-imperialist sentiment. Erisman (1985:152) and del Aguila (1984:102) concurred that nationalism is intrinsic to the Revolution and a driving force behind Havana's foreign policy. Heroes of Cuba's pre-revolutionary struggles against imperialism—such as Antonio Maceo, José Martí, and Máximo Gómez—sustain Havana's image of a nation seeking to control its own destiny at home and abroad.

If Castroites did not officially draw on Marxist-Leninist doctrine to spur internationalism during their first years of power, they subsequently did. There is no ambiguity about this. When Cuba took steps to institutionalize the Revolution in the mid-1970s it formalized its official commitment to world socialism, communism, and international proletarian solidarity. The First Party Congress Resolution on International Policy specified that Cuba subordinates its interests to the general interests of socialism and communism (and national liberation of peoples), so as to defeat imperialism and eliminate colonialism (*GWR* November 1980: supplement, p. 2). Similarly, the 1976 constitution expressed Cuba's commitment to "the principles of proletarian internationalism and the combative solidarity of the peoples." In the 1980s Castro continued to claim that "our actions have been inspired by feelings of solidarity, by the purest internationalist spirit" (Elliot and Dymally 1986:180). Proletarian internationalism—a commitment to help one's ideological brethren to seize and consolidate power—is embedded in Marx's famous dictum "workers of the world, unite" to destroy capitalism.

The moral basis of Cuban internationalism has also been attributed to international racial solidarity. Castro (1985:119), in his April 1976 speech commemorating the fifteenth anniversary of the Cuban Bay of Pigs victory, asserted that

> At Girón, African blood was shed, that of the selfless descendants of a people who were slaves before they became workers. . . . And in Africa, together with the blood of the heroic fighters of Angola, Cuban blood . . . also flowed. Those who once enslaved man and sent him to America perhaps never imagined that one of those peoples who received the slaves would one day send their fighters to struggle for freedom in Africa. The victory in Angola was the twin sister of the victory at Girón. . . . Angola represents an African Girón.

Here, racial and not merely revolutionary Marxist-Leninist, and nationalist sentiments are drawn upon to foster a commitment to internationalism.

Moral ideals may induce Cubans to serve willingly overseas and to legitimate the government's allocation of scarce resources to the foreign programs. However, ideological commitment alone cannot explain several aspects of the island's foreign policy. It cannot, for example, explain why Castro stepped up overseas activities so dramatically in the mid-1970s. The growth was grounded in changing global and domestic opportunities and (as will be argued in the following) in changing domestic needs, not in a sudden surge of moral rage.

This structural interpretation does not deny the importance of ideology; it merely implies that ideology alone cannot account for the foreign programs. Conditions in the mid-1970s that made large-scale international activism possible included improved domestic security; as a consequence, defense was a less pressing national concern. In addition, the island's armed forces were professionalized by then, undoubtedly increasing their confidence in their capability and their interests in strengthening their institutional importance. Changes in the domestic labor pool also made large overseas commitments possible at the time. Meanwhile, the disintegration of the Portuguese colonial empire in Africa offered new opportunities for Cuba to aid national liberation struggles. The U.S. isolationist mood after the Vietnam war and Watergate and the 1970s recession meant that the United States was not likely to subvert Cuba's internationalist endeavors. Thus, Cuba's ideological commitment may have predisposed the island to extend military and civilian aid to "progressive" governments and movements, but only when conditions were "ripe" could the ideology be put to practice on a large scale. The "necessary" structural conditions for internationalism to become a viable strategy included domestic political and economic, as well as global, geopolitical changes.

If moral motives were the necessary and structural prerequisites the sufficient condition for Cuban internationalism, Havana should only extend aid to countries with similar ideological leanings. Yet Havana has aided Equatorial Guinea, one of the world's most repressive regimes, and it has sided with Libya against Egypt, the Sudan, and Chad. Castro aided Ethiopia during its conflict with Somalia, even though the latter was a self-proclaimed Marxist-Leninist regime and a beneficiary of island aid up to two months before Cuba sent massive aid to Colonel Mengistu Haile Mariam (LeoGrande 1980:23). Cuba claimed it sought to help repel a conventional military invasion. As Jorge Domínguez noted (1979b:89), this is the language of high diplomacy, not of revolutionary solidarity.

The driving force of ideology must also be questioned because Cuba has charged countries since the late 1970s for some of the military and civilian services it provides and because the government relies on material and political incentives, along with moral exhortations, to induce Cubans to take on international assignments. If recipient countries pay for assistance, the programs cannot be viewed as entirely self-sacrificing and unmotivated by material concerns, and if Cubans are attracted to internationalism in part for private gain they too should not be assumed to be motivated by moral commitments alone. The government offers overseas civilian workers a bonus equivalent to 20 percent of their base salary, special pension benefits, and priority access to housing and scarce, valued consumer goods when they return to the island (Roca 1980:67). The government undoubtedly offers such incentives to induce otherwise reluctant Cubans to leave their jobs and family.

Yet even when the government has had material reasons for promoting internationalism, it has not ignored ideological considerations. Cuba charges countries for its foreign assistance on an ability-to-pay basis.

The same type of services that some countries pay for, others receive free of charge.

Material Bases for Cuba's
Overseas Involvements

In 1978 Castro declared that the "exportation of technical services is becoming an important factor in the economic development of the country" (Roca 1980:67). Why might this be so? And do the economic benefits of Cuba's overseas programs exceed costs? Most studies of Cuban internationalism do not address economic aspects, and the few that do fail to pinpoint the structural dynamics shaping the changes in the island's foreign assistance program in the late 1970s. I will show that economic limitations—and not merely the political military strength— of the Soviet bloc have induced Cuba to expand its overseas programs and that the overseas programs make use of one of the Revolution's greatest accomplishments, its human resource development. Paradoxically, some programs portrayed as advancing socialist solidarity are designed also to improve Cuba's economic relations with the West.

Cuba could benefit economically from overseas military and civilian programs in several ways. Programs could open up new trade and investment opportunities, and they could generate revenue if host countries pay for the services rendered. Also, the Soviet Union might reward the island economically for advancing the superpower's hegemonic interests: The Soviet Union might, as a result, guarantee Cuba markets, subsidize trade, and provide the island with capital assistance. If Cuba benefits economically from the programs, the material gains might or might not be known in advance. If the economic gains are known when the assistance is extended, the programs cannot be purely grounded in moral sentiments, regardless of what the government and party publicly proclaim. And if the economic gains include other aspects than increased Soviet material assistance, we have added evidence that Cuba has not "gone international" solely and possibly not even mainly at the behest of the COMECON superpower.

The Cuban government not only claims generally to be self-sacrificing in extending foreign assistance; it also publishes no regular information on the economics of its foreign assistance programs. Therefore, material considerations and the material impact of the programs can only be inferred, and estimates are necessarily rough approximations. With such methodological limitations in mind, I will assess the economic import of the island's internationalist programs.

Domestic Economic Gains

Whatever Cuba's intentions, thus far the island derives limited trade payoffs from its aid programs. Since the Revolution Cuba has traded mainly but not exclusively with COMECON countries. In the late 1970s, when the island's overseas involvements became extensive, Third World countries accounted for merely 4 to 7 percent of total Cuban trade (LeoGrande 1982:179). Only 3 percent of Cuba's exports went to Africa, and less than 1 percent of its imports came from Africa (Roca 1980:64). Moreover, Cuba's trade with Angola and Ethiopia decreased between 1975 and 1977 as its aid to those countries increased. In the late 1970s the island's principal African trade partners were not the main recipients of island military and civilian assistance.

Although Cuba's overseas activities did not generate significant trade in the late 1970s, they might have been designed with future markets in mind. Ethiopia, for example, has wheat, and Angola, Algeria, and Libya have oil which Cuba must import. In the late 1970s, when Cuban internationalism increased significantly in scale, Cuba received oil from the Soviet Union at below world market rates. Consequently, it had no reason to buy oil elsewhere. However, as long as domestic energy sources remain inadequate, friendly relations with possible alternative suppliers is expedient. Moreover, because Soviet oil prices are determined for five-year periods, when world oil prices plunged in the mid-1980s the economic advantage of Soviet oil purchases disappeared (probably only temporarily, until the next five-year period). The Soviets may even want Cuba to find other providers so that it can market its petroleum surplus elsewhere, for foreign exchange if not for more money.

Angola, in addition, might be coveted for future metals and agricultural trade. Imports of staples would allow Cuba to concentrate on sugar production, an area in which it has a comparative advantage. Cuba is one of the world's most efficient sugar producers, and the crop is a major source of export earnings.

Already in the late 1970s Third World countries accounted for 15 to 20 percent of Cuba's non-Communist trade. Moreover, by the 1980s some evidence actually suggested that aid previously provided gratis had opened up markets. In 1981 cement exports reached an undisclosed record volume (EIU February 26, 1982:10). Overseas construction assistance may have opened up Cuba's cement export market. Countries that contract Cuba for building aid may purchase cement from the island; the aid, in this respect, may be "tied," although there is no publicly available evidence acknowledging that it is. Cuba's medical assistance program may be opening up markets for Cuban medicine. In the middle of the decade Cuba produced 83 percent of the medicines domestically consumed, and it exported some 12 percent of total production (*GWR* January 19, 1986:12). Although the Cuban government claims that its medical program exemplifies socialist internationalism, it earns revenue from the sale of certain medicines overseas and it has developed those markets with the assistance of Western firms.

In 1983 the French agreed to form a joint venture company to manufacture vaccines; the company was to serve Cuban markets in developing countries as well as domestic Cuban needs. British medical equipment suppliers tried to increase their supply of equipment to Havana with the hopes that it would be used by Cuban medical teams abroad (EIU no. 3, August 22, 1983:16, 17; no. 4, December 5, 1983:14). Similarly, in 1985 Cuba planned to export paper for the first time. About half of its paper production (utilizing sugarcane bagasse) that year was earmarked for export (*GWR* July 7, 1985:12). Cuba's educational assistance program may open up markets for Cuban paper products. In 1986 Cuba planned to export 14 million books. It exported textbooks to Angola and Nicaragua and reported demand for books on medicine, science, and pedagogy in Latin America (*GWR* July 6, 1986:7). Here too Western capital and technology were instrumental in developing export markets tied to Cuba's civilian assistance program. The French firm, Creusot-Loire, had been contracted to help manufacture paper, with repayment to be based on production (undoubtedly production for export, generating convertible currency).

There is no evidence that the Cuban government promoted aid with the explicit intent of generating trade, for, as we have seen, the aid is purportedly given for moral reasons. With time the government has at least attempted to make use of its aid programs to open up trade opportunities.

Gonzalez (1980:44), Roca (1980:60–63), and LeoGrande (1980:9) have argued that the main economic benefit accruing to the island from its overseas programs is not trade but increased Soviet aid. Though the Cuban economy unquestionably benefits from Soviet assistance, there is little evidence substantiating the authors' claims that Soviet aid has been contingent on Cuban overseas involvements; if the aid were so contingent, it would validate the Soviet surrogate thesis, adding only that the Soviet Union uses a carrot as well as stick strategy to mobilize the Cubans to assume a proxy role. In the 1970s Soviet technical assistance to Cuba increased, and the Soviet Union heavily subsidized sugar and nickel exports from and oil imports to the island. But the superpower cut back the oil subsidy following post-1973 Organization of Petroleum Exporting Countries (OPEC) price hikes, and it even charged above world market prices in the mid-1980s. Moreover, Soviet financial aid did not rise after Cuba stepped up its internationalist activities in Angola and Ethiopia. The superpower offered Cuba more new and inexpensive financing in 1972 than later in the decade. The two possible Soviet payoffs for the massive expansion of Cuba's internationalist commitments in the mid-1970s were a record high sugar subsidy and new military material. The Soviet Union had raised the sugar subsidy in the mid-1970s when the world sugar prices skyrocketed, and it did not lower the subsidy when world sugar prices plunged later in the decade. The Soviets provided Cuba, in turn, with major new weapons in the early 1980s. Though the new deliveries may be a reward for Cuba's overseas proxy activity, they may also have been designed to help Cuba fend off new Reagan administration security threats. Thus, there is no convincing evidence substantiating the claims that Cuban internationalism has resulted in Soviet subsidies that would otherwise not have been forthcoming or that Cuba has promoted foreign assistance so as to increase material payoffs from the superpower.

If the foreign aid program stimulated little trade, at least until the 1980s, and little Soviet aid that otherwise would not have been forthcoming, it has opened up some investment opportunities and more substantial foreign exchange–generating opportunities. The principal investment door that materialized from island aid programs was in Angola. There, Cuba acquired permission both to fish within the country's rich fishing waters and to establish a base for fishing off the Western African coast (Pérez-López 1980:81). Although fishing still accounts for a small portion of Cuba's national product, it is one of the island's most dynamic economic sectors.

Of greater economic significance is the hard currency that Cuba receives from foreign assistance programs, above all from civilian contacts. The precise revenue generated by the programs is not publicly known; available evidence undoubtedly underestimates actual earnings. The island began charging wealthier countries for projects in 1977. That year Cubans overseas generated an estimated $50 million in hard currency, the equivalent of 9 percent of the value of Cuba's 1977 commodity exports to Western countries (Theriot and Matheson 1979:556, 567). The revenue from programs and its importance as a source of hard currency earnings subsequently increased; however, the amount of money generated from the programs appears to vary considerably from year to year. Thus, in 1979 Cuba received $115 million for a construction and technical aid contract with Libya and $25 million for another contract with Angola (Roca 1980:66). The two agreements alone generated 18 percent of the value of Cuba's 1979 hard currency trade (Theriot 1981).

Available evidence suggests, though, that the earnings generated by overseas programs and their importance, relative to hard currency earnings from commodity trade, declined the following year: According to a Department of Commerce source, Cuba's overseas activities generated some $100 million in 1980, 6 percent of the value of the island's commodity exports to the West (Theriot 1981; Theriot, personal communication). In 1981 Cuba seems to have fared better: Cuba allegedly received $250 million just for its military and civilian operations in Angola (*New York Times* October 3, 1981:20).

Some aid initially provided free of charge has resulted in subsequent hard currency contracts. In particular, military aid provided gratis has paved the way for foreign exchange generating civilian contracts. This appears to have been true in Angola. However, free civilian aid has also resulted in revenue-generating contracts. In the Congo, for example, a donation of a plant to build prefabricated housing led to a contract to construct a highway and several farms and towns (*GWR* February 27, 1983:9).

Yet money-making ventures at times have been turned into donations. According to an official source, in 1983 the island received "favorable financing terms" for a contract to build a sugar mill in Nicaragua, primarily with Cuban machinery (*GWR* April 3, 1983:12). Two years later, though, Cuba reportedly converted a $73 million investment in a new Nicaraguan sugar factory into a donation; the loan was to have been paid back over twelve years (EIU February 1985:16).

Both technical assistance and construction work have been sources of invisible hard currency earnings. Cuba has established a special state agency, the Union de Empresas Constructoras Caribe (Uneca) to attain overseas construction projects. Uneca even advertises for foreign contracts. Between 1977 and 1984 Uneca secured assignments worth over $400 million (EUI Annual Supplement 1985:25, 26). The 1985 plan provided for overseas construction worth an additional 36 million pesos (with Uneca responsible for about half the work), along with 1,195.9 million pesos in convertible currency commodity exports.

Cuba needs foreign exchange to purchase goods from, and to repay debts to, Western countries. Trade with Western countries expanded markedly when world market sugar prices reached a record high in 1974, and Western bloc countries were willing, under the circumstances, to purchase Cuban sugar. Cuba took advantage of the opportunity to purchase Western products that CMEA either does not offer or offers only in inferior quality. But Cuba's capacity to pay for the Western imports with exports deteriorated in the latter 1970s when world sugar prices plunged. Cuba produces few goods, other than sugar, that it can market in the West. Political more than economic constraints limit its export options. In particular, its close, "natural" large market, the United States, refuses to trade with the island. Cuba's problems were also compounded in the late 1970s by soaring Western interest rates, which drove up the cost of servicing outstanding Western debts. As a consequence, the island's hard currency debt rose from $660 million in 1974 to $2.6 billion by 1980 (Eckstein 1986:515). Precisely when the debt became problematic Cuba expanded its foreign assistance program and began to charge, in convertible currencies, for some of its activities. Even though the aid programs are not the main source of hard currency earnings, they generate much needed and coveted foreign exchange. Moreover, Cuba would like very much to earn more foreign exchange from such programs.

Domestic Opportunity Costs

All countries experience domestic opportunity costs when they export goods, capital, and personnel, and Cuba, as an underdeveloped country, is no exception. The island unquestionably could benefit from use of all possible resources to improve its economy. Sergio Roca (1980) argued that the economic costs of Cuba's overseas ventures outweigh the gains, at least in Africa where Cuba has been most involved. In what ways are Cuba's overseas activities a drain on the economy?

The island incurs costs from its military program. Even though the Soviets provide Cuba and Cuban internationalists with weaponry free of charge, Cuba's military establishment is costly to maintain. Indeed, available evidence suggests that no other Latin American country commits as high a percentage of its gross product to military expenditures as does Cuba (Wilkie 1978:144). Even though a good portion of Cuba's military expenditures undoubtedly go to domestic defense, the military budget did increase more than the national budget between the eve of the Angolan war and 1978, when Cuba's overseas military commitments expanded considerably and domestic security was not a major concern (Domínguez 1980:24).

The military aid program, in addition, utilizes labor that could otherwise be deployed in civilian activity. Since overseas missions draw upon reservists, they drain the country of civilian human resources. For this reason, some enterprise managers have apparently been reluctant to release employees for internationalist assignments (Domínguez 1978b; 1979a; 1979b:84–85).

Although output in some enterprises may suffer when reservists go abroad, the foreign aid program expanded at a time of growing unemployment. Unlike in the 1960s when there was a shortage of labor (largely because of low labor efficiency and a smaller percentage of the labor force economically active), in the late 1970s around 5 percent of the labor force was estimated to be unemployed (Brundenius 1984:135). Since the Cuban government (unlike governments in other Latin American countries) pays generous unemployment compensation, internationalist costs do not necessarily significantly outweigh labor costs that it otherwise would incur, and the economic gains from the programs may exceed the costs in the long if not the short run.

By the 1970s, when the foreign aid program came to involve tens of thousands of cadre, the quality as well as the size of the labor force had changed. The educational level of the children of Castro's Cuba by then had been significantly upgraded. Thus, the civilian component of the foreign aid program, which draws on skilled labor, expanded at a time when the supply of skilled labor was at a record high. Skilled labor had been in short supply in the early revolutionary years not merely because the average educational level was then much lower but also because many professionals emigrated during Castro's first years of rule.

In terms of island shortages, Cuba can least afford to export construction workers. The government sends construction workers abroad despite housing shortages at home. The number of housing units constructed dropped as the size of overseas building brigades increased. The number had reached a record annual high of about 21,000 in 1973 (surpassed, under Castro, only in 1961), but it ranged between about 14,200 and 20,000 from 1974 to 1980 (Brundenius 1984:95). Sergio Roca estimated that the building personnel sent abroad could have built at least 8,000 units on the island in the late 1970s had they stayed at home (1980:73). However, he was incorrect in assuming that the internationalists would have expanded the housing stock had they remained in the country. Building depends not only on labor but also on material supplies and government construction priorities. And indeed, building supplies are scarce on the island. This material constraint became apparent in 1980 when the government announced that the only restriction on the use of work center profit funds would be housing construction, because of insufficient building supplies; the fund was established to stimulate enterprise productivity.

The Castro government sends large numbers of builders and supplies abroad, though they are in short supply domestically, because it can thereby generate foreign exchange. Its international building program is profitable, producing more hard currency revenue than other civilian programs (Roca 1980:60). To take advantage of the earning opportunities abroad the government not only allocates scarce domestic supplies to overseas projects but also sends its best workers abroad. It otherwise risks losing contracts, since the island must compete for foreign building contracts (Pérez-López 1980:83). Although in sending workers abroad the economy incurs undeniable losses and domestic demand for housing remains unresolved, the fiscal costs of a more isolationist strategy would be greater. The foreign exchange can be used for interest payments on the government's unpaid Western debt.

The island's supply of medical personnel and teachers, in contrast, is large by Third World standards. Consequently, the medical and educational components of the overseas programs probably have less direct negative effects on the economy than the internationalist construction projects. Nonetheless, health care and education standards can still stand to be improved. Cuba needs more teachers, for example, for the planned expansion of its secondary school system and more cadre for its ambitious family doctor program initiated in the 1980s.

Cubanologists have argued that both the civilian and the military programs have adversely affected the country's overall development capacity (see Roca 1980:74–75; Mesa-Lago 1979:178; Blasier 1980:38; Domínguez 1980:25). The domestic economic growth rate, which had reached a record postrevolutionary high in the early 1970s, indeed declined when the island's overseas commitments expanded. However, the drop in export earnings, with the decline in world market sugar prices from over $.60 a pound in November 1974 to $.08 two years later, plus the rapid rise in import costs and interest payments on the country's Western foreign debt, undoubtedly contributed more to the economic contraction than the expansion of overseas programs. Moreover, the economy experienced a comeback in 1978, the peak year of the island's overseas military commitments (Roca 1980:57, 74). That year the island's growth rate, as measured by the gross social product, reached one of its highest postrevolutionary levels (9 percent). Although the growth rate might well have been higher had the tens of thousands of internationalists remained at home—because the large aid missions occurred at a time of growing domestic unemployment—their impact was kept at a minimum. Also, it must be kept in mind that the internationalists engaged in foreign exchange–generating programs contributed directly and immediately to the health of the economy, and internationalists who worked gratis may have helped pave the way for subsequent trade and money-making service contracts.

Finally, an assessment of the economic effect of Cuban internationalism must also consider foreign responses to the island's overseas involvements. Cuba would benefit, in particular, from an end to the U.S. trade embargo. In the mid-1970s Castro and U.S. businesspeople had begun to discuss trade and investment possibilities, and political relations between the two countries had begun to thaw. However, by the end of the decade business and diplomatic discussions cooled. Cuba's widescale aid to Ethiopia unquestionably contributed to the diplomatic tensions, but the response of the business community was rooted primarily in deteriorating economic opportunities in Cuba. Although Cuban trade with the West expanded dramatically in the mid-1970s, Cuba's hard-currency crisis compelled the government to restrict Western imports later in the decade. U.S. businesses had benefited from the Western opening because they had traded with Cuba through their overseas subsidiaries.

Certain of Cuba's overseas involvements seem, in contrast, to have impaired Havana's relations with other Western countries. In particular, Cuba's military involvements in Africa may have contributed to the suspension, reduction, or nonrenewal of island economic and technical aid from Sweden, Holland, Norway, West Germany, and Canada between 1976 and 1978 (Mesa-Lago 1982:140).

In sum, Cuba's overseas programs entail certain domestic costs, but they generate needed foreign exchange earnings and they seem to have opened up, with time, some trade channels. Since the Soviet bloc does not provide all the goods and services that the Cubans want, Cuba has material interests in maintaining and expanding at least its money-making overseas programs. In this respect, the weakness of the Soviet economic bloc has been a driving force behind Cuban internationalism, not the strength of the Soviet Union to impose its will on Cuba, as proponents of the Soviet surrogate thesis contend. There is no evidence that Cuba's aid programs during Castro's first decade and a half of rule were premised on such economic considerations, but once faced with a Western debt crisis in the latter 1970s Cuba sought to promote internationalism for economic and not merely moral or geopolitical ends. Recognizing the limits of its Western commodity export market, Cuba ingeniously restructured and expanded its ideologically legitimated "international proletarianism" to improve its economic relations with the West. The Cuban government obviously has a vested interest in promoting a program that serves such diverse interests simultaneously.

Future Prospects of Cuba's Foreign Exchange–Generating Overseas Involvements

Given Cuba's failure to diversify commodity exports, its persistent need for foreign exchange, and the qualities of the domestic labor force, the overseas civilian program is creative and sensible. The revolutionary government has been exceptionally successful at human resources development, to the point that Cuba can afford—more than other Third World countries—to export trained personnel. Also, it can do so at a low cost. How viable, though, is the foreign aid program as a long-term economic strategy? Although the continued impressive expansion of higher education implies that the country can afford, more than other Third World countries, to export its human capital, the prospects for expanding its money-making internationalist programs hinge more on global political events than on domestic resource developments and domestic priorities.

Domestic support appears to be no obstacle to the aid program. Though some Cubans may be averse to additional overseas military activities, especially as friends and family are killed on overseas assignments, the island's overseas civilian programs seem to have widespread domestic support. Cuban surveys report that more than 300,000 persons had been willing to go to Angola and Ethiopia (*GWR* March 16, 1980:2) and, when Castro called for volunteers to serve in Nicaragua in 1980, 29,500 teachers offered to go (*GWR* March 16, 1980:2). Official sources also report that when some Cuban teachers were murdered by counterrevolutionaries in Nicaragua 100,000 Cubans volunteered to take their place—nearly all those up to thirty-five years of age (*GWR* June 22, 1986:2). Cubans no doubt rally to internationalist calls for moral reasons but also for adventure and material and political rewards. As previously noted, the government offers overseas workers a variety of economic incentives, and internationalists receive special consideration for membership in the highly selective Communist party.

Although there thus far appears to be domestic support for internationalism, the expansion of Cuba's foreign aid program requires a proliferation of friendly progressive governments in the Third World. Industrialized countries are unlikely to be interested in Cuban technical assistance; they have their own trained personnel. The non–left-leaning Third World regimes are likely to feel threatened by at least certain of Cuba's programs, and the capitalist development models to which they adhere generally assign low priority to the very social services that Cuba can best afford to provide. Third World capitalist countries generally emphasize short-run economic gains, not long-term investment in human resource development. The governments opposed to Castro's politics are undoubtedly reluctant to allow Cubans to work in the economically depressed rural areas of their countries. The Cubans might foment revolutionary turmoil there.

Yet the world recession of the early 1980s contributed to a cutback in contracts even from friendly governments. In 1984, Cuba reduced its troop strength in Ethiopia, both because the cadre were no longer needed and because they were too costly for the Ethiopian government to support. That same year the Cuban government considered withdrawing troops from Angola, apparently in part because the war-torn impoverished nation had trouble meeting its payments (*Boston Globe* March 13, 1984:1, 6).

Cultural barriers further limit Cuba's internationalist options, especially in the field of education. Cultural barriers are least in Spanish-speaking

Latin America. The common religious, linguistic, and general Spanish heritage that the Cubans and Nicaraguans share may help explain the speed with which the Sandinistas turned to Cuba for aid after Anastasio Somoza was ousted. However, cultural as well as political differences have kept Cuba from getting many Middle Eastern labor contracts. Oil-rich Arab states have hosted millions of foreign laborers and their families since 1973, following OPEC price hikes.

Global political constraints also constricted Cuba's internationalist options in the 1980s. The U.S. invasion of Grenada in 1983 brought the 784-person operation there to an abrupt halt, and the Sandinistas soon after reduced the size of their Cuban mission out of fear of a U.S. invasion. The Grenadian experience also prompted Suriname's president to order all Cuban diplomats and advisers to leave and to suspend all educational and cultural agreements with Havana. Government officials and outside observers reported that the Cuban ambassador had been involved in all aspects of government (*New York Times* January 10, 1984:2).

U.S. pressure threatens Cuban projects in other parts of the world as well. In particular, the Reagan administration insists that Angola oust all Cuban troops before it will either support Namibian independence or establish diplomatic relations with the former Portuguese colony. Although Angola has thus far refused to acquiesce to the pressure, since 1984 the Cuban government has considered withdrawing its troops from Angola in conjunction with peace agreements for southern Africa (*Boston Globe* March 13, 1984:1).

Thus, Cuba's capacity to advance both its ideological commitment to internationalist solidarity and its material interests in hard currency–generating overseas activity accordingly depend on the proliferation of Third World governments that both want and can afford to contract Cuba for assistance. It is contingent, in turn, on reduced U.S. pressure to isolate, in Reagan's words, the "communist virus."

References

Adams, Gordon. 1981. "Cuba and Africa: The International Politics of Liberation Struggle—a Documentary Essay." *Latin American Perspectives* (winter):109–112.

del Aguila, Juan M. 1984. *Cuba: Dilemmas of a Revolution.* Boulder: Westview Press.

Blasier, Cole. 1979. "The Soviet Union in the Cuban-American Conflict." In Cole Blasier and Carmelo Mesa-Lago, eds., *Cuba in the World.* Pittsburgh: University of Pittsburgh Press, pp. 37–52.

———. 1980. "Comment: The Consequences of Military Initiatives." *Cuban Studies* 10 (January):37–42.

Brundenius, Claes. 1984. *Revolutionary Cuba: The Challenge of Economic Growth with Equity.* Boulder: Westview Press.

Castro, Fidel. 1985. "Cuba's Internationalist Volunteers in Angola." *New International* 2, no. 2 (fall):119–135.

Domínguez, Jorge. 1978. "The Cuban Operation in Angola: Costs and Benefits for the Armed Forces." *Cuban Studies* (January):10–20.

———. 1979a. "The Armed Forces and Foreign Relations." In Cole Blasier and Carmelo Mesa-Lago, eds., *Cuba in the World.* Pittsburgh: University of Pittsburgh Press, pp. 53–86.

———. 1979b. "Cuban Military and National Security Policies." In Martin Weinstein, ed., *Revolutionary Cuba in the World Arena.* Philadelphia: Institute for the Study of Human Issues, pp. 77–98.

———. 1980. "Political and Military Limitations and Consequences of Cuban Policies in Africa." *Cuban Studies* 10 (July):1–35.

Durch, William. 1977. "The Cuban Military in Africa and the Middle East." Occasional Paper no. 201. Arlington, Va.: Center for Naval Analysis.

Eckstein, Susan. 1980. "Capitalist Constraints on Cuban Socialist Development." *Comparative Politics* (April):253–274.

———. 1986. "The Impact of the Cuban Revolution: A Comparative Perspective." *Comparative Studies in Society and History* 28 (July):502–534.

Economist Intelligence Unit (EIU). 1976–1986. *Country Report: Cuba, the Dominican Republic, Haiti, Puerto Rico* (quarterly).

Elliot, Jeffrey, and Mervyn Dymally, eds. 1986. *Fidel Castro: Nothing Can Stop the Course of History.* New York: Pathfinder.

Erisman, H. Michael. 1985. *Cuba's International Relations: The Anatomy of a Nationalistic Foreign Policy.* Boulder: Westview Press.

Gonzalez, Edward. 1980. "Comment: Operational Goals of Cuban Policy in Africa." *Cuban Studies* 10 (January):43–48.

Granma Weekly Review (GWR). 1978–1986.

LeoGrande, William. 1980. "Cuban-Soviet Relations and Cuban Policy in Africa." *Cuban Studies* 10 (January):1–37.

———. 1982. "Foreign Policy: The Limits of Success." In Jorge Domínguez, ed., *Cuba: Internal and International Affairs.* Beverly Hills, Calif.: Sage, pp. 167–192.

Maingot, Anthony. 1983. "Cuba and the Commonwealth Caribbean: Playing the Cuban Card." In Barry Levine, ed., *The New Cuban Presence in the Caribbean.* Boulder: Westview Press, pp. 19–42.

Marcus, Bruce, and Michael Taber. 1983. *Maurice Bishop Speaks: The Grenada Revolution, 1979–83.* New York: Pathfinder Press.

Mesa-Lago, Carmelo. 1979. "The Economy and International Relations." In Cole Blasier and Carmelo Mesa-Lago, eds., *Cuba in the World.* Pittsburgh: University of Pittsburgh Press, pp. 169–198.

Pérez-López, Jorge. 1980. "Comment: Economic Costs and Benefits of African Involvement." *Cuban Studies* 10 (July):80–85.

Roca, Sergio. 1980. "Economic Aspects of Cuban Involvement in Africa." *Cuban Studies* 10 (January):50–80.

Smith, Wayne. 1985. "U.S.-Cuba Relations: Twenty-Five Years of Hostility." In Sandor Halebsky and John Kirk, eds., *Twenty-Five Years of Revolution: 1959 to 1984.* New York: Praeger, pp. 333–351.

Theriot, Lawrence. 1981. "1980 Estimated Cuban Hard Currency Income." U.S. Department of Commerce, International Trade Administration, Department of East-West Trade. Typescript.

Theriot, Lawrence, and Jenelle Matheson. 1979. "Soviet Economic Relations with Non-European CMEA: Cuba, Vietnam, and Mongolia," Soviet Economy in a Time of Change. Washington, D.C.: Joint Economic Commission of the U.S. Congress (October).

10

Revolution and Paradigms:
A Critical Assessment
of Cuban Studies

Nelson P. Valdés

Things are not what they seem.
—Peter Berger

Ideas and categories are not more eternal than the relations which they express.
They are historical and transitory products.
—Karl Marx

No existe nada químicamente puro.
—Edmundo Desnoes

The Cuban Revolution is twenty-eight years old. So is the profession that has dedicated its efforts to studying it. Today, we know much more about the Revolution than about the scholars who have written about it. We do not possess a history or a sociology of Cubanologists—the body of professionals who dissect, describe, and explain the Cuban Revolution.

This chapter seeks to raise some pertinent questions about Cubanology. The intention is not to present a thorough and systematic history or sociology of the field. Nor is this an ideological critique of the authors reviewed. Rather, the chapter raises questions related to the concepts, models, theories, and methods found in the study of the Cuban Revolution. I hope that this discussion will initiate the necessary process of self-knowledge and self-criticism required in any area of the social sciences and the humanities.

Classifying Cubanology

The literature on the Cuban Revolution has grown by leaps and bounds since 1959. Over the years numerous authors have offered different ways of organizing this vast literature. As a rule, works have been classified on the basis of the authors' political preferences or the subject described.

In 1969, two authors Nelson P. Valdés and Edwin Lieuwen organized a bibliography on the Revolution using a simple geopolitical perspective. They classified works on the basis of whether they were for or against the Revolution. They went further to engage in a sort of geographic determinism. They wrote, "In fact, the place of publication usually indicates the bias of the author" (Valdés and Lieuwen 1969:1). A few years later, James Nelson Goodsell suggested that the published material on Cuba available in the United States was of three types: (1) the exploratory personal journalistic-witness type; (2) the detailed studies that answered why Cuba became Communist and joined the USSR; (3) what he described as the sophisticated and dispassionate approach. Sadly, he gave us no examples of any of the types.

In 1978 an informal classification was introduced by Anthony Maingot, who divided works into four clusters. He said,

> The first [cluster] is composed of those works written between 1959 and 1962 with the central concern being "why the Revolution" and "why it is or why it isn't going Communist. . . ." A second cluster is composed of the work of the disillusioned, disappointed, and or defeated. By 1970, there appeared a third cluster: foreigners basically sympathetic to the revolutionary process but critical. . . . A fourth and final cluster is not identified by time or specific theme but rather by the fact that the authors are Cuban exiles bent on producing serious scholarship on it. (Maingot 1978:227)

The problem with this particular classification is that it used totally different categories to differentiate works: subject matter (first cluster), political stance (second cluster), national origins and political stance (third cluster), and situational status and nature of scholarship (fourth cluster). Maingot only provided examples of the fourth cluster.

By 1981 William LeoGrande made the point that "the study of Cuba has traditionally been more ideographic than analytic," but he did not apply these categories to the literature available then (LeoGrande 1981:188). Four years later, the historian Louis A. Pérez surveyed twenty-five years of scholarship on Cuba. He concluded that there had been several stages in the study of the Revolution. He classified those stages and their nature as follows: (1) polemical works with a policy orientation (early years of the Revolution), (2) emigre literature (also in the early years), (3) scholarly works with a polemical tint (in the 1960s), (4) scholarly synthesis with an emphasis in history (during the 1970s), and (5) specialized works (from the mid-1970s to the present). According to Pérez, "it has been the literature of specialization that has prevailed in the last 15 years" (Pérez 1985:401).

There seems to be a consensus that a significant shift has taken place in Cuban studies: The field is now dominated by professional scholars. It is unclear, however, whether professionalism here means a more scientific or objective comprehension of the Revolution. The question, however, is whether the emergence of a professional language hides in a more complex and sophisticated mantle of political/ideological preferences.

The Absence of Explicit Method

Scholars dealing with the Revolution, or those reviewing their work, have shared a strong aversion to considering or even discussing the premises, concepts, logic, framework, or theoretical perspectives their works had. This is not surprising. The literature on Cuba has been permeated by so much political polemic that scholars have preferred to remain silent about the method they have utilized or the paradigm guiding their investigation and analytical logic. Declaring such method has become tantamount to losing objectivity or to lacking serious scholarship.

Maurice Halperin in his book, *The Rise and Decline of Fidel Castro*, expressed this attitude well. He wrote: "The book needs no further explanation. . . . It should 'explain' itself, and if it fails to do so, no extended commentary on my part concerning aims, methods . . . and so on will be of much value" (M. Halperin 1972:ix). Bias, supposedly, was avoided by this decision. Objectivity, it was assumed, would be achieved by just presenting "the facts." The myth of empiricism thus reigned supreme.

Others equated a stated methodology or theoretical clarity with value preferences. Cole Blasier wrote:

> My approach to this subject was not facilitated or burdened by explicit doctrinaire predispositions. Conservative, liberal and radical writers all have made arguments of one sort or another which I consider persuasive, but I do not identify totally with any single school—no doubt partly because these terms are vague labels which serve as useful shorthand. (Blasier 1976:xvi)

Thus, theoretical paradigm and political positions have been defined as identical. Authors often prefer to be unattached and consequently "free and objective." Whether the truth of an argument is the result of the persuasive power of an argument or the product of accuracy, validity, and verification does not seem to be part of the scientific method.

Again, all that is necessary is to "gather the facts," and the facts will speak for themselves. The context in which the facts take place, or why some facts may be more significant than others, is not as important. Andrés Suárez in his 1967 book disclosed in his preface the approach: "The analysis and description of the sociological milieu has been reduced to the strictly necessary, while major emphasis is placed on the events, both external and internal, of the development of the revolution" (Suárez 1967:xiv).

Empiricism does not free us from philosophical assumptions or from ideological preferences; it merely hides them from the reader and perhaps even from the writer. E. H. Carr in his famous essay, "What Is History?" disposed of such assumptions many years ago, but Cuban studies are somewhat provincial on such matters.

The Search for Impartiality

Studies on the Cuban Revolution have not been classified by method, model, or theory. The majority of the authors have not disclosed any of these. Some, however, have felt compelled to let us know their value preferences. This is a welcome practice, one that appears to take seriously the call made by Gunnar Myrdal many years ago.

In the 1978 preface to one of his books, Jorge I. Domínguez stated,

> Since all works of scholarship, even those that strive for impartiality, as this one does, are affected to some degree by the writers' own views, biases, and ideology, the reader of this book may find it helpful to know a few pertinent facts about my life. . . . Awareness of my ideological framework may be important in judging the information offered here. (Domínguez 1978:ix)

A similar approach was used by Carmelo Mesa-Lago in a book dealing with the Cuban economy in the 1980s. He wrote,

> In my writing, I have tried to assume a relatively detached, balanced, and objective attitude. And yet my value framework and legal training favors political pluralism and civil freedoms as well as social justice, while my economic training emphasizes efficiency and economic rationality. (Mesa-Lago 1981:207)

A few authors, from a left political position, have informed the readers of their value choices. But they have not claimed that by doing so they were attempting to achieve some higher level of objectivity and impartiality. Instead, they recognized that their perspectives shaped the very nature of their work. Samuel Farber is a case in point. He noted that he owed it to his readers to state clearly his political standpoint "from which I have examined and analyzed the data" (Farber 1976:xii).

The critical issue, however, is not to simply state one's values in a preface and then go on with the scholarly work. A. R. Louch pointed out that many social scientists tend to think of values as "subtle and dangerous" obstacles in the business of "objective description of human action." Authors may "feel that if they set their values to one side, articulate them, and isolate them in a preface all will be well" (Louch 1969:56).

But all is not well. Values shape academic work, including the subject matter to be investigated, the definition of the problem, the concepts used to deal with it, the material gathered to support the argument, and even the conclusions reached. Yet, in Cuban studies these are questions seldom raised. Adrienne Cheasty and Carlos F. Díaz Alejandro did so, in passing, in a review essay on the Cuban economy. They stated that "few people can be neutral on Cuba." And added that "ideology may be expected to influence not only the authors' conclusions, but also the way they tackle their subject" (Cheasty and Díaz 1983:80–81).

Cubanologos, like many political scientists, want to collect facts, organize them, and make some sense of them all. They are not concerned with disputing theoretical foundations that justify or support their work. Consequently, no one talks of paradigms or theories (Wolin 1968:131).

Cuban Studies: Levels of Analysis and Research Agendas

The study of the Cuban Revolution can be characterized as encompassing three levels of interest. From 1959 to the late 1960s the dominant level was the international dimension of the Revolution. Works abound on U.S.-Cuban relations, Soviet-Cuban relations, or the overall impact that exogenous political or economic variables had on Cuba's internal economy or politics. In the late 1960s and early 1970s a totally different level began to attract interest. Cuba was studied on its own internal context, tracing the continuity of its history or the peculiarities of its development. The Cuban Revolution as a national phenomenon became very important. Numerous studies were produced dealing with the economy, politics, culture, or society. Of less impact we find a third variant: studies that concentrated on local matters. This is the least developed line of study. It began in the late 1960s and has continued, with some difficulty, to the present.

Works dealing with international and/or national issues have not relied on research inside Cuba. The same is not true for local studies. Consequently, most of the works of a local type have had a very different methodology than the other two. Moreover, as a rule, they have been fairly "radical" (in a political sense).

By the 1980s a veritable explosion of works on Cuba appeared. It was no longer possible to identify the historical moment with a given set of issues and questions. The number of scholars involved in the study of Cuba increased as well. The virtual monopoly exercised by Cuban emigre scholars in the 1970s began to be challenged by North American as well as European analysts.

Interestingly, the center of gravity of Cuban studies—which had been located at the Latin American Studies Center at the University of Pittsburgh under the direction of Carmelo Mesa-Lago—also began to change. Two new university contenders appeared: Johns Hopkins University created its own Cuban studies program under the guidance of Wayne Smith, former U.S. representative to Cuba during the Carter years. The other contender had the backing of the U.S. government under the Reagan administration and established close ties with the Radio Martí Program at the University of Miami. The director of the Cuba Project there is Jaime Suchlicki. Thus, the search for "impartiality" represented by Pittsburgh was challenged by a liberal program at Johns Hopkins and a conservative one at the University of Miami.

It remains to be seen, nonetheless, which of the three programs determines the agenda of Cuban studies in the future. If money is to be the key determinant, then the University of Miami should be in command. It should be noted that the program directed by Mesa-Lago publishes the highly regarded journal *Cuban Studies*. Johns Hopkins University produces occasional papers. The University of Miami seems to be much more active, sponsoring conferences, symposia, and a monograph series.

Finally, two private institutions should be mentioned as well: the Instituto de Estudios Cubanos, presided over by Maria Cristina Herrera, and the Center for Cuban Studies, under the direction of Sandra Levinson. Both institutions were established in 1969 and function on the basis of donations. The Instituto de Estudios Cubanos (IEC) began as an effort to understand the Cuban Revolution through the efforts of Cuban emigre scholars in the United States and elsewhere. The Center for Cuban Studies (CCS), based in New York City, has been a strong supporter of the Revolution. Most of the work by Cuban emigre scholars (such as Carmelo Mesa-Lago, Jorge Domínguez, Sergio Roca, Jorge Pérez-López, Juan del Aguila, Marifeli Pérez Stable, and many others) is discussed within IEC before it is published or discussed elsewhere. Recently IEC opened its membership to non-Cubans. The CCS is possibly the most active of all Cuba-related concerns. It organizes conferences, film showings, tours, and numerous other activities. It also publishes a newsletter, "Cuba Update."

Cuban Studies and the Importance of Paradigms

Whatever the focus of analysis or the research agenda, it is essential to be aware of the importance paradigms have in analytical work. Such paradigms have been present in the literature on the Cuban Revolution but only in an implicit form. It is the intent of this chapter to point out some of the features of the dominant paradigms in the fields of international relations and political power in Cuba. The treatment given here is not exhaustive. The intention is to initiate discussion on these issues.

A paradigm is understood as a single, generally accepted view about a phenomenon and the proper procedure of investigating and researching it. A paradigm provides a set of concepts, assumptions, and even ways of getting data on a subject. Once the paradigm is accepted, it rules the discipline and defines any further practice. (If some people do not accept the paradigm, they are not accepted by the community of scholars or if accepted only in a peripheral manner; because they are dissidents their work may be considered naive or, worse yet, "ideological" by those who accept the paradigm.)

A paradigm, once accepted by a significant majority within a discipline or area of study, is assumed to be scientific and objective. The language and the logic of the paradigm is borrowed by the practitioners (Bernstein 1976:84–90). A paradigm determines what is to be considered a fact as well as the criteria for what is important. Robert W. Friedrichs wrote:

> With the paradigmatic base thus secured, the group or community [of scholars] turns its attention to what is essentially mop-up work. Members focus on those facts and theories that are seen as most relevant in the paradigm's terms. . . . The few who would still operate in terms of other paradigms are simply ignored, for the discipline has concluded that there is no other scientifically justified stance for the given area. . . . A scientist perceives little of this process self-consciously. His professional education takes place, typically, within the confines of a single paradigm. The structures

that guide him are simply the way his science is. . . . The "rules" he lives by are raised to the level of consciousness only if and when the paradigm itself is shaken. Only then does he begin to subject them to critical examinations and admit debate about them (Friedrichs 1970:5)

Do we then find a dominant paradigm in the study of the Cuban Revolution? A negative answer would appear to be the logical reply. Often those who have written on the subject have made no reference to any explicit theory of society or politics. But a paradigm can exist even if there is no explicit statement about any theoretical framework. We can determine the existence of a paradigm by searching for some of the domain assumptions in a given work or, at least, by looking for some indications of assumed premises.

In a paradigm we have domain assumptions. By domain assumptions is meant "beliefs about the world that are so general that they may, in principle, be applied to any subject matter without restriction" (Gouldner 1970:30). Domain assumptions provide the terms of reference with which the world is interpreted. They refer to the dispositions to believe a particular thing and then the search for data to prove that the belief is correct.

To understand the character of Cubanology it is imperative to understand the domain assumptions with which it functions and works. Or as Alvin Gouldner told us, "The most basic changes in any science commonly derive not so much from the invention of new research techniques but rather from new ways of looking at data that may have long existed" (Gouldner 1970:34). The answer, consequently, has to be in the affirmative: There is a paradigm in Cuban studies. Let us then look at some of the domain assumptions found in studies of Cuban foreign policy as well as in the nature of the revolutionary political system.

Cuban Foreign Policy Studies:
Basic Postulates

Studies on Cuban foreign policy are not guided by any explicit theory. Works are narrative, descriptive, and inductive. The literature tends to neglect the socioeconomic basis of foreign policy. More often than not, foreign policy has been construed as the expression of a static internal order. If there are changes in Cuban foreign policy, and there have been many, they do not result from changes within the socioeconomic system; rather they are the manifestation of Fidel Castro's decision or of pressure from the Soviet Union.

Most studies on Cuban foreign policy, in fact, appear to share a series of postulates. Among them are the following:

POSTULATE 1: Fidel Castro is the key to understanding Cuba's relations with the world.

This particular view has had a long and healthy life in Cuban studies. A representative and succinct formulation of foreign policy as biography can be found in the recent work of Edward Gonzalez and David Rondfeldt (1986) where they stated, "To understand Cuban foreign policy, one must first understand Fidel Castro" (Gonzalez and Rondfeldt 1986:1). Jorge Domínguez expressed the same sentiment when he stated that Fidel Castro "has been decisive for most issue areas" (Domínguez 1978:420).

Subsumed under this postulate is the view that Cuba's foreign policy is guided by the logic of personalism, but the foreign policies of the superpowers are not. Former U.S. representative to Havana during the Carter years, Wayne Smith, stated that U.S.-Cuban relations were "a mix of Castro's goals and U.S. reaction to them that initially led him to align with the USSR" (Smith 1985:334). Cole Blasier, another scholar who has written on U.S. policy toward revolutions in Latin America, asked, "How did U.S. officials respond to Madero and Castro?" (Blasier 1976:7). Thus, the Third World has individuals shaping foreign policy while the developed countries possess unnamed, impersonal officials and, by implication, institutions.

POSTULATE 2: Fidel Castro's perceptions of the outside world are much more important in shaping foreign policy than the actual reality of those relations.

This view is known in the social science literature as the Thomas Theorem. U.S. sociologist W. I. Thomas once observed that "If men define situations as real, they are real in their consequences" (Merton 1967:19). Cole Blasier, following this theorem, asserted,

> The fact that the United States posed the greatest potential threat to Castro . . . does not mean that the United States actually did threaten Castro or use these pressures in 1959 and early 1960. . . . The United States government was relatively accommodating. . . . Castro's reason for concern during the early period was not so much due to what the United States had done, as to what it could do. . . . In a way, he [Castro] was already responding to what the United States would do, not to what it had done, thereby helping to fulfill his own dire prophecies (Blasier 1973:57)

Foreign policy turns out to be the manifestation of erroneous subjective perceptions by one person. In such "analyses" the United States, with a more realistic outlook, merely reacted to Fidel Castro. Cuban foreign policy, then, is personalistic, subjective, and erroneous. And to boot Fidel Castro acted in such a way that he compelled the United States to do what he wanted to avoid.

Some authors, although accepting the "perception" argument, end up asserting that the Cubans had a fairly realistic understanding of the world. W. Raymond Duncan wrote,

> Cuban perceptions of the Caribbean flow from operating principles in foreign policy held by Havana's decision-making elite. . . . In pursuance of power politics in foreign policy, the decision-making elite in Castro's government . . . can be characterized as basically realist in their perceptions of the external world. (Duncan 1979:141)

How these authors know what the perceptions of the Cuban authorities are we are not told. How the authors know whether those perceptions are erroneous or correct is never discussed. Epistemology is still a central part of Cubanology.

POSTULATE 3: *Cuban foreign policy is autonomous.*

There seems to be a fairly widespread consensus among scholars that Cuba has a worldwide foreign policy not consonant with its limited material resources. This is explained on the basis that the policy concurs with that of the Soviet Union. But Cuba's policy is not dictated by the Soviets. Even conservative scholars adhere to this view (Thomas et al. 1984b:11–13).

The concurrence of Cuban-Soviet interests thesis acknowledges that the USSR has influence over the revolutionary government in Havana, but nonetheless Fidel Castro (or Cuba) has a certain relative autonomy. What the structural basis of that autonomy is has never been clearly explained. Jorge I. Domínguez is perhaps the best exponent of the concurrence/autonomy thesis. He stated,

> This relationship [between Cuba and the USSR] has two fundamental characteristics each in some tension with the other: hegemony and autonomy. Evolving gradually since 1960, but most clearly since 1968, the Soviet Union has established its hegemony over Cuba. This has meant that a framework surrounds Cuba's foreign policy; Cuba will not transgress these boundaries. Differences between Cuban and Soviet policies, which surfaced in the 1960s, have gradually been eliminated (with some relatively minor exceptions).

Within that hegemonial framework, however, Cuba exercises considerable autonomy. Cuba launches important foreign policy initiatives and often leads the Soviets. . . . Hegemony means that Cuba takes no initiatives against Soviet interests; hegemony means, also, that there is extensive consultation, and that the hegemonial power provides considerable political, military and economic support for Cuba. But autonomy also means that Cuba exerts some leverage over the Soviet Union, at least enough to get the Soviet Union to behave differently than it would have, or did, otherwise. (Domínguez 1985:27)

How we know this to be the case is anyone's guess since Cuban-Soviet relations remain an area immersed in secrecy. Nonetheless, this is an impression that Cuba scholars seem to share—obviously a domain assumption.

POSTULATE 4: Cuban foreign policy expresses a set of unchanging principles and goals.

This postulate is perhaps the most widespread. It is accepted by people from all political perspectives. Authors may disagree on the specific principles or their ranking, but no one questions the existence of the principles or their constancy. The Cuban government itself proclaims that such principles exist. For example, a Cuban government official has noted that "general propositions . . . form the structure of our foreign policy." And he goes on to add that "the foreign policy of the Cuban revolution responds to an unyielding line of principles" (Yanez 1984:202, 204).

Some authors refer to these principles as "objectives" (William LeoGrande, Jorge I. Domínguez, Pamela Falk), "motivating factors" (W. Raymond Duncan), or "goals" (Edward Gonzalez). The terms may vary, but the principles, we are told, shape foreign policy. And the principles have not changed since 1959. Domínguez wrote, "Cuban foreign policy has had certain continuing characteristics" (Domínguez 1984:167). And Gonzalez stated, "Since coming to power in 1959, Castro's foreign policy has been characterized by a set of minimum defensive interests" (Gonzalez 1985a:74). Hugh Thomas stated the same: "Since coming to power Castro's priorities remain unchanged" (Thomas et al. 1984b:5).

What are those principles? There is no agreement on their number, ranking, or content. Those who tend to be friendly toward the Revolution usually stress security and "system maintenance," whereas those who are critical emphasize "personal power maintenance."

The system maintenance outlook can be found in the work of William LeoGrande. In a recent essay he affirmed that "since 1959, the first and foremost objective of all Cuban foreign policy has been the survival of the revolution. There have been other objectives, to be sure, but all have necessarily been subordinate to survival" (LeoGrande 1985:167). The priority given to survival is related in the literature to the threat posed by the United States. Consequently, we are told, all foreign policy matters revolve about that important goal.

On the other hand, critics of the Revolution do not seem to be very concerned with the security needs of the revolutionary regime or how the United States may threaten it. Critics place much greater stress on the preservation of power. Instead of national security, personal power is the key to foreign policy. English historian Hugh Thomas, for example, believed that the main principle in foreign policy has been to maintain "undiluted" Fidel Castro's power (Thomas 1984a:5). Similar views were held by Edward Gonzalez (Gonzalez 1985a:74) and Carmelo Mesa-Lago. The latter asserted, "Castro's record shows that, whenever there has been a choice between his country's independence and his own power, he has sacrificed the first for his own gain" (Mesa-Lago 1974:136). Statements of this kind may reveal much more about the domain assumptions of students of Cuba than the actual reality of the subject under analysis.

It would be an error to assume, however, that only conservative critics or self-professed detached scholars adopt the "preservation of personal power" outlook. At least one liberal commentator offered the same argument. Pamela S. Falk in her recent book on Cuban foreign policy maintained that "Castro has attempted to channel the Cuban perception of national interest . . . into a foreign policy that suits his personal ambitions, fosters Cuban unity and nationalism, and by and large, suits the Soviet Union" (Falk 1985:171).

Some disagreement also exists on the ranking of the revolutionary principles. If we were to use the two most representative exponents of each of the two perspectives (system maintenance as espoused by Jorge I. Domínguez and power maintenance as elucidated by Edward Gonzalez) we end up with two sets (see Table 10.1).

Domínguez suggested that the first two principles in the system maintenance outlook are primary whereas the rest are of a second order; they are subordinate to security and economic development. Personal power does not appear to play a significant role. Gonzalez disagreed. He distinguished between "maximum defensive interests" and "maximum goals." The first four principles constitute inmediate/minimum interests, whereas the last one is part of a long-range maximum goal (i.e., world revolution). Consequently, the power maintenance argument suggests that Cuban foreign policy is offensive in nature and stems from Fidel Castro's desire to control other countries.

TABLE 10.1
Principles in Cuban Foreign Policy

System Maintenance	Power Maintenance
1. Revolutionary survival	1. Maintain and enhance Castro's power
2. Economic development	2. Regime security
3. Influence governments abroad	3. Increase system autonomy from external control
4. Influence political movements abroad	4. Economic development
5. Support revolutions abroad	5. Foreign interventionism

In an article dealing with the Cuban and Soviet "challenge" in the Caribbean, Edward Gonzalez claimed that "Castro's imperial ambitions are the heart of Cuba's interventionist imperative" (Gonzalez 1985:75). Foreign policy or intervention thus is not the byproduct of some internal social, economic, or political dynamic. The ideas of neither John Hobson nor Vladimir Lenin are necessary to understand the process, for it is not structural. Nor is it based on a desire for national aggrandizement. Rather foreign policy arises from a psychological drive.

Oddly, both outlooks agree that Cuban foreign policy, which despite its shifts and turns has been constant in its adherence to the presumed principles. Domínguez said,

Over the years, Cuba has chosen, rather consistently, among alternative policies and paths as if it were following this hierarchy of goals. While the specifics of Cuban foreign policy have changed enormously since the revolutionary government came to power in January 1959, the pattern of choosing has remained remarkably steady. (Domínguez 1984:167–168)

Even if one were to grant that the Revolution has a set of principles that determines the framework for foreign policy, that hardly exhausts the issue. In fact, the literature under review assumes there is a harmony of interests among those principles. More important, those principles, if they exist, are mediated not only by their interpretation but by the very reality they address. The real question is how and why those principles, in whatever hierarchical order, are translated into particular policy options. What determines the choice of a given option over another? If Cuban security or power is the highest priority, why does the set of principles lead to closer relations with the United States at one point and not at another point.

POSTULATE 5: Cuban foreign policy has changed over time. As the Revolution gets older its foreign policy becomes more "mature."

This postulate suggests a relationship between foreign policy and the age of the Revolution. In other words, a sort of biological model has been used to describe the history of the policy. The "older" the Revolution gets, the less radical is its foreign policy. In the early years of the Revolution, we are told, Cuba had a "romantic and relatively unsophisticated policy" (LeoGrande 1985:169). Or as Mesa-Lago described it, foreign policy was "idealist" and "irrational" (Mesa-Lago 1981:179). But as the years went by, the Revolution matured and so did its foreign policy. Consequently, foreign policy became "realistic," "pragmatic," and "mature" (Robbins 1983).

Biological interpretations assume that time, by itself, has an impact on policy or those who make policy. But the relationship is inferred rather than demonstrated. It is possible that the Revolution has created a more complex and experienced foreign policy establishment with more training and division of labor. If professionalism has taken root within the realm of foreign policy formulation and application, it remains to be shown how that process has affected the content of policy.

Any assessment of works on Cuba and foreign policy will have to recognize that the literature is often overtaken by events. Every shift and turn in the relations between Cuba and the rest of the world has surprised scholars. No one predicted the Revolution's conflict with China (1966) or with the Communist parties of Latin America (1967–1968) or the clash with the USSR (1968) or its reversal soon thereafter.

The fact that Cuba had an African foreign policy was not obvious until troops were sent to Angola. Then many scholars rushed to look at this matter. The relations between Cuba and the nonaligned countries began in 1959. We did not notice for almost twenty years. Fidel Castro had to become the head of the Nonaligned movement before any studies were produced on the subject. And even now the gaps remain extraordinary. We do not yet have any works on Cuba's relations with Latin America, Western Europe, or Eastern Europe. The Cuban role in international organizations, including the United Nations, remains a virgin region. The reactive nature of scholarship is fairly evident in the flurry of current works concentrating on Cuba and Central America. Once a crisis disappears, the number of works on the subject dwindle. In a way this is to be expected: Cuban studies, like other area studies, are often conducted to answer immediate pressing questions.

Not long ago, Damian J. Fernández commented that the literature on Cuba and foreign policy, although often claiming to discuss and explain foreign relations, has little to say about the process of policymaking and decisionmaking: "Far from gaining insight into the origins and development of Cuban policy, we are left with a description of its obvious manifestations and a rationale for its motivation" (Fernández 1986:147–153). He could have added that behind the descriptions or after-the-fact rationales could be found many shared domain assumptions.

Future works on foreign policy need to question the domain assumptions that have shaped the tenor of the research agenda. More attention should be paid to the institutions and organizations involved in foreign policy as well as the connection that might exist between different regional policies. It is important to understand also the relationship between foreign policy and the economic needs of Cuban society. (The ties to Eastern Europe, Western Europe, or Japan in those terms have not been explored.) It is essential to challenge the implicit assumption that foreign policy is shaped only in a political arena without inputs from parts of the Cuban social system. And last, inference has to give way to concrete evidence.

National Studies on Cuba:
Main Assumptions

In the early years of the Cuban Revolution numerous works were produced that attempted to describe the nature of the political system. As a rule the works were polemical and only tangentially dealt with economic issues. The fundamental question that dominated scholarly (and not so scholarly) production was the "revolution betrayed" thesis. That debate attempted to study the social and political origins of the revolutionary movement (prior to 1959) and then to compare them with the political system that emerged after 1959.

The "revolution betrayed" thesis represented by Theodore Draper and Andrés Suárez countered the rightist claim by conservative Cuban exiles who charged that the Revolution had been a "Communist conspiracy" from the onset. A third, but less influential, perspective suggested that the Revolution had been "pushed into communism" by the United States. The latter thesis had adherents such as William Appleman Williams (Williams 1961). The Marxist interpretations of Robin Blackburn or James O'Connor went unnoticed, which was to be expected when paradigmatic questions shape a debate and some of the participants raise a whole set of different questions (Blackburn 1963; O'Connor 1970).

From the early 1960s until the early 1970s, the "revolution betrayed" thesis reigned supreme in Cuban national studies. Theodore Draper became the representative par excellence of this view. It should be noted that Draper had done previous work on the American Communist party, and he had been a Marxist years earlier. Consequently, Draper brought to the debate a high respect for theory as well as an interest on matters of social class. Draper, in other words, was aware of the theoretical framework he worked with—something forgotten by later scholars.

Draper was not an empiricist or an eclectic borrower of concepts and theories. In his book *Castroism: Theory and Practice*, he wrote:

> In this search for a more tenable social theory [of the Cuban Revolution], I have not always attempted to follow any chronological historical order. I have rather explored aspects of Cuban society or cited various events and statements as the need for them arose to clarify or support some point in the social analysis of the revolution. (Draper 1965:viii)

Soon after this work was published, however, Draper's explicit concern with theory was forgotten. An illustration is provided by Andrés Suárez who, in 1967, wrote a book that also greatly influenced Cuban national studies until the early 1970s. In his book Suárez adopted a chronological and descriptive approach and reduced the analytical and theoretical "to the strictly necessary" (Suárez 1967:xiv).

Ernst Halperin asserted in his foreword that "modern sociological interpretations of history, according to which the course of events is determined not by the discussion of individuals, but by the clash of powerful forces" cannot be applied to Cuba. "One man alone, Fidel Castro, is responsible for the course of events in Cuba" (Halperin, in Suárez 1967:viii). This kind of thinking set a trend for many years.

Despite their methodological differences, Draper and Suárez, as well as many who followed in their footsteps, shared some basic premises. A significant portion of the literature on the politics of the Cuban Revolution has concentrated on (1) Fidel Castro as the critical variable; (2) the ways by which he has held onto power, and (3) the ways in which he has dealt with internal crisis. A similar situation seems to hold for the study of the Soviet Union and Eastern Europe until fairly recently. Fred H. Eidlin told us:

> This descriptive literature reflects a central theoretical interest in the way East European leaders keep their hold on power. It reflects theoretical assumptions about where the principal threats to his control are likely to come from and the assumption that the question of "who rules?" in a Communist state and how he maintains his rule is one of the most important questions one can ask about such regimes. (Eidlin 1979:136)

This penchant for stressing the role of one individual in a historical process is not necessarily the result of the system under investigation, although that is what those who have adopted this particular mode of analysis usually claim. Juan Martínez Alier, in a trailblazing work, showed how social forces shaped agrarian reform policy in the early years of the Cuban Revolution (Martínez Alier 1972). In other words, Martínez Alier demonstrated the existence of interest groups in Cuba, the methods by which they articulated their interests, and the manner in which policy was affected. If others have not noticed this scholar's work, it may be because their paradigm assumptions forestall perceiving certain aspects of the political system.

All these indicate that authors are working with a set of premises about the nature of Cuban politics and society as well as about what aspects are significant. And those premises as well as the determination of significance are not value free. In fact, the literature suggests that numerous authors have worked with an implicit (and sometimes explicit) "totalitarian model."

The totalitarian model assumes that the entire social, economic, and political fabric of Cuban society is dominated by the state; that the state (depending on the period in question) has been dominated by the Communist party; and that the party is controlled by the Central Committee. The Central Committee follows the dictates of the Political Bureau, and the Political Bureau is a tool of Fidel Castro. Hence, the totalitarian model reduces every fact of the Cuban revolutionary process to the will of one person. With such a model politics actually disappears. (For a discussion of the totalitarian or directed-society model applied to the Soviet Union, see Hough 1972.)

There may be other elements at work here. First, it is much easier to trace political developments—in any society—by merely relying on the statements made by the leaders. Second, the nineteenth-century tradition in which history was merely biography may have some adherents as well. Thus, charismatic authority is turned into a modernized version of "the great men make history" approach.

Regardless of the reasons, the literature on the Cuban political system is often characterized by a series of premises and concepts. Among them can be found the following.

1. *The Cuban Political System Is Dominated by Fidel Castro.* Scholars, regardless of their specific treatment of the Cuban Revolution, seem to be part of a fairly widespread consensus. Early on Herbert Matthews wrote that "the Cuban Revolution is Fidel Castro's revolution" (Matthews 1969:15). A similar view was expressed by James Nelson Goodsell when he said, "In the first place, the Cuban revolution is in considerable measure a personal revolution, so much so that it is difficult to disassociate Castro and the revolution. . . . Almost all decisions of consequence in Cuba today depend on Castro personally" (Goodsell 1975:5).

And Lee Lockwood wrote, "Contemporary Cuban society is dominated in every conceivable way by Castro's mind and personality" (Lockwood 1969:xix). The same theme is echoed by Maurice Halperin when he affirmed that Castro's "personality, style and leadership have dominated the Cuban Revolution" (Halperin 1972:19).

Jorge Domínguez began his magnus opus on Cuba by saying, "Fidel Castro remains at the center of all politics and is the decisive figure not only for the legitimation of the system but often for affecting the minutiae of policy implementation" (Domínguez 1978:7). Juan M. del Aguila (1985:51) characterized the role of Fidel Castro within the political system as "hegemonic authority," and Robert A. Packenham (Packenham 1986:80) asserted that "within Cuba itself power centers, first and foremost, on Fidel Castro." Edward Gonzalez in 1985 wrote that "he still plays a vital role in the everyday governing of Cuban society" (Gonzalez 1985b:3). Finally, Tad Szulc in his 1986 biography of Fidel Castro claimed that in the very first stage of the Revolution, Castro assumed "total power" and still had it (Szulc 1986:478).

Assuming that Fidel actually exercises such a dominant role in Cuban society, how can this phenomenon be explained? The ready-made answer is always the same: Fidel Castro has charisma. But in the social scientific literature charisma is not an inherent individual quality but rather a structural social relationship. In other words, charisma is a form of authority that emerges in a given sociopolitical system when a number of conditions are present. The literature on Castro's charisma, more often than not, seems to be unaware of these basic sociological discoveries. Richard Fagen is one of the few notable exceptions. He said, "The charismatic leader is always the creation of his followers" (Fagen 1972:158).

Domínguez discussed some of the aspects of charismatic authority. According to him charisma "provides an authority that rests upon the extraordinary quality of the ruler as a person as it is perceived by the citizenry." He goes on to add that charisma "depends on the leader's conviction that he is not dependent on election by his followers but has been 'elected' by a supernatural authority, either God or some 'historical force,' and on the citizenry's sharing that conviction" (Domínguez 1978:197). An enunciation of this kind reduces charisma to a subjective state that leader and followers share. But in stressing subjectivity, the critical sociological facet of charisma, as Max Weber stated it, is missed. For charisma is a form of authority that appears under very special social circumstances (see Valdés 1976:7–13). The reference to charisma often fails to define what it is. Even those who offer the reader a definition fail to use the concept in the proper Weberian fashion. This is, of course, only one illustration of the conceptual confusion prevailing in Cuban studies.

Although the literature seems to show no interest whatsoever in the sociology of charismatic authority, it has, nonetheless, a particular desire to investigate the psychological motives behind Fidel Castro's exercise of power. This leads us to the second shared assumption.

2. *For Fidel Castro Power Is an End in Itself.* This premise suggests that Fidel Castro exercises power only in order to maximize it and to remain in absolute control.

The premise has gone through a number of stages over the years. Four major variations on the same theme can be outlined. At first, power maximization was attached to personal self-interest. This is a selfish but conscious effort. This view was replaced by the coming together of power maximization and ideology. The latter in turn was supplanted by a biological model of Fidel Castro's motives. Conscious self-interest or ideology gave way to the awesome logic and power of aging. Last, Fidel Castro's policies were interpreted on the basis of subconscious drives and forces. Let us review each of the four variations on the same theme.

a. Fidel Castro and Self-interest. This particular perspective began with the work of Theodore Draper, who portrayed Castro as an opportunist merely trying to justify his hold on power with different ideologies. In 1965 Draper stated, "Historically, then, Castroism is a leader in search of a movement, a movement in search of power, and power in search of an ideology" (Draper 1965:48–49).

The thesis of Castro as the power-hungry opportunist who merely used ideologies to rationalize his control was adopted by Hugh Thomas in his 1970 book on the history of Cuba. In a recent work Thomas expressed the same thought as follows:

> In analyzing Castro's rule, it is evident that his primary motive and objective has always been to maintain the undiluted power needed to carry out his destined historical role as a great revolutionary torch bearer. Everything else is of a lesser priority, and he has opposed any activity, law, or reform . . . that involves a diminution of his political power. Over time, Fidel Castro, as a political opportunist, has changed and adapted to circumstances whenever necessary to preserve his power and enable him to pursue his unchanging primary goals. (Thomas 1984a:3)

b. Fidel Castro, the Ideologue. The Draper-Thomas thesis of Fidel Castro as ideological opportunist did not fare very well soon after it was proclaimed. This was the case because the development model established at the time (the so-called Sino-Guevarist route) seemed to indicate a strong dose of ideology. However, that particular turn of events hardly served to dissuade Cuba scholars to reconsider the central premise of

personal power maintenance. Instead, a revised version of power maximization was introduced.

The new version, stressing ideology, appeared first in those works
dealing with the Cuban economy. Carmelo Mesa-Lago is representative
here. According to Mesa-Lago, Cuban economic policy was the result
of ignorance as well as "naive," "irrational," and highly ideological
views on matters of economic policy (Mesa-Lago 1981).

In this new version ideological opportunism is just replaced by
ideological "naivete," and everything is kept as usual. A good example
of this was offered by Antonio Jorge and Jaime Suchlicki in their review
of one of Mesa-Lago's books. They wrote:

> The varying ideological stances adopted by the leaders of the revolution
> go far to explain the wide swings in preferred growth strategies and the
> magnitude of economic failures. Only ideological naivete and gross ig-
> norance of the lessons of economic history—combined with power politics
> and the personality and ambitions of key Cuban leaders—can explain the
> blind adherence, in quick succession, to the Stalinist economic model, the
> Maoist experiments in radical human and socioeconomic change, to Soviet
> economic reformism, and finally, to an uneasy mix of the latter with the
> persistent anti-organizational traits and charismatic mass mobilizational
> ethos of the Cuban revolution. (Jorge and Suchlicki 1984:102)

c. Fidel Castro and Biology. The literature of the Cuban political system
has changed from imputing to Fidel Castro a nonideological stance to
defining him as ideological (or ideologically naive). Interestingly, once
the Cuban Revolution moved away from the Sino-Guevarist model in
the 1970s, it became again necessary to address the question of Fidel
Castro's relationship to ideology.

Again, Carmelo Mesa-Lago, in his works on the Cuban economy,
provided a way out of the paradigmatic morass without actually discarding
its dominant premises. Mesa-Lago merely borrowed the interpretation
that the Cuban revolutionaries offered at the time. Thus, the Sino-
Guevarist experiment was just an expression of idealism. To this argument,
Mesa-Lago attached a biological dimension. He suggested that the Cuban
Revolution had "matured" in the 1970s and consequently was more
"pragmatic," "realistic," and "rational" (Mesa-Lago 1981:64, 179). Mesa-
Lago wrote, "My contention is that the Revolution has come of age
and, learning from its mistakes and under Soviet influence, has become
increasingly pragmatic and institutionalized. . . . The romanticism of
the 1960s has apparently come to an end" (Mesa-Lago 1974:ix).

Fidel Castro has been characterized differently over the years in order
to be in accord with whatever authors have claimed was happening in

Cuba. Castro has been portrayed as an opportunist (pre-1965), a naive and idealist revolutionary (1966–1970), and a pragmatist (1970–1986). Implicit in some of the characterizations has been a certain biologism. That is, the changes in Fidel seem to parallel his getting older. In brief, in his early years he was an opportunist or an idealist because he was too young. His pragmatism, on the other hand, exemplified a coming of age or maturity. Policy thus mirrored the evolution of Castro's aging process.

In his biography of the Cuban revolutionary, Tad Szulc carried this biological determinism to its logical conclusion: Maturity had to be followed by degeneration. Szulc asked, "Who is Fidel Castro?" at the end of his book. He then answered, "Since around 1980 his behavior suggests that he has few fresh ideas for his aging revolution. . . . Castro faces the dangers that his revolution may be decaying" (Szulc 1986:651–652).

Decay, of course, will end with death. And some eager Cuba scholars, in 1985, met at the University of Miami to discuss the problems of succession in Cuba. Irving Louis Horowitz, present at the conference, noted that "the question of political succession is at its core an issue of psychological wishful thinking" (Horowitz 1985:21). Perhaps he should have added that it was also a logical expression of the very model that has dominated the thinking of scholars dealing with Cuba.

The biological model (with its stages of youth, adulthood, maturity, and decay) works as long as political events can be fit into that frame of reference. But in early 1985 Cuban reality again began changing in ways contrary to the model's expectations. Fidel Castro, as in earlier periods, sounded like an idealist rather than a mature statesman.

This new turn of events led Jorge Domínguez to write,

> Cuba is at a turning point. President Fidel Castro has been using his power boldly during the past two years to reshape internal affairs along lines not seen since the late 1960s. Instead of delegating authority to powerful subordinates, as he had done since the early 1970s, he has recentralized it. Instead of liberalizing the economy, he has reversed several market-reliant policies of the past decade. And instead of stressing pragmatic policy goals, he has again been emphasizing the need to follow the "correct ideological route in building socialism." (1986:118)

Perhaps it is not just Cuba that finds itself at a turning point: The study of the Revolution is in a state of analytical crisis. The interpretative models utilized until the present simply cannot account for what is happening in Cuba.

Some attempts have been made at a rescue operation. Domínguez, for example, has collapsed the old dichotomy of idealism versus maturity into a new category "ideological maturity," a belief he says Castro adheres to. Domínguez wrote, "He [Castro] believes that the regime is today more ideologically mature and better organized, and thus able to achieve these [revolutionary] goals without the costs incurred in the 1960s" (1986:121).

d. *Fidel Castro and the Unconscious.* The biological model is in trouble, and some Cubanologos have begun to recognize the problem. Edward Gonzalez and David Rondfeldt deserve special mention on this account. In June 1986 they published a study for the Rand Corporation entitled, *Castro, Cuba, and the World.* The work demonstrates how much Cuban studies has changed since Theodore Draper began to raise important theoretical questions about the nature of the Cuban political system.

These two authors decided to challenge the biological model while remaining true to the view that Fidel Castro is the key to the country's political system. They wrote,

After 27 years in power, has Fidel Castro become a mellower revolutionary, no longer rebellious radical of the past? Now approaching 60 years of age, he has displayed signs of moderation. . . . He has, however, also shown flashes of his earlier self. . . . Still, it was an older Fidel who recently discoursed extensively on religion and commenced a "dialogue" with the Catholic church at home and abroad. (Gonzalez and Rondfeldt 1986:v)

Gonzalez and Rondfeldt concluded that there is no new Fidel. Aging has not affected his politics or his ideology. These two elements remain a constant. But then how about the policies initiated in the 1970s that had been interpreted as "mature" pragmatism? They answer, "Pragmatism is . . . a short-term tactic" used merely to "buy time, conserve power, and protect realized gains" (ibid.:ix).

At first glance it may appear that the authors wished to stress the role of ideology or perhaps self-interest as in earlier works, but that is not the case. Self-interest and ideology concentrate on the conscious levels of Fidel Castro's personality, and these two scholars have embarked on explaining the unconscious instead. Hence they stated: "Castro continues to exhibit the same ambitions and behavioral patterns that have characterized his rule for more than a quarter of a century. The reasons for such constancy are in his extraordinary mindset and a mode of behavior that has served him well since childhood" (ibid.:v).

Instead of social, economic, political, or cultural forces shaping Cuban society and its leaders, we are told that the drama of politics is really unfolding inside Fidel Castro's mind. Gonzalez and Rondfeldt claimed that they had written an in-depth study of Castro's personal nature in order to ascertain its relevance to policy analysis. And to enhance "our understanding of and ability to predict Castro's (and thus, Cuba's) future international behavior" they invented the "hubris-nemesis complex" and postulated a set of "idiosyncratic behavior patterns" (ibid.:2).

> To analyze Castro as a political actor, this study begins by turning to two concepts from Greek mythology, hubris and nemesis. These concepts illuminate the core of Castro's mindset, and in combination they enable the identification of a "hubris-nemesis complex" that reflects two of Castro's most basic drives: his unrelenting ambition for power and his continuing animosity turned toward the United States. (ibid.:v)

One may ask whether two political scientists writing for the Rand Corporation are intending to rely on psychological literature, particularly those works dealing with political leadership, as a way of getting into this subject. But this is not the case. The hubris-nemesis complex is the invention of David Rondfeldt, who applied it to the Mexican military in 1985. In fact, we are told that "the concept is not derived from existing psychological, psychiatric, or psychoanalytic" works. The hubris-nemesis complex, we are also told, "is in an early state of formulation and development," and consequently the "discussion is exploratory" (ibid.:4). The conclusion, nonetheless, ignores these caveats.

Historian Arthur Marwick once wrote that as long as historians continued to back their own psychological insights without reference to the discoveries of modern psychology their intellectual production should be considered, at best, works of fiction. Perhaps the same could be said of the recent work of Gonzalez and Rondfeldt. But that would be insufficient. The work under consideration betrays in a fairly clear fashion the weakness in methodology found in Cuban studies.

Let us look at the hubris-nemesis categories. The authors noted that these two terms originate in Greek mythology. Hubris refers to "the capital sin of personal pride, a pretension to act like a god while failing to observe the established balance of man and nature" (Gonzalez and Rondfeldt 1986:5).

We are told that hubris finds expression in "overweening pride, self-exaltation, arrogance, defiance, and an extreme overconfidence in one's ability and right to get away with whatever one wishes, to the point of overstepping established boundaries and disdaining the cardinal virtues of life" (ibid.:5). Hubris, in other words, sounds much like Freud's instinctual desires, the id, or George Herbert Mead's concept of the I. (The authors did not make the connection.)

Nemesis, on the other hand, refers to "the obscure goddess of divine retribution, righteous anger, and Olympian vengeance" (ibid.:vi). According to the authors, nemesis personifies "moral reverence for law." Nemesis was a deity that "intervened in human affairs to restore equilibrium when it had been disturbed, usually by persons who had attained excessive power and wealth" (ibid.:5). Thus, nemesis is concerned with "proper conduct, behavior, and equilibrium in human affairs" (ibid.:5).

This concept of nemesis, as defined by the authors, is the equivalent of the Freudian superego or Margaret Mead's concept of the me. Nemesis, like the superego and the me, is the conceptual expression of social norms and values. This is how the Greeks understood the term. In other words, nemesis is the antithesis of hubris in the sense that hubris refers to the individual whereas nemesis exists outside the individual. Nemesis, then, is society as a whole.

What is peculiar about Gonzalez and Rondfeldt's work is that despite the correct definition of nemesis, they applied it incorrectly. Nemesis is not an individual drive or instinct: Like the superego and the me, nemesis refers to the social realm of existence. That they misunderstood the categories utilized in their own work was evident when they equated hubris with "ambition for power" and nemesis with "vengeance" (ibid.:6, note 5).

Let us assume that hubris is an acceptable concept. How do we operationalize or measure it? The authors did not say. Yet, we were told that Fidel Castro has often "shown great hubris" (ibid.:6) and that Castro "clearly exudes hubris." Next, the authors stated that Castro's "statements and actions" provided the evidence of his hubris (ibid.:13). These are assertions. But assertions and proofs are two different things in the social sciences. Where is the evidence that the statements cited reveal "hubris," that is, demonstrate validity? These methodological issues are simply not dealt with. Instead, the assertions of others are simply used to "prove" the authors' case. (Thus, if Herbert Matthews or Carlos Franqui stated that Fidel Castro is such, it must be so, and is also an example of hubris.) Curiously, Castro's statements that could be construed as a negation of the hubris argument are cited to demonstrate that he possesses it but dismisses its existence (ibid.:22–25).

The most glaring and damning flaw in this work, however, is in the very application of the nemesis concept. For the goddess Nemesis, to the Greeks, symbolized the role that society played when individuals did not recognize social rules and laws. In such a situation, Nemesis (society) intervened and punished the individual. Nemesis, in other words, was the goddess that punished individual deviance. Nemesis means social punishment of individuals. Yet, in the hands of Gonzalez and Rondfeldt, the term nemesis means something else. Nemesis is no longer social nor is it Freud's superego or Mead's me. Instead, nemesis has been transformed into the Freudian Thanatos (without its counterpart, eros).

Fidel Castro, like Thanatos, is violent, aggressive, and irrational. In this scenario, the Cuban revolutionary has appointed himself the force that is to bring down U.S. power. For "long ago [he] committed himself to being the nemesis, in this case, of the United States" (ibid.:6). Castro, we are told, has a strong desire for vengeance and sees himself as housing an "anti-American destiny." Consequently, he "remains ready to put Cuba at risk for his own purposes" (ibid.:32). And this "requires him to possess absolute power at home and relentlessly seek to expand it abroad" (ibid.:41). In other words, Fidel Castro's mindset requires the establishment of a totalitarian state, power maximization, and an imperial foreign policy agenda.

Epithets and pejoratives permeate this work. Thus, Fidel Castro is characterized as "violence-prone," "manipulative," "extortionist," "vengeful," "self-interested," and "deceitful," to mention a few. What impact the U.S. economic blockade, now over twenty-four years old, may have had on the Cuban people and their revolutionary leaders seems to be of no consequence to these two analysts. To imagine the subjective and unconscious influence that hidden drives may have on nationalism apparently is much more interesting than studying the concrete impact that U.S. foreign policy has exerted over this small island. This is the poverty of subjectivism.

The Soviet Union, Sovietization, and the Political System

Within the Cuban political landscape Fidel Castro is the unquestioned power, with no other contending autonomous national force. Instead, the only other serious power center is external to national forces: the Soviet Union. According to Jorge Domínguez, "Politics in Cuba is organizationally based. The things that count in gaining power are proximity to Fidel Castro or to power in the Soviet Union" (Domínguez 1978:7). Fidel Castro and the Soviet Union then are characterized as polar opposites. Thus, if Castro symbolizes charisma, the Soviets represent bureaucracy and institutions—the "irrational" versus "the rationality of routine" (Gonzalez 1976a).

Soviet influence on Cuban society, thus, has meant the establishment of institutionalization—an outcome that Cuba analysts often have welcomed at the same time that they have criticized this new dependence (on Sovietization) (see Fitzgerald 1978). This Manichean approach (Castroite independence with irrationality versus Cuban dependence on Soviets with rationality) put scholars in an unenviable and ridiculous position. Mesa-Lago acknowledged this when he wrote: "In the last decade, the increasing influence over Cuba . . . has helped to moderate the island's foreign policy. Sad as it is, the United States is better off dealing with a Soviet-dependent Castro than with him loose" (Mesa-Lago 1974:135).

Sovietization as a moderating influence did not last long as a thesis. It simply made everyone working on Cuba uncomfortable. Once Havana deployed some of its soldiers to Africa in 1975 a more appealing and politically agreeable interpretation began to surface. Sovietization began to mean that the USSR had with Castro a patron-client relation in which the island operated "within the parameters set by the Kremlin" (Duncan 1985; Duncan 1986:46). In other words, the image of the Soviet role shifted from moderating Cuban policies to using Cuba to serve its own geostrategic interests. Obviously, the latter has a much more appealing message.

Conclusion

Studying social revolutions has never been an easy task. In the case of Cuba the enterprise has been exceedingly difficult because of the ongoing clash between Cuba and the United States. Scholarship, as a consequence, has suffered. This is obvious when we see that a fairly large portion of the works dealing with the Revolution tend to rely on content analysis of printed matter, as well as on secondary sources. Scholars, who as a rule do not have access to policymaking authorities, archives, or even some primary sources, have used inference to fill the vacuum. Inference, at times, has been accompanied by vivid imagination. But this route, imposed by circumstance, has serious drawbacks.

A case in point is the role of Fidel Castro in the Revolution. It would be farfetched to even dare to question the influence exercised by the "maximum leader." But perhaps it would be a healthy endeavor to begin with the statement that Fidel Castro's power needs to be demonstrated. Every major policy or policy change, as a rule, has been announced by Castro; also Castro has occupied strategic roles in the Cuban government and in the Communist party. But we should be aware that appearance and reality do not always coincide. Perhaps in the Cuban case the two are one and the same, but what is the evidence? Is it possible that Fidel Castro is the "great communicator" of Cuba but other forces are at work that he simply expresses?

The same set of questions can be raised about the process of policymaking. Jorge I. Domínguez noted that "the study of policy formation in Cuba is among the more inaccessible topics for research by outsiders" (Domínguez 1982:33). If this is true, can we be certain about how and who makes policy in Cuba? Apparently the dearth of information does not stop many of us from making assertions about the policy; but it may be worthwhile to recognize that we are involved in scholarly guesswork.

Cuban studies have moved slowly away from a totalitarian model to an elite model of the political system. But the elite model is not very well defined. If there are elites or interest groups in Cuba it is imperative to accurately identify and define them and ascertain what are their internal structure and their interests and how they are articulated. It is to be expected that at some point scholars will begin to study interest groups (or institutional interests).

There is a certain resilience in stressing the role of the "great man" in history. But biography and history are not one and the same. Psychological studies of Fidel Castro and other revolutionaries may be worthwhile and even fruitful. But they should be infused by a deep knowledge of psychology, and other works should be used as guidelines. It would be extremely useful to analyze the character structure of the "little men and women" of Cuba as well.

A community of scholars has grown around the study of the Cuban Revolution in the last two decades. Much has been gained from their work. This chapter has not mentioned their scholarly contributions to a better understanding of the Cuban Revolution. I had a different objective: to understand those who study the Revolution.

Seven years ago I noted that the time had arrived to look beyond mere assertions, the simple use of data, and conclusions. "We must delve much deeper into the relations that exist, in the works of analysts, between concepts, assumptions, the logic of arguments, the premises, and the values. We require, in other words, an explicit understanding of everyone's method and the paradigm they work with" (Valdés 1979:84). In this chapter I have attempted to evaluate some aspects of the work of colleagues. I hope that others will join the effort.

References

Aguila, Juan del. 1985. *Dilemmas of a Revolution*. Boulder, Colo.: Westview Press.
Bernstein, Richard J. 1976. *The Restructuring of Social and Political Theory*. New York: Harcourt, Brace, Javanovich.
Blackburn, Robin. 1963. "Prologue to the Cuban Revolution." *New Left Review* (London), October.

Blasier, Cole. 1973. "The Elimination of United States Influence." In Carmelo Mesa-Lago, ed., *Revolutionary Change in Cuba*. Pittsburgh: University of Pittsburgh Press.

_____. 1976. *The Hovering Giant: U.S. Responses to Revolutionary Change in Latin America*. Pittsburgh: University of Pittsburgh Press.

Bonachea, Rolando, and Nelson P. Valdés, eds. *Cuba in Revolution*. New York: Anchor Books, 1972.

Cheasty, Adrienne, and Carlos F. Díaz Alejandro. 1983. "Cuba: An Appraisal of Two-Decade Appraisals." *Cuban Studies*, winter.

Domínguez, Jorge I. 1978. *Cuba, Order and Revolution*. Cambridge, Mass.: Harvard University Press.

_____. 1982. "Revolutionary Politics: The New Demands for Orderliness." In Jorge I. Domínguez, ed., *Cuba: Internal and International Affairs*. Beverly Hills, Calif.: Sage Publications.

_____. 1984. "Cuba's Relations With Caribbean and Central American Countries." In Alan Adelman and Reid Reading, eds., *Confrontation in the Caribbean Basin: International Perspectives on Security, Sovereignty and Survival*. Pittsburgh: University of Pittsburgh.

_____. 1985. "U.S.-Cuban Relations in the 1980s: Issues and Policies." *Journal of Interamerican Studies and World Affairs*, fall.

_____. 1986. "Cuba in the 1980s." *Foreign Affairs*, fall.

Draper, Theodore. 1965. *Castroism: Theory and Practice*. New York: Praeger.

Duncan, W. Raymond. 1979. "Soviet and Cuban Interests in the Caribbean." In Richard Millet and W. Marvin Well, eds., *The Restless Caribbean: Changing Patterns of International Relations*. New York: Praeger.

_____. 1985. *The Soviet Union and Cuba: Interests and Influence*. New York: Praeger.

_____. 1986. "Castro and Gorbachev: Politics of Accommodation." *Problems of Communism*, March-April.

Eidlin, Fred H. 1979. "Soviet Studies and 'Scientific' Political Science." *Studies in Comparative Communism*, summer-autumn.

Fagen, Richard. 1972. "Charismatic Authority and the Leadership of Fidel Castro." In Rolando E. Bonachea and Nelson P. Valdés, eds., *Cuba in Revolution*. New York: Anchor Books.

Falk, Pamela S. 1985. *Cuban Foreign Policy: Caribbean Tempest*. Lexington, Mass.: Lexington Books.

Farber, Samuel. 1976. *Revolution and Reaction in Cuba, 1933–1960: A Political Sociology from Machado to Castro*. Middletown, Conn.: Wesleyan University Press.

Fernández, Damián J. 1986. "Scholarship and Double Standards." *Journal of Interamerican Studies and World Affairs*, summer.

Fitzgerald, Frank T. 1978. "A Critique of the 'Sovietization of Cuba' Thesis." *Science and Society*, spring.

Friedrichs, Robert W. 1970. *A Sociology of Sociology*. New York: Free Press.

Gonzalez, Edward. 1976a. "Castro and Cuba's New Orthodoxy." *Problems of Communism*, January-February.

————. 1976b. "Political Succession in Cuba." *Studies in Comparative Communism,* spring-summer.

————. 1985a. "The Cuban and Soviet Challenge in the Caribbean Basin." *Orbis,* spring.

————. 1985b. "After Fidel: Political Succession in Cuba." In Jaime Suchlicki, ed., *Problems of Succession in Cuba.* Miami, Fla.: University of Miami.

Gonzalez, Edward, and David Rondfeldt. 1986. *Castro, Cuba, and the World.* Santa Monica, Calif.: Rand Corporation, June.

Goodsell, James Nelson. 1975. "Introduction." In *Fidel Castro's Personal Revolution in Cuba: 1959–1972.* New York: Alfred A. Knopf.

Gouldner, Alvin W. *The Coming Crisis of Western Sociology.* New York: Avon Press, 1970.

Halperin, Ernst. 1967. "Preface." In Andrés Suárez, *Cuba: Castroism and Communism, 1959–1966.* Cambridge, Mass.: MIT Press.

Halperin, Maurice. 1972. *The Rise and Decline of Fidel Castro: An Essay in Contemporary History.* Berkeley: University of California Press.

Horowitz, Irving L. 1985. "Commentary." In Jaime Suchlicki, ed., *Problems of Succession in Cuba.* Miami, Fla.: University of Miami.

Hough, Jerry F. 1972. "The Soviet System: Petrification or Pluralism?" *Problems of Communism,* March-April.

Jorge, Antonio, and Jaime Suchlicki. 1984. "Castro's Costly Path to Dependency." *Problems of Communism,* September-October.

LeoGrande, William. 1981. "Two Decades of Socialism in Cuba." *Latin American Research Review* 16, no. 1.

————. 1985. "Foreign Policy: The Limits of Success." In Jorge I. Domínguez, ed., *Cuba: Internal and International Affairs.* Beverly Hills, Calif.: Sage Publications.

Lockwood, Lee. 1969. *Castro's Cuba, Cuba's Fidel.* New York: Vintage Books.

Louch, A. R. 1969. *Explanations and Human Actions.* Berkeley, Calif.: University of California Press.

Maingot, Anthony. 1978. "A Question of Methodology: Review Essay on Recent Literature on Cuba." *Latin American Research Review* 13, no. 1.

Martínez Alier, Juan, and Verena Martinez Alier. 1972. *Cuba: Historia y sociedad.* Paris: Ediciones Ruedo Iberico.

Matthews, Herbert. 1969. *Fidel Castro.* New York: Simon and Schuster.

Merton, Robert K. 1967. *On Theoretical Sociology.* New York: Free Press.

Mesa-Lago, Carmelo. 1974. *Cuba in the 1970s: Pragmatism and Institutionalization.* Albuquerque: University of New Mexico Press.

————. 1981. *The Economy of Socialist Cuba.* Albuquerque: University of New Mexico Press.

Nelson Goodsell, James. 1975. "Introduction." In *Fidel Castro's Personal Revolution in Cuba: 1959–1972.* New York: Alfred A. Knopf.

O'Connor, James. 1970. *The Origins of Socialism in Cuba.* Ithaca, N.Y.: Cornell University Press.

Packenham, Robert A. 1986. "Capitalist Dependency and Socialist Dependency: The Case of Cuba." *Journal of Interamerican Studies and World Affairs,* spring.

Pérez, Louis A. 1985. "The Cuban Revolution—Twenty-five Years Later: A Survey of Sources, Scholarship and State of the Literature." In Sandor Halebsky and John M. Kirk, eds., *Cuba: Twenty-five Years of Revolution, 1959–1984.* New York: Praeger.

Robbins, Carla Anne. 1983. *The Cuban Threat.* New York: McGraw-Hill.

Smith, Wayne. 1985. "U.S.-Cuba Relations: Twenty-five Years of Hostility." In Sandor Halebsky and John M. Kirk, eds., *Cuba: Twenty-five Years of Revolution, 1959–1984.* New York: Praeger.

Suárez, Andrés. 1967. *Cuba: Castroism and Communism, 1959–1966.* Cambridge, Mass.: MIT Press.

Szulc, Tad. 1986. *Fidel, A Critical Portrait.* New York: Morrow.

Thomas, Hugh. 1984a. "Coping With Cuba." In Irving L. Horowitz, ed., *Cuban Communism.* New Brunswick, N.J.: Transaction Books.

Thomas, Hugh, George A. Fauriol, and Juan Carlos Weiss. 1984b. *The Cuban Revolution—25 Years Later.* Boulder, Colo.: Westview Press.

Valdés, Nelson P., and Edwin Lieuwen. 1971. *The Cuban Revolution: A Research-Study Guide.* Albuquerque: University of New Mexico Press.

———. 1976. "Revolution and Institutionalization in Cuba." *Cuban Studies,* January.

———. 1979. "Reply." *Cuban Studies,* July.

Williams, William Appleman. 1961. *The United States, Cuba and Castro.* New York: Monthly Review Press.

Wolin, Sheldon. 1968. "Paradigms and Political Theories." In Preston King and B. C. Parekh, eds., *Politics and Experience.* Cambridge, Mass.: Cambridge University Press.

Yanez, Hernan. 1984. "Comments." In Alan Adelman and Reid Reading, eds., *Confrontations in the Caribbean Basin: International Perspectives on Security, Sovereignty and Survival.* Pittsburgh: University of Pittsburgh.

11

Cubanology and Crises: The Mainstream Looks at Institutionalization

Carollee Bengelsdorf

The deeply ingrained political illiteracy concerning Cuba in the United States has been framed by various factors. Not the least among these factors has been scholarly work on Cuba. The voice of the dominant Cubanologists in the United States has provided a number of critically important services: It has furnished the rationale and justification for the aggressively hostile policies which, with few brief exceptions, the U.S. government has pursued with regard to Cuba since the inception of the Revolution. In much the same manner, it has infused and distorted the public's conception of the Cuban Revolution, thereby assuring a general atmosphere of popular acceptance of these policies.

The centrality of the role of the leading Cubanologists is all the more ironic, given the quality of their product: The study of Cuba in the United States has been characterized, above all, by its limitations. Its practitioners have, with almost startling consistency, molded their analyses into interpretive models that have remained intact and unaltered for the duration of the Revolution. These models borrow from the social science literature that was predominant in U.S. universities in the 1950s and 1960s and that, by and large, has been discredited or has fallen into disuse.

The fact that these models continue to be applied to the Cuban situation says something about the literature dealing with Cuba. These models have distinguished themselves by their dubious relevance. In hindsight, the categories on which they are based have demonstrated little capacity to elicit an understanding of Cuba that would give some insight into its future course of development. Further, they have been, and continue to be, fundamentally misleading. The hastily drawn and erroneous interpretations of Cuba's activities in the Angolan war of 1975–1976, which almost universally assumed that Cuban actions came in response to Soviet initiatives (as it turned out, an exact reversal of what actually took place), provide perhaps the most striking and accessible example of this.

The models fall essentially into three nonexclusive categories. The first of these categories involves a revival of elite theory. The old mode of operation of the "Kremlin watchers"[1] has been resuscitated and applied wholeheartedly to Cuba, within the context of searching for factional conflicts between what is variously called the "Raulistas" and the "Fidelistas," and even the "Carlos Rafael Rodriguistas" (representatives of the pre-1959 Cuban Communist party, or PSP) to explain any given policy. Who is sitting next to whom at a meeting or rally and what was their affiliation as of 1959 when the Revolution took power become the determining factors in situating people in the different camps.

The problems with this model of interpretation are readily apparent. An ever-increasing number of people cannot be categorized because they were not in circles of power in 1959. But most important, we are given a fundamentally static interpretation of a society that has been anything but static. We are left with an ahistorical interpretation of the history of the Cuban Revolution, ahistorical in the sense that the crucible for interpreting the Cuban reality of 1968 or 1978 or 1986 remains always the Cuba of 1959. Our contention is that such a mode of analysis by definition—because of its purposeful discounting of the very notion of change—must be inherently misleading. And, like all elite theory, it denies a priori a role to anybody in the society other than the top ranks of the leadership. It entirely ignores the relevance of another critical dynamic at work, a dynamic that requires consideration not simply of the leadership but of the broad spectrum of the population and of the interaction between the leadership and the people.

The second model involves the application to Cuba of the universal paradigm of what is a "developed" society, which was used so widely in the 1960s in political development literature.[2] Here, Cuba is measured against an invisible but universally accepted model of democratic performance (which, as has been pointed out by numerous critics of political development literature, bears a strong resemblance to a totally idealized version of the United States, or more generally of Western democracies) and is found wanting.

Finally, both these models are frequently set forth within the framework of the "Sovietization thesis."[3] The core of this thesis is the idea that, in both foreign and domestic policy, Cuba has become little more than a dupe, a copy, and an agent of the Soviet Union. Scholars emphasize different moments at which the Soviet Union took hold in Cuba. Theodore Draper, who wrote the first critiques of the revolution within this mode, traced Cuban subordination back to the early years of the Revolution. All, however, agree that by 1970 the Soviet Union was essentially in charge in Cuba.

The Sovietization thesis is pervasive: It characterizes both the scholarly and the popular understanding of Cuba. Its pervasiveness gives it enormous significance. In its very essence, it effectively excludes the need for any serious examination of the dynamics of Cuban internal development as the starting point for understanding the logic of the course the Revolution has taken.

The treatment of the 1970s transition in Cuba and the institutional process that it initiated provide the most fertile ground in the literature for a more extensive examination of these three models. Here we witness a real flowering of each side: The Havana watchers and the Sovietization theorists come into their own and blend together in their critiques, while the neomodernization theorists find confirmation of the basic lines of their argument. Let us consider the interpretation each has given to this institutional process in order to reveal more clearly their basic frame of reference, assumptions, and methodology.

For both the elite theorists—the Havana watchers—and the Sovietization theorists, the institutionalization process that Cuba has undergone since 1970 is nothing more than the internal manifestation of its wholesale passage into the Soviet orbit. It is, as Carmelo Mesa-Lago phrased it, "institutionalization a la Soviet."[4] The two groups work from a common base of evidence. Their assertions are rooted in a series of conclusions they have drawn about the nature of the institutionalization process in Cuba. They see this process as one marked, first, by an increasing level of social and economic inequality, reflected in a return to material in place of moral incentives; second, by a further verticalization of the political process; and third, by a conscious effort to depoliticize the Cuban population as a whole.[5] Mesa-Lago perhaps best captured this vision of the 1970s in Cuba when he asserted:

> The appealing, quixotic attempt to skip the transitional phase of socialism and rapidly create a "New Man" in an egalitarian communistic society through the device of development of consciousness, the use of moral incentives and labor mobilization has been quietly halted. The talk of the day in Cuba is economic incentives, wage differentials and building the material base through the use of cost-benefit analysis and raising capital efficiency and labor productivity. The uniqueness of the Cuban Revolution, so much praised by Sartre, has gradually dulled and the more conventional features of socialism "a la Eastern Europe" appear increasingly stronger on the island.[6]

If both elite theorists and Sovietization theorists agree with these conclusions, the path they have followed to reach them has differed, in emphasis if not in content. Mesa-Lago, dean of the Sovietization theorists, sees the reconstruction of the political process within Cuba as the result and reflection of Cuba's ever-growing economic dependence, in terms of both trade and aid, upon the USSR. His argument is that, given the 1970 economic debacle and what he understands as the consequent erosion of Castro's "charismatic" hold upon the Cuban population, Castro "had no other alternative but to yield to Soviet pressure," even if that meant "relinquishing part of his power, and Cuba its independence."[7] He could not allow the certain continuing deterioration inherent in the Sino-Guevarist" model; alternatively, the United States was not, for reasons Mesa-Lago supplied, willing to attempt a rapprochement that might have opened Cuba to other sources of economic assistance. Therefore, acceding to Soviet wishes and formulas was the single alternative open to Castro, if he wished to continue in power, albeit at a diminished level. By 1972, Mesa-Lago argued, economic dependence on the Soviet bloc had "reached the point of no return": The year 1972 marked Cuba's entry as a full member of COMECON.[8] The integration of Cuba into the Eastern bloc economic sphere, the increasing and unfavorable balance of payments deficit, the enormity of the Cuban financial debt to the Soviet Union—all these pointed, for Mesa-Lago, to Cuba's structural dependence upon the Soviet Union.[9]

Within the framework of this structural dependence the entire process of institutionalization has taken place: Every phase of it, Mesa-Lago argued, has been indelibly marked by the imposition of Soviet forms to Cuban reality. The "institutionalization trend," he argued, "has been characterized by central controls, dogmatism, administrative bureaucratic features, and limited mass participation resembling the Soviet system."[10] Trade unions, he asserted, have been revived in the classic Soviet image as "conveyor belts." The 1975 Cuban constitution, he declared, is little more than a copy of its Soviet counterpart: Thirty-two percent of its articles are taken directly from the 1936 Soviet constitution, and another 18 percent are heavily influenced by that constitution.[11] Furthermore, every political body set forth by that constitution, according to Mesa-Lago, is mirrored in the Soviet Union: "The National Assembly of People's power is equivalent to the Supreme Soviet; the Council of State corresponds to the Presidium of the Supreme Soviet, and the Council of Ministers, the judiciary and the Organs of Popular Power can also be paired with similar institutions in the U.S.S.R."[12] The restructuring and growth of the Cuban Communist party reflect lines set out in the Soviet party model. That is, he charted, essentially the imposition in

Cuba of what we might call "official Marxism-Leninism," both ideologically and in practice.

The Havana watchers do not disagree with this litany. They likewise
argue that a "client-state" relationship exists between Cuba and the
Soviet Union[13] and that the "institutionalization of the revolution has
proceeded toward the 'sovietization' of Cuba's domestic order."[14] Nor
do they disagree with the Sovietization analysis of the economic basis
for what they call the "heightened Soviet tutelage after 1970":[15] "fi-
delismo" and "charismatic hardship-communism," Edward Gonzalez
argued, were "economically dysfunctional."[16]

But if the Sovietization theorists stressed the economic roots of
"institutionalization a la Soviet," elite theorists tended to place particular
emphasis upon superstructural, more political factors. The failure of the
1970 harvest signaled, above all, that, in the words of Andrés Suárez,
"Castro's political resources were almost exhausted."[17] Gonzalez articulated the nature of this exhaustion with greater specificity: The failure
of the harvest made it "difficult to maintain . . . the illusion of the
omnipotent and omniscient charismatic caudillo" because

> Fidel's charismatic authority had stemmed from his proven ability to
> perform extraordinary deeds (such as overthrowing Batista) and to produce
> remarkable and beneficial results (such as the agrarian reform, and defeat
> of the United States at the Bay of Pigs, and the successful defiance of
> Moscow) thereby winning over and maintaining the devotion of the popular
> masses and immediate followers alike. These triumphs were largely in the
> past, however. With the harvest failure, Fidel had to admit . . . that he
> could no longer perform "miracles."[18]

The unbreachable abysses now corroding the fiber of "charismatic
hardship communism" made institutionalization necessary, if Castro was
to retain even part of his former power. Whether the result, as Suárez
argued, of direct Soviet imposition or simply of internal political jock-
eying, this institutionalization, for elite theorists, was synonymous with
a formalization of the Soviet model, as reflected in the reemergence of
factions besides the Fidelistas in positions of influence. Indeed, Suárez
argued that after 1970 the combined forces of the PSP (referring to the
old pre-1959 Cuban Communist party) and the "Raulista" factions
"enjoyed an easy majority in the Party secretariat" and that the monopoly
of power held by the July 26th faction had eroded so seriously after
1968 that it had virtually "vanished" from government.[19]

Gonzalez, at least in his writings prior to the 1975 Congress of the
Cuban Communist party, by and large agreed with this assessment.
Although he was far more ambiguous in his assessment of the Raulistas

(he left open the question, in his pre-1975 work, of whether they were a subgroup of the Fidelistas or a force on their own), he emphasized the rise of PSP faction to prominent positions and went so far as to argue that "it may well be that future historians will write that the Fidelista revolution—as we have known it—began with the Moncada assault on July 26, 1953, and ended exactly seventeen years later with Fidel's speech on July 26, 1970."[20]

The logic of the Havana watchers' thinking gets them into some trouble in their own terms. In the factional competition model they employed, the flow of their argument after 1970 had to lead to the conclusion that after that date the PSP faction had the upper hand. And indeed this is exactly what they argue. Yet they are forced to reverse themselves when they reassess who from what faction is really where, when the institutionalization process has been more fully laid out. Once more, according to Gonzalez—and despite his 1974 predictions—the Fidelistas seem to be back in control. They have reasserted their dominance through an alliance with the Raulistas, who turn out, after all, not to be a competing faction but a complementary one. Somehow and without any justification, Gonzalez argued that "these once mutually antagonistic tendencies have now been reconciled, and, in fact, seem to be mutually supportive."[21] Gonzalez, again by the logic of his own evidence and despite his assertion that 1970 might mark the end of the "Fidelista revolution," was forced to argue in 1976 that Castro had "succeeded in turning the process of institutionalization to his own political advantage."[22]

Fidel and Raul, he explained, clearly manipulated the institutionalization process, and, as Max Azicri summarized Gonzalez's argument, "by placing their followers ('Fidelistas' and 'Raulistas') in key leadership positions such as the Political Bureau and the Central Committee of the P.C.C. (the Cuban Communist Party) they were able to retain control of the political and state organs in spite of the structural changes that took place."[23] Again, the evidence for Gonzalez's argument is drawn from an assessment of who is where after the 1975 First Party Congress: The newly elected Central Committee, he argued, "shows continued dominance by the Fidelista-Raulista and M-26-7 coalition": "Of the 91 members in the previous Central Committee, 64 came from the ranks of the M-26-7, 23 from the PSP and 4 from the DR-13-M the Revolutionary Student Directorate."[24]

The most startling part of this analysis is that, more than fifteen years after the victory of the Revolution, Gonzalez and other elite theorists were still using as their sole criterion for determining the various "actors" allegiances as they formally stood on January 1, 1959. Gonzales did not seem to take into account that the DR-31-M effectively dissolved or disappeared on January 8, 1959 or that various members of the old PSP had stood by Castro, following his policies since before the victory or that by his own admission Gonzales could not identify some 21 percent of the Central Committee members (since they did not "belong" to any of his factions in 1959—mostly because they were "born too late").[25] The fact that the elite theorists were essentially caught with their pants down in their predictions for the 1970s—predictions that they would be forced to reverse—demonstrates the bankruptcy of their model.

More recently, Gonzalez and his team attempted to add some complexity to their model by introducing a four-part division within elite ranks and to enliven its static quality by suggesting the possibility of "generational cleavage."[26] They based their identification of four tendencies, according to Gonzalez, upon "soft data": Each is classified according to "institutional and group affiliations" and "respective issues orientations imputed according to the regime's past and current policies."[27] Thus, they identified the "Fidelista tendency"; the "technocratic tendency" led by Carlos Rafael Rodríguez; the "bureaucratic tendency" led by Osvaldo Dórticos (who died shortly after Gonzalez assigned him this position); and the "party cadre tendency."[28]

Gonzalez's divisions seem rather unimaginatively to be based more upon the standard categories of the Moscow watchers than were his earlier categories, which were almost entirely personality based. This revision of categories follows naturally from Gonzalez's statement that "fundamentally . . . institutionalization meant the restructuring of the Cuban regime along the lines of a Soviet political order."[29] If this is so, Gonzalez's new divisions seem to have little more to do with Cuban realities than his old ones, in terms of both the artificiality of the divisions and the substantive bases upon which they rest.

Thus, for instance, one of the defining characteristics of the Fidelista tendency is its "isolation from other elite elements in the past, because of its opposition to institutionalization and to normalization of relations with the U.S."[30] But this characterization floats in a time vacuum. The questions become, How much in the past? Who supported institutionalization before 1970? When did Castro oppose normalization of relations with the United States and what were his options at the time? Indeed, if anything, and on the basis of an avalanche of different kinds of reports, Castro would like nothing more than the normalization of relations with the United States.

The "technocratic tendency" led by Carlos Rafael Rodríguez, seemingly forever branded by Gonzalez as a major source of opposition to Castro despite the role he has played since 1957 because of his pre-1959 membership in the PSP, stands for "greater institutionalization and for rationality in the economy."[31] Again, this argument is derived from the past and apparently from Rodríguez's role in the famous great debate with Ché Guevara; it has nothing to do with post-1970 reality. Gonzalez did not provide, nor could he provide, any evidence of divisions or conflicts in the leadership over the need for planning and for institutionalization. Rodríguez seemed to be elected head of the "technocrats" partly because he has always played a central role in economic planning. But so has Castro—Gonzalez certainly would not deny this.

Dórticos's "bureaucracy tendency," Gonzalez implied, is infused by those elements of the July 26th movement that are historically less committed to Cuba's socialist goals and that "in particular, might favor some liberation of Cuba's political and economic policies."[32] Dórticos, like Rodriguez, seemed to have acquired his title simply because he was in a traditional sense the chief bureaucrat, as president of the Republic. He and his group (the very existence of which is not supported by evidence) are perhaps identified as more liberal because in the years immediately after 1969, Dórticos was not a vocal and visible socialist (he was somewhere behind the scenes, where every good bureaucrat presumably knows he/she belongs). But again, no evidence indicates that Dórticos for the entire period since the Revolution took power did not support Fidelista policy; nor did Gonzalez provide any evidence to prove otherwise. Finally, about the party "cadre tendency," Gonzalez could tell us only that it is "too new to tell."[33]

After an analysis of Raul Castro and the Revolutionary Armed Forces, which led Gonzalez to assert that "the veteran Raulistas share an affinity with the Fidelistas in their international perspective, particularly with respect to Castro's confrontation posture toward the U.S."[34]—and again, we must question whether Castro's posture has indeed not been the reverse of confrontation—Gonzalez concluded that the future looks bright for the technocratic and bureaucratic tendencies. These, he argued "are the ones most likely to coalesce in that they share broad areas of agreement on most domestic and foreign policy issues."[35]

Gonzalez's "tendencies," by their own definition, have nothing to do with Cuban reality. Gonzalez seemed literally to be inventing separations between tendencies, and his categories collapse when one considers them in the light of the "issues" he saw separating them or the people identified inhabiting them. Although his mention of generational cleavages is suggestive, he did not develop the idea. Rather, Gonzalez and the scholars who work in this mode seem increasingly intent upon importing external modes of analysis and applying them to Cuban reality, with results that are important only because they are taken seriously in various influential quarters of the U.S. academic and political world. Ironically, in terms of their frame of reference, it is really they who have fallen under the aura of Sovietization. Their scholarship seems to borrow from the weakest Western analyses of Soviet reality, a factor that becomes even more obvious when applied wholesale to Cuba.

The neomodernizers offer a more complex and sophisticated version of the institutionalization process than that of the Sovietization theorists or the Havana watchers. Jorge Domínguez, in his study *Cuba: Order and Revolution*,[36] provided an exploration of both prerevolutionary and revolutionary Cuba that touched upon an enormous variety of subjects, draws (as William LeoGrande correctly pointed out) upon a range of different modes of analysis, and attempts to bring to bear the approaches of such disparate thinkers as Weber, Apter, and Davies and Gurr.[37] But he did not attempt a real synthesis; rather he haphazardly intercut categories of analysis without a substantial attempt to interrelate them. As a result Domínguez's book is characterized by its surprisingly choppy and unintegrated style and substance. And this analytical choppiness frames and accentuates the jumbled and jumpy presentation of his massive date base. Domínguez filled hundreds of pages with facts and figures, but the reality of Cuba, particularly in the book's treatment of the revolutionary period, is not convincingly portrayed.

The unifying themes that run through the book are taken in a fairly straightforward fashion from modernization paradigms, most clearly from the work of Domínguez's teacher and mentor, Samuel Huntington. The very title of the book points to this by its emphasis on "order." (The Huntington book that Domínguez borrows most directly from is *Political Order in Changing Societies*.[38]) And the theme of order as the goal of modernization in revolutionary Cuba remains at the center of Domínguez's more recent piece on the subject, an extended essay entitled, "Revolutionary Politics: The New Demands for Orderliness."[39]

In his discussion of the institutionalization process itself, Dominguez's measuring rods of the long-term success of the effort were drawn directly from Huntington: These involve complexity, coherence, adaptability, and autonomy.[40] The result, we would argue, is an analysis that is frequently misplaced and misleading because it accepts unquestioningly the objectivity of the universalistic pretensions of classical modernization theory. In accepting these pretensions, Domínguez's analysis is subject to the entire range of critique that served, in the late 1960s and 1970s, to discredit the key premises of the modernization formulation, a critique that focuses upon its ahistoricity, its unilinearism, and its particularism and its nonobjective nature.[41]

Let us consider, for instance, Domínguez's discussion in his book of the nature of the Popular Power elections in Cuba. (Here, he based his exposition on the first two rounds of these elections: the 1974 experiment in Matanzas Province and the first nationwide elections in 1976.) His assertion that these elections were "rigged"[42] is based upon his assessment of the nature of the electoral process itself and his subsequent conclusion that "the rules governing these elections [make] the manipulation of the election by the Communist Party itself easy."[43] The criteria upon which he based his conclusion center first around the idea that a fair election must involve "autonomy and competition," that the absence of these features in Cuba is defined by the fact that self-nomination is impossible, that there is no campaigning as such by candidates or any discussion of the issues, and that the party, the government, and the mass organizations rather than the individual candidates distribute information and organize meetings concerning the elections.[44] Second, he asserted that "fair and representative elections should show some correspondence between the distribution of political affiliations among electors and the same distribution among elected public officials" and that the "rules governing the election should not be biased so that members of certain organizations are much more likely to be elected than others."[45]

What becomes clear in Domínguez's formulation of the criteria and the measuring rods for a fair campaign and a fair election is that there is an implicit model operating close to the surface of his discussion. That model is the idealized electoral process of the idealized society at the apex of the modernization paradigm—in this case, the United States. We leave in abeyance questions that might be raised by a thorough application of these measuring rods to the United States—that is not our task here. Rather, we suggest that the conclusion that the Cuban elections are rigged because the campaign process and the electoral structure are not comparable to those in the United States fails to take into account that the Popular Power system has been conceptualized within a framework that explicitly rejects, both in its purposes and in its operations, the type of representative form inherent in Domínguez's model and consciously pretends to be seeking something else entirely. Domínguez can critique this conceptualization, and he can evaluate the validity of its pretensions. But, as LeoGrande concluded, he cannot call it rigged "simply because it does not conform to North American conceptions of what functions an election ought to perform."[46]

Domínguez's application of a modernization paradigm to Cuba is misleading not only in its own terms but also because he seeks to apply it wholesale to a system consciously formulated with an entirely different frame of reference, as if that other frame of reference did not exist or had no validity. It is telling, as Lourdes Casal pointed out, that, despite the fact that the Domínguez study is concerned with a revolution that has explicitly defined itself as Marxist-Leninist and that it draws, if haphazardly and unevenly, upon multiple theoretical streams, there is not a single reference in over 650 pages to either Marx or Lenin.

Domínguez's framework, is, in Casal's words, "alien": It suffers fundamentally from an "inability to consider the Cuban revolution in its proper setting" and thus "leads to endless distortions and misinterpretations."[47]

In the final analysis, although Domínguez asserted elsewhere that, contrary to the Havana watchers' assertions, "there is no evidence that the historical factional split has much relevance in Cuban politics in the 1980's"[48] and although he spoke (elsewhere again) far more of the effects of external threat, in the form of the United States, upon Cuban development than do the Sovietization theorists in general, his basic analysis of Cuba and of its internal evolution since 1970 differs very little from that of either Mesa-Lago or Gonzalez. That is, he essentially understands politics in Cuba as the prerogative of a small group of individuals who effectively exercise control within a centralized and bureaucratic system whose parameters have been "powerfully" determined by the Soviet Union (which, Domínguez stated, "successful[ly] reassert[ed] hegemony over Cuba" in 1970).[49] In the end Domínguez's work on Cuba is based upon the same assumptions and characterized by the same inability to get at the reality of revolutionary Cuba that so limit the work of the Sovietization theorists and the Havana watchers.

Such scholarship has managed so totally to dominate the study of Cuba in the United States for several reasons. The almost continuous hostile attitude of seven U.S. administrations toward revolutionary Cuba has clearly provided an appropriate environment for such scholarship, much as the academics who produce these studies have provided the rationale and justification for this hostility. Moreover, the Cubanologists' refusal to look to the internal dynamics of the Revolution as their starting point echoes a more general and deep-rooted theme in U.S. policy concerning Cuba. Successive administrations have refused, in the most unbending terms, to recognize either the legitimacy or the originality of both the Revolution and its leadership. Any serious consideration of the Revolution in its own terms would inherently acknowledge Cuba's right to exist as a sovereign, independent nation—a right that has never, in the history of U.S.-Cuban relations, been honored by the United States.

But the dominance of the Cubanologists must also be traced to the absence of an alternative scholarship of any quality that might challenge their posture and their interpretations in a convincing fashion. With the exception of a few articles and books produced largely in the early years of the Revolution, the study of Cuba by those U.S. scholars sympathetic, or at least not hostile to, the Revolution, has been distinguished by its lack of distinction. It has taken a basically defensive posture and has focused overwhelmingly upon descriptive rather than analytical categories. As a result, this work has tended to paint a picture of Cuba as a static utopia rather than an underdeveloped island struggling with the complex and often contradictory problems of a transition to a new largely uncharted political, economic, and social system. In portraying Cuba in such unreal and unrealistic terms, these commentators and writers have not enunciated viable alternate paradigms that might effectively counter the models of interpretation that at present so pervade the study of Cuba in this country. An apologistic line of argument does no service either to the Revolution or to those in the United States who might actually be seeking to understand Cuban reality. It is to be hoped that the new generation of Cuba scholars coming into its own in the United States will be able to address the vacuum of solid analyses of the Cuban Revolution and to begin to facilitate a richer, more complex discourse concerning Cuba. It falls to these young scholars to "explode" the category of Cubanology itself: It is their task to transform the limited and limiting terrain that has so stunted the study of Cuba in this country by becoming, themselves, the dominant Cubanologists.

Notes

1. The primary exponents of this interpretation are Edward Gonzalez and Andrés Suárez. Gonzalez's work includes *Cuba Under Castro: The Limits of Charisma* (1974), articles dealing with the Cuban leadership in the journal *Problems of Communism*, and an article on "Political Succession in Cuba," in the 1984 edition of *Cuban Communism*, edited by Irving Horowitz. Suárez's *Cuba: Castroism and Communism 1959–1966* (published in 1967) is his major work.

2. The principal figure in this mode is Jorge Domínguez. Domínguez laid out this perspective in *Cuba: Order and Revolution* (1978), in a number of articles that he produces regularly for several journals, and in edited collections, including *Problems of Communism and Cuban Studies/Estudios Cubanos*.

3. In this regard, see the work of Irving Louis Horowitz, Leon Goure, and Julian Winkle, and in particular, Carmelo Mesa-Lago. Mesa-Lago's *Cuba in the 1970s* (1978) is the work most relevant to our discussion.

4. Carmelo Mesa-Lago, *Cuba in the Seventies: Pragmatism and Institutionalization* (New Mexico: University of Albuquerque Press, 1978), p. 112.

5. For discussion of this, see Frank Fitzgerald, "A Critique of the Sovietization Thesis," in *Science and Society* 42, no. 1, 1975. Fitzgerald's piece is the best overall critique of the Sovietization thesis thus far published.

6. Carmelo Mesa-Lago, *Cuba in the Seventies*, p. x.

7. Ibid., pp. 153, 156.

8. Ibid., p. 18.

9. Ibid., see discussion, pp. 10 and 25.

10. Ibid., p. 115.

11. Ibid., p. 72. Mesa-Lago drew upon the work of Leonel de la Cuesta, "The Cuban Socialist Constitution: Its Originality and Role in Institutionalization," in the journal that Mesa-Lago founded and coedits, *Cuban Studies/Estudios Cubanos* 6, no. 2 (July 1976):15–30.

12. Ibid., p. 73. What is perhaps most remarkable about the consideration and discussion of the Popular Power system by the entire range of dominant Cuba specialists in this country is the absence of such discussion. The Sovietization theorists, as we have seen, were quick to situate Popular Power within their catalogue of evidence that Cuba is tripping obediently down the Soviet path. Neomodernization theorists, in reviving the old continuum from traditional to modern society, have judged Popular Power by measures such as the absence of competition in the form of electoral campaigns and concluded that crucial aspects of a good electoral system have not yet come to Cuba. Consider, for instance, the two major academic studies dealing with Cuba in the 1970s. Mesa-Lago's *Cuba in the Seventies* dismissed Popular Power with a two-page description, a chart giving graphic form to this description, and an additional two pages outlining its limitations and the manner in which it duplicates the Soviet system. Jorge Domínguez's *Cuba: Revolution and Order* (Cambridge: Belknap Press, 1978)— a book that goes into extensive detail on about everything in the course of its 650-odd pages—allotted Popular Power only a small portion of a chapter. Indeed, from the time of the 1974 experimental elections in Matanzas province, critiques have agreed with reporter George Ann Geyer's 1975 *Chicago Sun Times* description of Popular Power as merely "window dressing." The critique appears to run along three parallel axes. The first line of the critique deals with representativeness. Mesa-Lago argues that Popular Power is not representative of the population, as measured by occupation, race, sex, education, and party membership. The second line argues that Popular Power institutions at the "base" level have no real power: They deal only with petty secondary concerns that are handled by a form of "machine politics and ward bosses" (Jorge Domínguez, *Cuba: Revolution and Order*, p. 286). This assessment, of course, contrasts directly with the Cubans' assertion that Popular Power represents a fundamental decentralization of power, allowing for the active participation of the people in the decisions that most affect their lives. The final line of critique understands the National Assembly, which stands structurally at the apex of the Popular Power system, as merely a rubber stamper of policies formulated by a small group of people at the center of the system. In his most recent discussion of this subject, Domínguez qualified this conclusion: He declared that "debates in the National Assembly have become somewhat open." In assessing five case studies of debates, as reported in the Cuban newspaper, "discussion," he wrote, "has been rigorous. . . . it is extremely unlikely that these were staged or prearranged." It would therefore be "an error . . . to consider the National Assembly to be only an adornment" (see "Revolutionary Politics: The New Demands for Orderliness," pp. 33, 34, 37, in Domínguez, ed., *Cuba: Internal and International Affairs*, Beverly Hills, Calif.: Sage Publications, 1982). The Neo-Modernization theorists argue that this conclusion is self-evident in the fact that the National Assembly (like its prototype in the Soviet Union) meets only twice a year, for three-day sessions each time. Again, such a conclusion directly

contrasts with the Cuban view that the fundamental authority at the national level rests entirely with the National Assembly. We will consider in some form each of these lines of critique.

13. Edward Gonzalez, *Cuba Under Castro: The Limits of Charisma* (Boston: Houghton Mifflin, 1974), p. 217.

14. Edward Gonzalez, "The Party Congress and Poder Popular: Orthodoxy, Democratization and the Leader's Dominance," in *Cuban Studies/Estudios Cubanos* 6, no. 2 (July 1976):10.

15. Gonzalez, *Castro Under Cuba*, p. 218.

16. Ibid., p. 197.

17. Andrés Suárez, "Soviet Influence on the Internal Politics of Cuba," in Alvin Rubinstein, ed., *Soviet and Chinese Influence in the Third World* (New York: Praeger, 1975), p. 193.

18. Gonzalez, *Cuba Under Castro*, p. 212.

19. Suárez, "Soviet Influence," pp. 191–193.

20. Gonzalez, *Cuba Under Castro*.

21. Gonzalez, "The Party Congress and Poder Popular," p. 1.

22. Edward Gonzalez, "Castro and Cuba's New Orthodoxy," in *Problems of Communism*, January-February 1976, p. 14.

23. Max Azicri, "The Institutionalization of the Cuban Revolution: A Review of the Literature," in *Cuban Studies/Estudios Cubanos* 9, no. 2 (July 1979):71.

24. Edward Gonzalez, "The Party Congress and Poder Popular," p. 12.

25. See Table 1.2: Composition of the P.C.C. Central Committee According to Political Affiliations, in Edward Gonzalez, "Institution, Political Elites and Foreign Policies," in Cole Blasier and Carmelo Mesa-Lago, eds., *Cuba in the World* (Pittsburgh: University of Pittsburgh Press, 1979), p. 11.

26. See Edward Gonzalez, "Political Succession in Cuba," in Irving Louis Horowitz, ed., *Cuban Communism*, fifth ed. (New Brunswick: Transaction Books, 1984), pp. 419–451.

27. Ibid., p. 442.

28. Ibid., pp. 442–444.

29. Ibid., p. 442.

30. Ibid., p. 442.

31. Ibid., pp. 442–443.

32. Ibid., pp. 442–443.

33. Ibid., p. 444.

34. Ibid., p. 444.

35. Ibid., p. 445.

36. Jorge Domínguez, *Cuba: Order and Revolution* (Cambridge: Belknap Press, 1978).

37. William LeoGrande: "Two Decades of Socialism in Cuba," in *Latin American Research Review* 16 (1981):189.

38. Samuel Huntington, *Political Order in Changing Societies* (New Haven: Yale University Press, 1968).

39. Jorge Domínguez, "Revolutionary Politics: The New Demands for Orderliness," in Jorge Domínguez, ed., *Cuba: Internal and International Affairs* (Beverly Hills, Calif.: Sage Publications, 1982), pp. 9–70.

40. Domínguez, *Cuba*, p. 237.

41. The literature critiquing the modernization formulation is vast and beyond the purview of this chapter to review. For a useful summary and brief overview of modernization theory, its critique, the various critiques of the critique, and the alternative constructs, see Ian Roxborough, *Theories of Underdevelopment* (London: Macmillan, 1979). For our purposes, the configuration of the critique of modernization provided by Suzanne Bodenheimer in "The Ideology of Developmentalism: American Political Science's Paradigm Surrogate for Latin American Studies," *Berkeley Journal of Sociology* 95, no. 137 (1970), has been particularly helpful.

42. Domínguez, *Cuba*, p. 287.

43. Ibid., p. 287.

44. Ibid., p. 289.

45. Ibid., p. 287.

46. LeoGrande, "Two Decades of Socialism in Cuba," p. 194.

47. Lourdes Casal, "Review: Jorge Domínguez, *Cuba: Order and Revolution*," in *Cuban Studies/Estudios Cubanos* 9, no. 2 (July 1979):94.

48. Domínguez, "Revolutionary Politics," p. 29.

49. Domínguez, *Cuba*, p. 259.

About the Editor
and Contributors

Carollee Bengelsdorf is associate professor of politics and feminist studies at Hampshire College in Amherst, Massachusetts. Her work has centered on questions of democracy and socialism in both theory and practice. She has carried out extensive research in Cuba.

Claes Brundenius is director of the Research Policy Institute at the University of Lund, Sweden. He is former president of the Scandinavian Latin American Studies Association. He has authored three books on Latin American development, most recently, *Revolutionary Cuba: The Challenge of Growth with Equity.*

Susan Eckstein is professor of sociology at Boston University. She is author of *The Poverty of Revolution: The State and Urban Poor in Mexico* and *The Impact of Revolution: A Comparative Analysis of Bolivia and Mexico.* She has written numerous articles on the outcomes of revolutions in Latin America and is currently completing a book on the Cuban Revolution and editing a book on protest and resistance movements in Latin America.

Frank T. Fitzgerald is associate professor of sociology at the College of Saint Rose in Albany, New York. He has written many articles on Cuba and on social change in the Third World, and he has authored a forthcoming book entitled *Politics and Social Structure in Revolutionary Cuba: From the Demise of the Old Middle Class to the Rise of the New Professionals.*

José Luis Rodríguez is deputy director of the Centro de Investigación de la Economía Mundial in Havana. He has written several books and dozens of articles on the Cuban economy. He is a member of the editorial board of *Economía y Desarrollo.*

Sarah Santana works in epidemiology at the Center for Population and Family Health and the G. H. Sergievsky Center at Columbia University. She has done research in cancer mortality, reproductive epidemiology, and the health of Hispanic and Chinese minorities in

New York City. She is presently investigating the determinants of the decrease in infant mortality in Cuba during the 1970s.

Nelson P. Valdés was born in Cuba in 1945 and came to the United States in 1961. He is professor of sociology at the University of New Mexico and editor of the Latin American Data Base, which publishes two semiweekly newsletters, *Central American Update* and *Latin American Debt Chronicle*. He has edited the selected works of Fidel Castro and of Ché Guevara and has written extensively on the sociology of the Cuban Revolution.

Andrew Zimbalist is professor of economics at Smith College. He has written widely on the Cuban economy and has published several books in the fields of comparative economic systems and Latin American development. He is editor of the Series in Political Economy and Economic Development in Latin America, published by Westview Press.

Index

229

participation, 69–70
rights, 69, 125
shortages, 123, 174
skilled, 175
women in, 121, 122–124, 125, 126, 128, 130
See also Agricultural sector, workers; Bonuses; Incentives, material and moral
Labor productivity, 61
Land use, 6
Lange, Oskar, 12
Laos, 157
Latin America, 137, 139
Communist parties, 195
and Cuba, 155, 156, 159, 160, 179, 195
external debt, 149
GDP, 2
GSP, 59
investment ratio, 61
national income, 4
and Western economic aid, 9
Latin American Political Economy: Financial Crisis and Political Change (Hartlyn and Morley), 58
Laundry services, 125, 126, 127
Lebanon, 157
Lenin, Vladimir, 194, 221
LeoGrande, William, 61, 163, 171, 183, 192, 220, 221
Leprosy, 110
Levesque, Jacques, 148
Liberalization period (1976–1985), 10, 11, 12
Liberman reform-type model, 12, 18–19(n27)
Library of Congress (U.S.), 27
Libya, 157, 168, 170, 172
Lieuwen, Edwin, 183
Life expectancy, 98, 110, 142
Light industry, 126
Literacy Campaign (1961), 121
Lockwood, Lee, 199
Louch, A.R., 186

Maceo, Antonio, 166
Machine tool/heavy industry, 6
Machista heritage, 16
Macroeconomic imbalance, 12, 15
Macro-indicators, 40

Maingot, Anthony, 183
Malaria, 97, 98, 110, 111
Malnutrition, 89, 110
Manley, Michael, 156, 158
Mariel exodus (1980), 31
Market economies, 67, 165
Market socialism, 12, 70
Martí, José, 166
Martínez Alier, Juan, 198
Marwick, Arthur, 204
Marx, Karl, 167, 221
Marxism, 130
Marxism-Leninism, 167, 216, 221
Mass participation, 145, 147
Matanzas, 128, 220
Maternity Code (1973), 125
Matthews, Herbert, 198, 205
Mead, George Herbert, 204
Mead, Margaret, 205, 206
Measles, 98, 111, 112
Media, 14
Medical assistance, 158, 159, 165, 170, 171, 176
Mengistu Haile Mariam, 163, 168
Meningitis, 98, 112
Meningococcal infections, 111
Mergers, 40
Mesa-Lago, Carmelo, 1, 4, 8, 15, 25–26, 27, 28, 31, 39, 44, 58, 62, 66, 73, 74, 77, 83, 84–86, 90, 97, 98, 100, 138, 142, 143, 144, 145–146, 185, 187, 188, 195, 201, 207, 214, 215, 222. *See also* Economic growth, Vanderbilt conference paper; Economic growth, World Bank study
Metals products, 50, 51, 52(table), 55(table), 56
Mexico, 155, 157
Microbrigades, 12
Middle class, 121
Middle East, 157, 160, 179
Military aid, 154, 155–157, 160, 162, 164, 165, 173, 174, 176
Military budget, 174
Military ventures abroad, 86. *See also* Angola; Ethiopia; Somalia
Minimum wage, 15
Minsap. *See* Public Health, Ministry of
Mixed economies, 71